Plant
Churc
Cross-
Culturally

Planting Churches Cross-Culturally

A Guide for Home and Foreign Missions

David J. Hesselgrave

Foreword by Donald A. McGavran
Contributions by Earl J. Blomberg

BAKER BOOK HOUSE
Grand Rapids, Michigan 49506

Scripture quotations are from the New American Standard
Bible, © The Lockman Foundation 1960, 1962, 1963,
1968, 1971, 1972, 1973, 1975, and are used by permission.

Fifth printing, April 1986

Copyright 1980 by
Baker Book House Company
ISBN: 0-8010-4219-4
Printed in the United States of America

To
Gertrude
loving wife and mother,
faithful companion and helpmate,
devoted Christian and layperson

Foreword

Here is a great book on Christian mission—lucid, wide-ranging, and biblical. David Hesselgrave of Trinity Evangelical Divinity School knows mission theory, theology, methodology, and history—and describes them well.

Hesselgrave puts the missions of many churches in many lands in his debt as he expounds what mission is and how it should be carried out in the enormously different settings found in the multitudinous societies which comprise our world. Missiologists will rejoice in this book. Teachers of missions will make it required reading for their classes.

The structure of the book arises systematically from the key idea that *the essential task,* in a world where three-fourths of all men and women have yet to believe in Jesus Christ as God and only Savior, *is that of planting new churches.* The process of mission, commanded by Christ and demonstrated by Paul, is set forth as consisting of ten steps. Hesselgrave is far too competent a missiologist to allow readers to think that these steps are all there is to mission. But it is remarkable how much of mission in all six continents can be properly catalogued and understood under the following headings: Missionaries Commissioned, Audience Contacted, Gospel Communicated, Hearers Converted, Believers Congregated, Faith Confirmed, Leaders Consecrated, Believers Commended, Relationships Continued, Sending Churches Convened, and, finally, More Missionaries Commissioned.

Discrimination, good judgment, and unswerving dedication to the heart of mission, mark this book. Two examples will illustrate this excellence. In Chapter 16, Hesselgrave speaks of continuing relationships between churches and missions. After quoting Harvie Conn to the effect that *ultimately* church and mission are to be integrated, Hesselgrave agrees, and then quickly goes on to say:

> However, we must not forget two factors. First, most missions exist under the aegis of sending churches [and hence are already church]. Second, as long as governments allow missions the freedom to evangelize ... the responsibility ... to do so should not be forfeited in order to integrate with receiving churches which do not have a vision for that God-given task.

In Chapter 10, speaking of the contextualization of the gospel message, Hesselgrave exhorts readers to remember that "not only does Scripture reveal a salvific core, it also reveals that the salvific core was adapted to various audiences—not to their prejudice and taste in order to make the message *palatable,* but to their world view and knowledge in order to make it *understandable.*" One longs for such discrimination in some who write and speak on contextualization. The ambassador never changes the message. He must, however, make sure it is understood.

A special merit of this book is its systematic development of each major topic. The framework, varying only slightly from chapter to chapter, keeps thought focused on the basic objectives. Career missionaries and candidates-in-training will profit from this masterly presentation.

Church leaders busily engaged in redefining mission to mean "everything God wants Christians to do" (our plain Christian duty) will not like this book, but churchmen and missiologists who define mission as cross-cultural propagation of the gospel will be pleased with it. The 75,000 missionaries at work on all six continents will acclaim its clarity, breadth, and depth. As congregations, denominations, and missionary societies multiply churches and carry out the Savior's will in the most responsive world ever to exist, they will do their task better for having read *Planting Churches Cross-Culturally*.

Donald A. McGavran
School of World Mission
Fuller Theological Seminary
Pasadena, California

Preface

Christ loved the Church and gave Himself for her. Though in seemingly inconsequential ways by comparison, I too have loved the Church and given myself to her. For thirty-five years it has been my high privilege to serve Christ in the fellowship of the Evangelical Free Church, in local churches in North America, in church-planting ministries in Japan, and in a teaching ministry at Trinity Evangelical Divinity School.

This book, therefore, grows out of thirty-five years of pioneering and pastoring, reading and researching, and learning and lecturing in company with literally thousands of people who have been my instructors and inspiration in service for Christ and His Church. The following are but representative of the larger number.

I thank congregations in Radisson (Wisconsin), Minneapolis-St. Paul, Rockford (Illinois), and Chicago, and in Urawa, Warabi, and Kyoto (all in Japan), for their patient support and prayers. Heartfelt gratitude is expressed to my colleagues on the faculty at Trinity—

Professors Arthur Johnston, J. Herbert Kane, and Victor
Walter—who have provided stimulation and inspiration.
The personnel at Free Church Headquarters, including
Dr. Lester Westlund and the Reverends Robert Dillon,
Wesley Gustafson, Vernon Anderson, R. Dean Smith,
and Lewis R. Wimberley, have been supportive. Trinity
students—and especially Greg Best—have been most helpful. Mrs. Carol Chmela typed the manuscript. Over the
years I have enjoyed a number of contacts with Dr. Donald
McGavran and on each occasion I have been the bene-
ficiary. His Foreword to this book is most appreciated.
As has been the case in every endeavor—directly and
indirectly—my wife, Gertrude, and my children, David
Dennis, Ronald Paul, and Sheryl Ann, have made irre-
placeable contributions.

Professor Earl Blomberg of Evangelico Seminario As-
sociado in Maracay, Venezuela, deserves special mention.
As a student in our Doctor of Missiology program at Trinity Evangelical Divinity School–School of World Mission
and Evangelism, missionary Blomberg did such outstanding work in research on church-planting that I requested
that he join me in the writing of this book. I was most
gratified when he agreed to do so, and most disappointed
when the pressures of his deputation schedule and early
return to the field rendered full collaboration impossible.
As the manuscript stands, Mr. Blomberg is largely responsible for the biblical background sections of chapters nine
to thirteen. A perusal of those sections will convince the
reader that the entire manuscript would have been enhanced had he been involved in the writing of every part.

Unless otherwise indicated, Scripture quotations are
from the New American Standard Bible. The other ver-
sions quoted are the King James Version (KJV), the Re-
vised Standard Version (RSV), and the New International
Version (NIV).

Numerous books on church growth have been published in recent years. Some books on church-planting

have also appeared. The Church of Christ has been strengthened by these literary contributions. The present volume is somewhat unique in its attempt to combine a biblical and step-by-step approach to church-planting with cultural and experiential data designed to facilitate the founding of new congregations in unreached areas of the world. As such, it can be successful only to the extent that the servants of Christ transmute its concepts into churches. I commend it, therefore, to the Lord and to His servants, in the hope that any strengths it may possess will aid them in their labors, and with the prayer that its weaknesses will not detract from their success.

David J. Hesselgrave
Deerfield, Illinois

Contents

PART FIVE
The Sending Church and the
Christian Mission (Continued)

PART ONE

The Christian and the Christian Mission

one

The Heart of the Christian Mission

The Church is a storm center of contemporary society. Communists view it as a chain anchoring the proletariat to the past. Secularists think of it as a vestigial organ without which society and individuals could function just as effectively, or more so. Many liberals see the Church as fulfilling its purpose when it permeates society and loses its separate identity. Most conservative Christians, on the other hand, place the Church at the heart of the divine purpose for the present age and view growth as one of its major responsibilities.

Adding to the confusion occasioned by these diverse views, theologians distinguish the visible Church and the invisible Church, the Church Militant and the Church Triumphant, and the Universal Church and local churches. Missiologists write about the indigenous church, the responsible church, older and younger churches, sending and receiving churches, and national and nativistic churches. Church analysts talk about formal and informal churches, traditional and innovative churches, and structured and unstructured churches.

We should make it clear at the outset that when we use the word *Church* (upper case) in this book, we refer to that body which is built upon the foundation of the apostles and prophets, which is composed of all true Christian believers, and of which Christ is the Head. When we use the word *church* (lower case), we refer to any duly constituted local body of Christian believers who corporately attempt to worship, witness, and serve in accordance with the Word of God. In fact, from a biblical point of view, these are the only entities that can rightly be called "church."

The thesis of this chapter is simple: *The primary mission of the Church and, therefore, of the churches is to proclaim the gospel of Christ and gather believers into local churches where they can be built up in the faith and made effective in service, thereby planting new congregations throughout the world.* Of course there are many other important tasks to be carried out by Christian believers both individually and corporately. But few of these objectives will be realized unless new believers are being added to local churches, unless new local churches are being added to the Universal Church, and unless existing churches are growing up into the fullness of Him who is their Head.

The Divine Plan for the Church

Countless pages have been written on the Church and its mission.[1] It can be demonstrated from the biblical record that God was not taken by surprise when Adam sinned. He had a prior plan that provided a way whereby man could be reconciled and restored to fellowship with God. As an

---

[1]See, for example, Johannes Blauw, *The Missionary Nature of the Church* (New York: McGraw-Hill, 1962), and Gary F. Vicedom, *The Mission of God* (St. Louis: Concordia Publishing House, 1965).

integral part of that plan God chose Abraham and his descendants in order that through them He might bless the world (Gen. 12:1–3). In one sense they failed, but the plan did not fail. Neither the continued provincialism of the Jewish people nor their ultimate rejection of the Messiah could obstruct the divine purpose. Rather, "by their transgression salvation has come to the Gentiles" (Rom. 11:11b). Believing Gentiles have been made "fellow-heirs and fellow-members of the body, and fellow-partakers of the promise in Christ Jesus through the gospel" (Eph. 3:6). And "this was in accordance with the eternal purpose [lit., purpose of the ages] which He carried out in Christ Jesus our Lord" (Eph. 3:11).

As Paul makes abundantly clear, the present "arrangement" whereby Jew and Gentile alike become members of a spiritual body by faith in Christ does not mean that the promises to Israel *as a nation* have been nullified. Certainly not. The "blindness of their eyes" and the "hardness of their hearts" are only partial and temporary until the "fulness of the Gentiles has come in." Then, "all Israel will be saved" (Rom. 11:25, 26). Israel will still have her day!

The present age, however, constitutes a unique period of history. It can correctly be called the "Church Age." When our Lord was ministering on earth He *prophesied* that He would build His Church and that the gates of Hades would not overpower it (Matt. 16:16–18). When He died on the cross He *provided* for the Church, giving Himself in death that the Church might be born and grow (Eph. 5:25). Now that He is in heaven He is *sanctifying* or "calling out" the Church and preparing it for its final presentation (Eph. 5:26, 27). When He comes again He will come for the Church to *glorify* it in the presence of the Father (I Thess. 4:13–18; Rev. 4–6).

Meaningful metaphors describe the Church in relation to Christ. It is His building—"built upon the foundation of the apostles and prophets, Christ Jesus Himself being the cornerstone" (Eph. 2:19–21). It is His spiritual body—"the fulness of Him who fills all in all" (Eph. 1:23; cf. also I Cor. 12:12, 13). It is, as it were, His bride—the object of His love and provision (Eph. 5:25-33).

The Church, therefore, is not an afterthought in the mind of God. He *planned* for it in eternity past and *provided* for it in the death and resurrection of His Son (Eph. 1:19-23). And the Son *prepared* for its formation and development by instructing His followers as to their mission and *empowering* them by His Spirit (Acts 1:4-8). The Church and the churches have no friend like their Lord! If Christians are to love what their Lord loves they must love the Church—and the churches! In the final analysis, Christology is closely allied with ecclesiology. When we inquire into a man's faith we do well to ask what he thinks of Christ and His Church!

The Great Commission

If there is any lingering doubt as to the central task to which Christ calls His people, it should be dispelled by an inquiry into the final command of Christ and the result of obedience to that command on the part of the early believers. Not that the Great Commission is overlooked! Perhaps no single passage of Scripture is more widely used to challenge Christians to faithfulness to their primary task than is Matthew 28:16-20. Nevertheless, the exhorters seldom take the time to carefully exegete the passage and compare it with parallel passages. As a result, the essence and method of mission are often lost in the exhortations to undertake it!

It is important to recognize that the One who speaks on the mountain is the risen Christ to whom all authority (*exousia*) has been given. (The Holy Spirit will provide the power or might [*dunamis*] to fulfill the command [Acts 1:7, 8].) The commission is clearly related to Christ's authority by the word *therefore*. Two meanings are possible: (1) all authority is behind the command; and (2) all authority belongs to Christ so those commanded to go can do so in that assurance. Both are true. But though the former meaning is usually assumed in this case, the latter possibility should not be overlooked.

The word which is translated "go" is a participle in the original and not an imperative. It should probably be translated "going" or "as you go." But that should not be allowed to blunt the force of the word. The same construction is found in Acts 16:9: "Come over and [or, coming over] help us." Obviously, if Paul does not "come" he cannot "help"! And if we do not "go" we cannot accomplish our mission. On the other hand, the emphasis is not on the "going" but upon the reason for going.

"Make disciples" is the sole imperative and the central activity indicated in the Great Commission. To make converts and believers is certainly involved. But faith and discipleship can never be divorced. Obedience is required, not just on the part of the one who takes the message, but also on the part of the one who listens, repents, and believes the gospel. "Converts" and "believers" *as popularly conceived* might "do their own thing." But "disciples" obviously must do the will of their Master.

"Of all the nations" has reference to the Gentiles, who, as we have seen, are now to be brought into the Church on the same basis as the Jews. Previously, our Lord had sent His disciples to "the lost sheep of the house of Israel" (Matt. 10:6). Gentiles had not been included. Why? Because God was still dealing with Israel as a people. Christ had not been rejected and crucified. All was not ready. But following the crucifixion and the resurrection, the gospel could go to the Gentiles also.

"Baptizing them in the name . . ." has reference to the means or method by which disciples are made. In the original, "baptizing" is a participle which derives imperatival force from the main verb. Converts are to be baptized *into* [*eis*] the name of the Father, and the Son, and the Holy

Spirit. This implies that they come into the ownership of the Triune God.

"Teaching them to observe all..." is parallel to the former participial construction. Disciples are made by a process of baptizing *and* teaching. And what is to be taught? All that Christ has commanded. Man lives by "every word that proceeds out of the mouth of God" (Matt. 4:4).

"Lo, I am with you always...." No one who is sent, and goes, goes alone. Christ Himself accompanies His servants to the ends of the earth and until the consummation of the age.

Though the most complete and oft-quoted statement of the Great Commission is found in Matthew 28, parallel passages should not be overlooked. They serve to underscore its central motifs (see Figure 1).

A comparison of these varied statements of the Great Commission clearly shows that they are neither redundant nor contradictory. They are complementary. In an effort to make a case for a social understanding of the Christian mission some interpreters have concluded that the Johannine statement takes precedence over the Synoptic statements. These interpreters say that our Lord's use of the phrase "as the Father has sent Me" indicates that our commission is to continue the ministry that He began in the world. Of course, there is a sense in which we *are* to continue His ministry. But these interpreters quickly move on to the passage in Luke 7:19–23 where John the Baptist sent his disciples to Jesus to ask Him if He indeed was the one who should come (i.e., the Messiah). Jesus' answer was concise and clear: "Go . . . tell John . . . how that the blind see, the lame walk, the lepers are cleansed, the deaf hear, the dead are raised, to the poor the gospel is preached" (KJV). This, these interpreters say, is the work that we are to carry on. And so, putting the other statements of the Great Commission aside, they place ministries of healing and social betterment, and the struggle for justice, at the very heart of our mission.

FIGURE 1

Complementary Statements of the Great Commission*

The Statements	The Authority	The Enablement	The Sphere	The Message	The Activities
1. Matt. 28:18–20	The authority given to Christ ("all authority in heaven and earth")	Christ is with us to the very end of the age	The nations (Gentiles)	All things Christ has commanded	Disciple by going, baptizing, and teaching
2. Mark 16:15			All the world (". . . all creation")	The gospel	Go and preach (proclaim)
3. Luke 24:46–49	In His (Christ's) name	Promise of the Father . . . power	All the nations beginning from Jerusalem	Repentance and the forgiveness of sins	Preach (proclaim) and witness
4. John 20:21	Sent by Christ as He was sent by the Father				
5. Acts 1:8		Power of the Holy Spirit	Jerusalem, all Judea, Samaria, and even to the remotest part of the earth	Christ	Witness

*From David J. Hesselgrave, *Communicating Christ Cross-Culturally* (Grand Rapids: Zondervan, 1978), p. 54.

Now there can be no question but that believers are created in Christ unto good works (Eph. 2:10) and that they are to "do good unto all men, especially unto them who are of the household of faith" (Gal. 6:10, KJV). And if one is disposed to say that all things that believers are commanded of God to do constitute their mission in the world, there is a sense in which we can agree. But to say that good works constitute the *Great* Commission, or the *heart* of our mission, or that the Johannine statement supersedes the Synoptic statements, is to fly in the face of sound exegesis and clear thinking. Neither the grammar nor the context of John 20 will support it. Furthermore, in Luke 7 Jesus was clearly substantiating His messiahship by reference to that miraculous ministry which John, familiar as he was with Old Testament prophecy, had been openly anticipating. The passage as such does not constitute a divine mandate for the continuing exercise of miracles or for the attempt to reproduce them as nearly as possible by the application of medicine or social and political redress.

In sum, the Johannine statement of the Great Commission does not change the direction of the statements in the Synoptic Gospels. Rather, it underscores the authority behind our mission to disciple the nations by preaching, baptizing, and teaching. To allow any understanding of mission to obscure the proclamatory, sacramental, and didactic responsibility of the Church is to put the knife to the heart of the Christian mission. To substitute other activities for those distinctly specified by our Lord is to attempt a "heart transplant"—one that sooner or later certainly will be rejected.

Pentecost

The event that was decisive for the expansion of Christianity was Pentecost. One would be hard put to argue successfully that the early Christians were inspired to carry out the Great Commission by reminding each other of its provisions and importance. Rather, the Holy Spirit came upon those early believers and transformed them into witnesses even as the Lord had promised. According to Acts 1:8, He had told them that when the Holy Spirit came upon them, they would (1) receive needed power or strength; (2) become witnesses or "testifiers" of the Christ whom they had seen and heard and in whom they believed; and (3) go to Jerusalem, Judea, Samaria, and the ends of the earth. After the Holy Spirit came, they discovered experientially that the *Holy* Spirit is also the "*Missionary* Spirit." *He* obeyed the Commission in and through them.[2]

And what was the result? Luke informs us that following Pentecost "the Lord was adding to their number day by day those who were being saved" (Acts 2:47). He tells us that when the Jerusalem disciples were scattered by persecution, they "went about preaching the Word" (Acts 8:4). After the persecution, the churches in Judea, Galilee, and Samaria "enjoyed peace, being built up; and, going on in the fear of the Lord and in the comfort of the Holy Spirit, continued to increase" (Acts 9:31). In Antioch, "a large number who believed turned to the Lord" (Acts 11:21).

Again, Luke reports that when Paul and Silas went through Syria and Cilicia, confirming the churches that had been established previously, the churches were "strengthened in the faith, and were increasing in number daily" (Acts 16:5). Francis Schaeffer has summed it up in unequivocal words: "'Now there were at the church that was at Antioch. . . .' Thus, here was a functioning local congregation called 'the church.' From here on the New Testament clearly indicates that churches were formed wherever some became Christians."[3]

---

[2]Harry R. Boer, *Pentecost and Missions* (Grand Rapids: Eerdmans, 1961).

[3]Francis Schaeffer, *The Church at the End of the Twentieth Century* (Downers Grove, IL: Inter-Varsity Press, 1970), p. 60.

Paul and the Mission of the Church

The man who was especially charged with the responsibility of taking the gospel to the Gentiles, and upon whose
missionary ministry the New Testament focuses, is the
apostle Paul. His ministry, therefore, is of special importance to an understanding of our mission.

Roland Allen, with his experienced eye as a true missionary statesman trained on the ministry of Paul in order
to bring the mission into clear focus, concluded:

> In a little more than ten years St. Paul established the
> Church in four provinces of the Empire; Galatia,
> Macedonia, Achaia, and Asia. Before A.D. 57 St. Paul
> could speak as if his work there was done, and could plan
> extensive tours into the far West without anxiety lest the
> churches which he had founded might perish in his ab-
> sence for want of his guidance and support.
> The work of the Apostle during these ten years can
> therefore be treated as a unity. Whatever assistance he may
> have received from the preaching of others, it is unques-
> tioned that the establishment of the churches in these prov-
> inces was really his work. In the pages of the New Testa-
> ment he, and he alone, stands forth as their founder. And
> the work which he did was really a completed work. So far
> as the foundation of the churches is concerned, it is per-
> fectly clear that the writer of the Acts intends to represent
> St. Paul's work as complete. The churches were really es-
> tablished. Whatever disasters fell upon them, in later years,
> whatever failure there was, whatever ruin, that failure was
> not due to any insufficiency or lack of care and complete-
> ness in the Apostle's teaching or organization. When he left
> them, he left them because his work was fully accom-
> plished.[4]

And why was Paul so successful? There were many reasons, of course. But one important reason was that Paul
considered the preaching of the gospel and the establish-

---

[4]Roland Allen, *Missionary Methods: St. Paul's or Ours?* (Grand Rapids:
Eerdmans, 1962), p. 3.

ment of churches as his primary task. The biblical record leaves no room for thinking that either Paul or the members of his team were basically engaged in raising living standards, ameliorating social conditions, imparting secular knowledge, ministering to medical needs, or dispensing aid from previously established churches. There can be little doubt that allegiance to Christ on the part of converts in the churches entailed some of these effects as by-products—even to the sending of needed aid *back* to the Jerusalem church (a kind of "reverse flow"). That the missionaries were concerned about social relationships, and the minds and bodies of men as well as their souls, is patently true. *But Paul's primary mission was accomplished when the gospel was preached, men were converted, and churches were established.* Obedience to the Great Commandment to love one's neighbor was part of the commission to teach *all* things Christ commanded. But good works were the *fruit*—not the *root*—of Paul's mission. As Paul Benjamin expresses it:

It would be well at this point to remember Paul's practice. Were there no poor in Corinth? Were there no race problems in Ephesus? Did all the children in Asia Minor have enough to wear? Paul's letters to the congregations in various cities demonstrate his deep concern for the poor and socially disenfranchised (Gal. 2:10). He exhorts the Christians in Corinth to follow the example of other congregations in taking up a generous offering for the poverty stricken saints of Jerusalem (2 Cor. 8, 9). Yet his uniform practice in spreading the gospel of love and brotherly concern was to establish congregations. To ignore the apostolic practice, then, is to overlook the very heart of the methodology whereby the gospel spread around the Mediterranean in the first century. Furthermore, it overlooks a vital way by which the spiritual and physical needs of people may be met.[5]

⁵Paul Benjamin, *The Growing Congregation* (Cincinnati: Standard Publishing, 1972), pp. 5–6.

No wonder Paul was so effective in multiplying believers and churches. Not only was he a gifted, Spirit-controlled man, he had a singleness and clarity of objective that have escaped many of his successors. He gave all of his boundless energy and unusual abilities to the building of the Church of Jesus Christ!

The Church and Its Mission in the Modern Era

If there is confusion as concerns the heart of our mission today, it does not stem from the Scriptures but from the blinders devised by history, and other blinders of our own making.

An Understanding of Mission
That Is Too Broad

The Reformers of the sixteenth and seventeenth centuries recovered the *message* of the Church, but (for the most part) were too preoccupied with the problems of Europe to give much impetus to mission in other parts of the world. It remained for the Pietists, Moravians, and a Baptist by the name of William Carey to recover the sense of urgency to take the gospel to the whole world.

The great missionary advance of the nineteenth century evidenced the fact that missionaries were not always clear as to their objectives, however. Mission took the forms of establishing schools and hospitals, opposing inhumane practices such as suttee and footbinding, and launching campaigns for sanitation. Christians can be justly proud of the great achievements of loyal sons and daughters who accomplished these tasks at the cost of great personal sacrifice. They deserve to be applauded by all people, and emulated by contemporary Christians. But in and of themselves, these worthy activities did not make disciples nor did they establish churches. Thus when history bequeaths to us either the misunderstanding that the mission of the Church consists in any worthy enterprise Christians may undertake, or institutions and enterprises that deter us from our *primary* task, history does us a disservice. For our own part, we moderns have tended to perpetuate confusion at this point. We have multiplied parachurch missions as "arms of the Church" in order to undertake every conceivable type of good work from feeding the hungry to immunizing populations against disease to introducing new strains of corn and cattle. These are worthy endeavors and according to Galatians 6:10 qualify as Christian undertakings. But organizations formed to accomplish them do not really qualify as *missions* unless upon entering needy areas they keep the "Church's primary *mission* primary." This is so important that, in areas where it is possible to proclaim the gospel and form churches, only organizations that support evangelism and church-planting in a significant way should be thought of as missions. If they do not engage in or support evangelism and church-planting, they are not only parachurch, they are paramission.

An Understanding of Evangelism That Is Too Narrow

If history sometimes affords us an understanding of mission that is too broad (in the above sense), it also provides us with an understanding of evangelism that is too narrow. In the last decades of the nineteenth century and in the present century, evangelism has become identified too closely with great campaigns or crusades designed to win individuals to a commitment to Jesus Christ. This on the one hand. And on the other hand there have developed a number of carefully-thought-out methods of personal evangelism with the same end in view. Both campaign evangelism and personal evangelism are to be encouraged. But as often practiced they do not place new

believers in vital contact with local churches. *Proportionately, too much emphasis has been placed upon multiplying converts—and not nearly enough emphasis has been placed on multiplying congregations.*
It is true that to evangelize means to "gospelize"—to spread the Good News of Christ. But in the New Testament, evangelism does not stand alone. Return to the statement of Francis Schaeffer referred to earlier and see what he has to say further on:

> Thus, here [at Antioch] was a functioning local congregation called "the church." From here on the New Testament clearly indicates that churches were formed wherever some became Christians.
>
> In a sense we have a complete picture of what the church ought to be: Individuals were becoming Christians, but not individualistic ones; the congregation covered the full spectrum of society; the members were all tellers, not only at home but abroad. And when the Holy Spirit said that Barnabas and Saul should be sent on the first missionary journey, the members did not function only as individual Christians, but as a unit, as a church.[6]

Schaeffer puts his finger on a crucial issue. If people had become individualistic Christians without a commitment to, and participation in, local churches, how would the Church have moved forward in her mission to disciple the nations? As Basil Mathews writes, one important reason why the Church of the early centuries triumphed in the Roman Empire was that

> the little "cells" or "societies of the Way of Jesus" enjoyed a community life never before achieved. Here was a new society with a new power to practice a new way of life, because it was living in fellowship with the perfect Man who is one with God.
>
> This Christian church became the best organized community in all the empire. Its local churches were living cells

---

[6]Schaeffer, *The Church at the End of the Twentieth Century*, p. 60.

in a far-flung body covering every part of the empire. They were linked together by the travels of the bishops. They found fellowship in smaller and greater councils, through common ways of worship, through reading the same Scriptures, and, above all, through burning loyalty to and communion with one ever-living Christ.[7]

So intimate is the relationship between gospel proclamation and church-planting that they cannot be divorced without doing violence to the mission of the Church. Notice how the church-growth specialist, Donald McGavran, defines evangelism: "Increasingly the primary assignment of missions is evangelism: the proclamation of the Good News and assisting in the emergence of churches which, rooted in the soil and with their own leaders, will be witnesses to the Good News."[8]

Putting Mission and Evangelism Together Again

We should be grateful for men like Bartholomew Ziegenbalg, Gustav Warneck, Henry Venn, Rufus Anderson, John Nevius, Roland Allen, and Donald McGavran. Spanning more than two centuries, they have reminded us that whatever else of good may issue from our obedience to the Great Commission, it must also result in the establishment of churches among the peoples of the world. We should thank God for Kenneth Strachan, Francis Schaeffer, Michael Green, and others who have reminded us that New Testament evangelism results in new converts coming into the Christian fellowship of congregations new and old, and in new congregations being established in communities around the world.

---

[7]Basil Mathews, *Forward Through the Ages* (New York: Friendship Press, 1960), pp. 17–18.
[8]Donald McGavran, *The Bridges of God* (New York: Friendship Press, 1955), Introduction.

It is instructive that Ralph Winter, who had earlier written about M-1, M-2, and M-3 *mission*, could so easily change the nomenclature to E-1, E-2, and E-3 *evangelism* at the International Congress on World Evangelization at Lausanne and mean essentially the same thing.[9] Does he not know that missionaries are often engaged in educational, medical, linguistic, and other ministries in which evangelists as we know them seldom become involved? Of course he does. But his primary concern is with *mission narrowly defined* as winning people to Christ and establishing churches. And he is concerned with *evangelism broadly defined* so as to include the same objective. Accordingly, he might well have used the designations ME-1, ME-2, and ME-3.

In this book we will use the hyphenated terms *mission-evangelism* and *missionary-evangelist,* and the designation *ME,* in order to communicate the idea that the two go together. When we are talking about the "heart of the Christian mission" and the larger implications of evangelism, the two are really inseparable. Although on occasion, in order to avoid redundancy, we may use these words separately, they are to be understood as having essentially the same meaning.

Winter has also made a helpful contribution by his use of numbers (ME-1, ME-2, ME-3) to indicate the cultural distance involved in carrying out our task. Geography as such does not affect the goal of the Church in mission. The words of our Lord in Acts 1:8 are important here. Grammarians are quick to point out that the Greek construction in Acts 1:8 binds "Jerusalem," "Judea," "Samaria," and the "uttermost parts" together in one inseparable entity. (Southern Baptists, therefore, are scrip-

---

[9]Ralph Winter, "The Highest Priority: Cross-Cultural Evangelism," in *Let the Earth Hear His Voice,* ed. J. D. Douglas (Minneapolis: World Wide Publications, 1975), pp. 213–25.

tural when they refer to a beginning church as a "mission" whether it is located in Asia or North America!) What changes as we go from place to place (and sometimes as we stay in one place) is the cultural adaptation that must be made in order to meaningfully communicate the message and "grow a church." With this in mind, Winter uses the numbers 1 to 3 in order to indicate the degree of cultural distance involved when a missionary-evangelist moves out to obey the Great Commission. Of course, the degree of cultural distance depends upon both the cultural orientation of the missionary-evangelist and that of his audience.

For example, when a Swedish-American in Los Angeles wins other Swedish-Americans to Christ and establishes them in churches, he has not surmounted any significant cultural barrier whatsoever. That is ME-1 mission-evangelism. If he were to win Los Angeles Latinos, the cultural distance traversed likely would be much greater. That would be ME-2 mission-evangelism. But if the Swedish-American were to go to Venezuela and learn an entirely new language and culture in order to communicate Christ and plant churches, the cultural distance would be greater still. That would be ME-3 mission-evangelism. Notice again that geographical distance per se has little to do with the difference. If the Swedish-American Christian were to learn Spanish and adapt to the culture of new Venezuelan immigrants in the Los Angeles area, that might still be ME-3 mission-evangelism.

We will use these designations in this book. In the first place, they constitute a neat sort of shorthand. Secondly, they are widely used by all who are familiar with church-growth materials. Thirdly, they bring mission and evangelism together in one formula. Finally, they call attention to the fact that while mission and message do not change, our methods will change as we encounter cultural differences. (It must be borne in mind that in assigning numbers 1, 2, or 3, we have taken a North American perspective.)

Today's Priority—Cross-Cultural Church-Planting

Ralph Winter's indefatigable mind did not stop with the distinction between ME-1, ME-2, and ME-3 mission-evangelism. At Lausanne and subsequently he has emphasized that the Church's highest priority today must be to cross cultural boundaries in order to win people to Christ and establish communities of Christians. If we are to fulfill the Great Commission we must recapture the pioneer spirit and move out to unreached people everywhere. To make clear what is involved Winter divides the world's population into four categories.[10]

First, there are 219 million "active Christians" in the world. They represent both a tremendous potential and an ever-present danger. The potential is that they can win others to the faith. The danger is that they may become ingrown and occupy themselves with nurturing their own faith rather than winning others.

Second, there are 1,000 million "inactive Christians." They are within the Christian tradition but are not committed Christians. They need renewal or what we might call "ME-0 mission-evangelism" since no significant cultural barrier has to be crossed in reaching them. They represent a great potential for the Church because they are relatively easily reached. But they also represent a danger because active Christians tend to expend most of their resources of time and money in reaching them.

Third, there are 500 million "culturally near non-Christians" in the world. They live within cultures that have already been penetrated by the Christian faith. They may be geographically distant from active Christian churches, but any cultural barriers that exist are minimal

---

[10]Ralph D. Winter, "Penetrating the New Frontiers," in *Unreached Peoples '79: The Challenge of the Church's Unfinished Business,* ed. C. Peter Wagner and Edward R. Dayton (Elgin, IL: David C. Cook, 1978), pp. 46–49.

and may be largely of the Christians' own making. Sensitive ME-1 mission-evangelism is needed here.

Fourth, there are 2,500 million "culturally distant non-Christians." These people may or may not be far removed from active Christians geographically. But they are far removed linguistically, socially, economically, and culturally. In no way can they be expected to come into existing congregations. New churches must be planted among them. But the cultural distance involved makes many of them all but invisible. They are the "hidden peoples"! We must first "see" them. Then, depending upon the situation, ME-2 or ME-3 mission-evangelism will be required to reach them.

This analysis is most perceptive. It graphically communicates the immensity of the task. It also indicates a strategy. Namely, identify cultural groupings, especially among the hidden unreached peoples of the world, and devise strategies for planting believing congregations among them. Priorities must be rearranged if the Church is to reach the whole world for Christ. It is all too easy to concentrate on those who are near us and most like us, while neglecting those who are far away. "Out of sight, out of mind," tends to be the case with believers as well as unbelievers.

But our task is both/and, not either/or. Many—perhaps most—of the 1,000 million "inactive Christians" are Christians only in name. Rather than being Christians who need renewal, they are unbelievers who need regeneration. Sometimes, the cultural barriers between evangelical ("active") Christians and nominals ("inactive Christians") loom as large as do the barriers between evangelicals and "culturally near non-Christians." Furthermore, though many cultural barriers between evangelicals and both of these groups are of our own making as evangelicals, we must recognize that Western culture as a whole is becoming post-Christian. This means that barriers erected out of the world views of naturalism and humanism are becoming very real. As Francis Schaeffer reminds us, unless we take these barriers into account, our evangelistic communication will be understood by an ever-decreasing number of people in the West. Thus we must keep our near neighbors in mind while we focus on more than 16,000 subcultures around the world where no Christian church yet exists.[11]

Let every denomination, every mission, every congregation, and every Christian take a fresh look at all four of Winter's categories and ask themselves what they are doing among these respective peoples. Where people are geographically and culturally accessible to existing churches, let us call them into fellowship with Christ and His Church. Where they are not, let us cross geographical and cultural barriers in order to preach Christ and plant the Church! This book is designed to aid true Christians in this latter task. In it we do not distinguish between ME-0 and ME-1 church-planting evangelism. The vast majority of church-planting situations today entail some measure of cultural adaptation.

Allow me to quote a recent graduate of Trinity Evangelical Divinity School (identified only as "B.A.") as he wrote in the school paper concerning Trinity and the Evangelical Free Church.

There's a new wind blowing, and it's wafting our way, soon to turn into a gale. Its theme is reflected in this simple little epigram:

If you want to grow something to last a season—
plant flowers.
If you want to grow something to last a lifetime—
plant trees.
If you want to grow something to last through eternity—
plant churches.

---

[11]Carl F. H. Henry, "Evangelicals: Out of the Closet but Going Nowhere?" *Christianity Today*, vol. 24, no. 1 (1980), pp. 16–22.

And that's the clarion the Holy Spirit is sounding louder and clearer each day: "I will build my church!"

Consider, for example, the situation at Trinity. Last year approximately a dozen grads applied for pastorates in the Free Church. This year almost four times that number appear to be following God's leading into the EFCA. Where are they going to put all of us? Or the projected fifty-plus for next year? Or the projected sixty-plus for the next year, and seventy-five for each year after that! There simply aren't enough churches to go around. Let us watch and pray that the Holy Spirit uses this situation to prod our beloved Free Church into an accelerated church-planting program.

Or how about your own local church? Let's think practically. Is it growing? Perhaps ten percent a year? Now, even without using banking terms such as "compounded annually," and so forth, a church of 500 could expect 750 in five years. If they put out 25 percent more effort in discipling, they could easily have 1,000 to 1,200 in seven years. Do they really want to be that big? Are they planning ahead for such numbers? Probably 750 is large enough for the mother church. How about starting three to five satellite congregations in the next five to seven years to handle the overflow and reach the community more effectively? AHA! Church planting.[12]

Call it, then, what you will. Call it "church-planting," "church development," "church growth," or "church extension evangelism." Or call it "mission-evangelism." The task is the same anywhere in the world. Any community of people without an accessible church—whether they reside in North America or South Africa—is a mission field. And it is the responsibility of believers in existing churches to fill those spiritual voids with believing congregations. As has often been remarked, neither a missionless church nor a churchless mission is in accordance with the plan of God. The same must be said for an unevangelistic church and a churchless evangelism. As Donald McGavran writes, mis-

---

[12]"The Free Church—Going to Seed. A Prophecy," *The Scribe* (Trinity Evangelical Divinity School), Spring 1976, no. 1, p. 7.

FIGURE 2
The Heart of the Mission

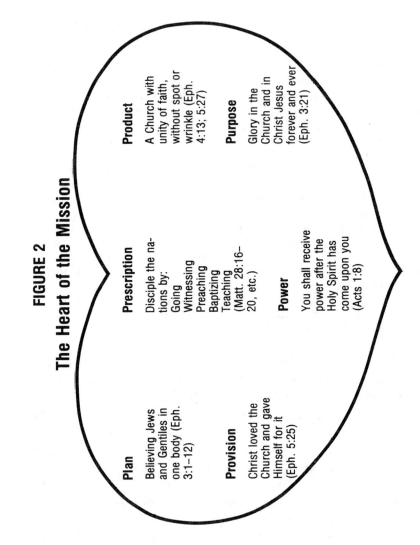

Plan

Believing Jews and Gentiles in one body (Eph. 3:1–12)

Provision

Christ loved the Church and gave Himself for it (Eph. 5:25)

Prescription

Disciple the nations by:
Going
Witnessing
Preaching
Baptizing
Teaching
(Matt. 28:16–20, etc.)

Power

You shall receive power after the Holy Spirit has come upon you (Acts 1:8)

Product

A Church with unity of faith, without spot or wrinkle (Eph. 4:13; 5:27)

Purpose

Glory in the Church and in Christ Jesus forever and ever (Eph. 3:21)

sion is "an enterprise devoted to proclaiming the good news of Christ and persuading men to become disciples and dependable members of his church."[13] And those who are sent to accomplish this basic task are missionaries and evangelists in the best sense of these words. To be sure, to win men of other world views, languages, and customs to Christ and to establish them in congregations of believers require special training and tools. And while it will be helpful, therefore, to use designations such as ME-1, ME-2, and ME-3 in order to denote the degree of cultural adaptation that will be necessary, we must keep in mind that, at its heart, our mission is the same irrespective of where it is performed or who constitutes our audience. And it is what the Church—and churches and missions—should be doing, and doing as effectively as they can, and doing now (see Figure 2)!

---

[13]Donald McGavran, *Understanding Church Growth* (Grand Rapids: Eerdmans, 1970), p. 34.

two

Method and Mission

Planning for the Task

The churches are "task forces." They have a job to do. But altogether too often the job is undertaken haphazardly and without thinking it through. A missionary once (probably facetiously) objected to planning on the basis that Abraham "went out not knowing whither he went." It was pointed out to the missionary that the analogy breaks down. Abraham didn't know where he was going, but he knew what he was going to do when he got there. If this missionary took his philosophy seriously, he knew where he was going but not what he was going to do when he got there!

The Bible has abundant evidence of God's plan. God is the greatest Planner of all! Before creation He devised a plan for man and history that took every contingency into account. When Christ was ministering on earth, He had a plan for deploying His disciples and getting the kingdom message to the "lost sheep of the house of Israel" (Matt.

10:1–42). After His death and resurrection He revealed the basics of His plan for the discipling of the Gentile nations (Matt. 28:18–20; Acts 1:8). During the period covered by the Book of Acts the Holy Spirit had a plan to fulfill the Great Commission even when the apostles didn't, and increasingly that plan became a matter of discussion and deliberation on the part of His people. Finally, Paul presents the Church in which Jew and Gentile participate on an equal basis, not as an afterthought or even a back-up plan, but as part of the eternal plan of God though only now fully revealed (Eph. 3:1–12).

Is it not peculiar that God had a plan for history; that ordered households make budgets, plan weekly schedules, and plan for the education of the children; but that the churches and missions often have no well-thought-out and prayed-about plan for the most important task of all? Is it not sad that, since God cannot count on obedience and wise stewardship in this matter, He often has to use church splits and ad hoc means to get new congregations of believers started? How much better it would be if we had a plan—His plan!

How does one develop a plan for winning men to Christ and planting growing churches? Experts tell us that there are six steps involved in planning for the accomplishment of any task:

(1) Understand the task.
(2) Compare the task with experience and research (identify helpful and useless approaches).
(3) Make an overall plan to accomplish the task.
(4) Gather the necessary resources.
(5) Execute the plan.
(6) Learn from experience (and use what is learned to modify the plan).[1]

---

[1] *Planning and PERT* (Program Evaluation and Review Technique) (Monrovia, CA: Communication Center, 1966).

The steps can be better understood if we plot them on a simplified planning chart. The chart helps us understand what is involved in the various steps. It is basically self-explanatory and needs no elaboration at this point. It should be noted that in this book we are primarily concerned with the first three steps of the planning chart. It should be borne in mind, however, that as important as planning is, the exercise will mean little until we go on to gather our resources, execute the plan, and learn from our own experiences so we can modify the plan as new understandings and circumstances may require (see Figure 3).

Three Sources of Missiology

Missiology is the study of the mission of the Church. There are three basic sources of information which are important for developing an effective missiology (see Figure 4):

(1) Revelation (Scripture investigation).
(2) Research (scientific observation).
(3) Reflection (sound thinking based on experience and knowledge).

Revelation

Notice that the Scriptures are first in order of importance. They are the only completely authoritative rule of faith and practice. Apart from them our understanding of God would be limited and our knowledge of His plan for the calling out of the Church of Christ would be negligible or nonexistent. If we are to do His work we must give attention to His Word. No true Christian would dispute this.

Of course, to settle the problem of ultimate authority

FIGURE 3

A Simplified Planning Chart*

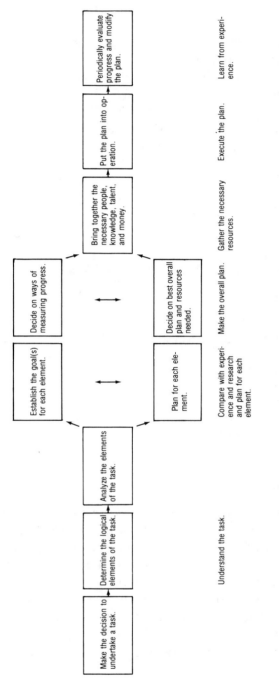

*Based upon PERT (Program Evaluation and Review Technique), developed by the Navy Special Projects Office in 1959 and elaborated by Missions Advanced Research and Communication Center, Monrovia, California.

FIGURE 4

Three Sources of Missiology

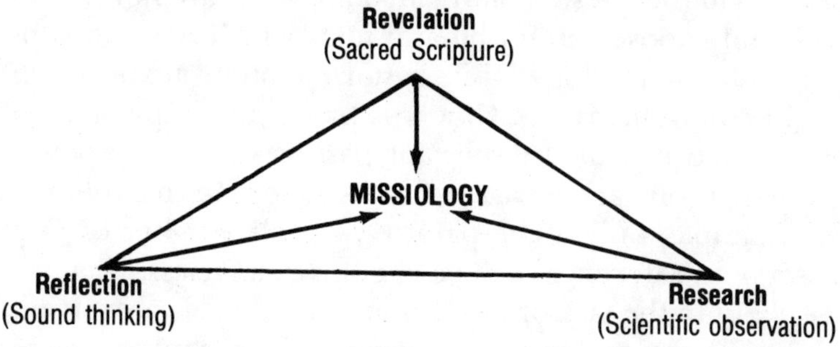

Revelation
(Sacred Scripture)

MISSIOLOGY

Reflection
(Sound thinking)

Research
(Scientific observation)

does not of itself produce a defensible hermeneutic. Sound hermeneutical principles must govern the determination of practice even as they govern the determination of doctrine. To adequately discuss those principles would take us far beyond the bounds of the present study. But before we proceed, we should mention three principles which have a bearing on "trouble spots" in missiology.

(1) Scripture must be interpreted within its own context. It is all too easy to fall into the trap of allowing our contemporary culture and experience to determine our understanding of the biblical text.

For example, recent Church Growth literature has made much of the reference to the *ethnē* in the Great Commission. Church Growth proponents have insisted that *ethnē* means the "tribes, castes, peoples, and families of mankind"—that is, the homogeneous units which are so important to Church Growth strategy. As Walter Liefeld and others have clearly demonstrated, however, this is to impose current anthropological and sociological understandings upon the Scripture. Of the various Greek terms which could have been used to refer to the tribes, castes, and other homogeneous groupings of mankind, the term *ethnē* is the weakest one. In the New Testament context *ethnē* clearly means "Gentiles."[2]

(2) The whole of relevant Scripture must be brought to bear upon the question at hand. That is, we are not free to pick and choose certain biblical texts which seem to support our conclusions while ignoring other texts which might contradict them. Now it is practically impossible to explicitly bring all the relevant passages to bear upon a given issue on each occasion it is discussed. In this volume, for example, only a comparatively small number of Old Testament references will be cited. Nevertheless, what we are about in the task of proclaiming the gospel, converting men to Christ, and building them into local churches rests upon the foundation of Old Testament revelation and is in no way antithetical to it. It is true to Old Testament teachings of creation, the fall of man, the redemptive purposes of God, and the mission of the people of God in the world. Similarly, even though a great number of New Testament texts will be cited, by no means can all of the relevant passages be brought to bear upon any given issue. That being the case, our conclusions are true only to the degree that they are consonant with all relevant texts. They are true only to the degree that we have cited basic representative texts and interpreted these texts correctly. They are true only to the extent that we have not ignored relevant texts that might lead us to modify our conclusions.

(3) The *teaching* of the Word of God concerning any given question must take precedence over the *record of events* that occurred in Bible times. This principle cuts to the heart of a crucial problem in missiology, and indeed, in theology. The issue has to do with distinguishing between that which is normative in Scripture and that which is purely descriptive. It has, and will, come into focus over and over again within these pages, especially in view of the

---

[2]Walter Liefeld, "Theology of Church Growth," in *Theology and Mission*, ed. David J. Hesselgrave (Grand Rapids: Baker, 1978), p. 175.

fact that we make numerous references to the Book of Acts.

The problem we face becomes apparent when we press any narrative portion of Scripture too far. For example, if the *experience* of the disciples on Pentecost is made normative we will be inclined to earnestly seek and wait for one of the gifts of the Spirit (glossolalia) which, according to the *teaching* of I Corinthians 12–14, is not for all believers and not to be coveted (i.e., eagerly desired).

Again, if we go too far and insist that the description of the Jerusalem church in Acts 2:41–47 be made normative for all churches, then private ownership on the part of Christians becomes suspect. But actually, of course, Christianity does not require communalism of this kind.

The same principle holds true in the case of the church of Antioch and the missionary strategy of Paul to which we will shortly turn. Descriptions of historical events and people furnish us with important information and examples (good and bad), but they yield norms only to the degree to which explicit doctrinal or teaching passages reinforce them.

Research

The word *research* in this context should not be viewed in the narrow sense of "controlled experiment" but as referring to understandings growing out of the social sciences. When it comes to this second source of missiology, however, many earnest Christians will be tempted to raise an objection. Their commitment to God as the Source of all wisdom and power seems to necessitate a rejection of the world's wisdom and its accomplishments. In a way, it is peculiar that this presents a problem to these Christians because they unhesitatingly utilize the airplanes, radios, and medicines that result from research in aeronautics, electronics, and chemistry. In another way, however, the problem is understandable. Social sciences such as history, management, communication, psychology, anthropology, sociology, and comparative religion seem to be of quite a different order than engineering and medicine. There is a different "feel" in using a radio wave than there is in using a principle of persuasion! In one case we are manipulating dials. In the other case we may be manipulating people! The problem is not new to the twentieth century. Many centuries ago Augustine faced the question of whether or not the knowledge that he had learned in the schools of his day (he was a rhetorician) could be used in building the kingdom of God.[3] His brilliant mind grappled with this problem, as it did with all the major issues of his day. His conclusion, therefore, is most important for us: *All* truth belongs to God and can be used for kingdom purposes. He drew an analogy from the experience of the children of Israel who were commanded to take some of the riches of Egypt for their use en route to the Promised Land. Since much of his knowledge of rhetoric had come from Alexandria, his analogy was particularly apt. Gold from Egypt is still gold! It can be utilized during our pilgrim walk with God. Augustine's works are a witness to the effectiveness with which "Egyptian gold" was utilized by that great scholar and saint.

Augustine did introduce three important cautions (two explicit and one implicit) concerning the use of the world's knowledge, however. First, in this "transfer of Egyptian gold" we should observe the maxim, "Nothing in excess." Second, we should remember that while some pagan knowledge is useful to the Christian, the amount is quantitatively small when compared to that which is derivable from the Scriptures. Third, it is everywhere apparent in Augustine's work in which the problem is treated (*On Christian Doctrine*) that the Scripture is the *standard of*

---

[3]Augustine, *On Christian Doctrine*, trans. D. W. Robertson, Jr. (New York: The Liberal Arts Press, 1958), Book II.

truth—Egyptian gold that does not measure up is not real gold but fool's gold!

Augustine's cautions should be taken seriously. Egyptian gold can be fashioned into golden calves! There is a real danger that when we come to understand what is happening on the plain, we will forget what is happening on the mountain! For example, there is real value in understanding what happens psychologically when a person becomes a Christian. But once we understand it, we must exercise care lest the psychological process involved becomes so absorbing that we forget that the all-important elements in conversion are conviction and illumination by the Third Person of the Trinity. No unsaved psychologist can understand or appreciate that fact. But the Christian can and must!

Reflection

Few would argue that thinking is unchristian! But that fact alone does not assure us that good thinking will occur—much less that it will prevail—in the service of Christ. Our Lord directed His first-century servants to be "shrewd as serpents and innocent as doves" (Matt. 10:16b). The simile of the dove seems appropriate enough, but why the simile of the serpent? Why, if not to get His point across? The fact of the matter is that those who rely on "Christ's sense" are often tempted to disregard "common sense." How often have I heard successful businessmen comment that if their businesses were run as the business of the Church is sometimes run, they would soon be bankrupt! To the degree that this is so, no credit accrues to the people of God. All shrewdness is not scriptural, but there is a scriptural shrewdness. Common sense mixes well with spiritual sense!

In his classic work *Planting and Development of Missionary Churches,* John L. Nevius emphasizes two tests of any plan for church-planting: "adaptability to the end in view, and Scripture authority."[4] He links adaptability to analysis of our past experiences. If we think clearly, history can serve as a guide to the future. Moreover, he insists that any plan which can pass *both* tests "has a much stronger claim upon our regard and acceptance than a plan which can claim the sanction of one test."[5] In other words, rely on God's revelation but do not neglect to reflect on past successes and failures. Much can be learned from them.

The Logical Elements of the Missionary Task

The missionary task of the Church must be understood in the light of biblical revelation. We have already touched upon this in a preliminary way, noting that the activities involved include witnessing, preaching, discipling, baptizing, and teaching. Just how these elements fit together in practice can perhaps best be seen in the ministry of the apostle Paul and his colleagues as they planted churches throughout the Roman Empire. Paul was the master builder of the Church in New Testament times (I Cor. 3:10). He was the church-planter par excellence!

Pauline Strategy and Methodology

There can be little doubt that insofar as we have in the New Testament an example of sound strategy for planting growing churches, we have it in the strategy of Paul. After giving us a brief record of the role of Peter and others in taking the gospel beyond the bounds of the Jewish community, Luke devotes the lion's share of his attention to the ministry of Paul and his coworkers. Much of the rest of

---

[4]John L. Nevius, *Planting and Development of Missionary Churches* (Philadelphia: Presbyterian and Reformed, 1958), p. 8.
[5]Ibid.

the New Testament is made up of Paul's correspondence with churches and their leaders. Certain basic questions have been raised concerning Paul's ministry, however.

Did Paul Actually Have a Strategy?

Our answer to this question will determine how we proceed from this point. If, as Michael Green seems to believe, Paul had little or no strategy, and "the Gospel spread out in an apparently haphazard way as men obeyed the leading of the Spirit, and went through doors he opened,"[6] then all we can learn is dependence upon that same Spirit. If, on the other hand, Donald McGavran is right when he says that while Paul was in Antioch he devised a strategy for reaching a great part of the Mediterranean world with the gospel,[7] then we can learn from Paul's strategy also.

A mediating position seems to square with the data. Green is quite right when he insists that we "must not organize him [Christ] out of the picture" and when he warns against the idea that "efficiency on the evangelistic production line will inevitably produce results."[8] But he seems to overstate his case. If Paul had *no* plan, the Holy Spirit could not have changed it (cf. Acts 16:6–10)! On the other hand, McGavran's argument concerning Paul's strategy for reaching "people on the bridge" (people related to believers) is fascinating and instructive. But at times, McGavran too seems to overstate his case.

J. Herbert Kane's words are worth pondering:

> We might begin by asking: Did Paul have a missionary strategy? Some say yes; others say no. Much depends on the definition of strategy. If by strategy is meant a deliber-

---

[6]Michael Green, "Evangelism in the Early Church," in *Let the Earth Hear His Voice*, ed. J. D. Douglas (Minneapolis: World Wide Publications, 1975), p. 174.

[7]Donald McGavran, *The Bridges of God* (New York: Friendship Press, 1955), pp. 25–35.

[8]Green, "Evangelism in the Early Church," p. 174.

ate, well-formulated, duly executed plan of action based on human observation and experience, then Paul had little or no strategy; but if we take the word to mean a flexible *modus operandi* developed under the guidance of the Holy Spirit and subject to His direction and control, then Paul did have a strategy.

Our problem today is that we live in an anthropocentric age. We imagine that nothing of consequence can be accomplished in the Lord's work without a good deal of ecclesiastical machinery—committees, conferences, workshops, seminars; whereas the early Christians depended less on human wisdom and expertise, more on divine initiative and guidance. It is obvious that they didn't do too badly. What the modern missionary movement needs above everything else is to get back to the missionary methods of the early church.[9]

We tend to agree with Kane's basic position, but we would modify his statement somewhat. Paul, of course, had comparatively little opportunity to base his strategy on observation and experience. But with two thousand years of missions history behind us we should have a "deliberate, well-formulated, duly executed plan of action based on human observation and experience." However, to be Christian, that plan should not be based primarily on human observation. It must be "developed under the guidance of the Holy Spirit and subject to His direction and control." As for flexibility, any strategy that is not flexible is simply bad strategy.

Let's agree, then, that "what the modern missionary movement needs above everything else is to get back to the missionary methods of the early church." That is the starting point. It would be as foolhardy for us to disregard the Holy Spirit-inspired record of the way in which the early Christians, and especially Paul and his cohorts, actually built up the churches of their day as it would have

---

[9]J. Herbert Kane, *Christian Missions in Biblical Perspective* (Grand Rapids: Baker, 1976), p. 73.

been for Paul to disregard the Holy Spirit's guidance received in Arabia and Antioch. At the same time, it would be as unthinkable for us to discount the understanding that has come to us through two thousand years of experience and study as it would have been for Paul to discount the processes of the Hellenization of culture and the religious penetration of Judaism in his own day. Nevertheless, Kane's warning is not to be ignored. If our dependence is on the overall strategy and the method of its implementation rather than on the wisdom and power of the Holy Spirit, we cannot claim to be true to New Testament precedent nor will our witness be as effective as was that of those first-century believers.

Is Pauline Strategy Applicable Today?

To say that Paul's missionary labors resulted from thinking as well as praying and working does not end the matter. We must ask whether or not Pauline strategy is applicable today. To that question we answer yes.

In the first place, the first-century world of Paul bears some remarkable similarities to our world of today. Of course, we must admit that the twentieth century is not a carbon copy of the first century, and that, when compared to the situation in which the modern foreign missionary usually finds himself, Paul's situation was quite different. Paul was a citizen of his missionary world. He learned no strange tongue in order to communicate. From the very beginning of his ministry he was familiar with the thought patterns of his audience. At the same time, as E. M. Blaiklock, professor of classics at Auckland University in New Zealand, is reported to have said, "Of all the intervening centuries, the twentieth is most like the first."[10] There was considerable intercultural flow of peoples of different races and backgrounds. There was a widespread bank-

---

[10]Quoted in Ray Stedman, *Body Life* (Glendale, CA: Regal Books, 1972), p. 129.

ruptcy of ideas and ideals. And there was a group of people scattered throughout the Roman Empire who, by virtue of their contact with or commitment to Jewish monotheistic and ethical ideas, constituted a "prepared audience" for the gospel.

In the second place, Paul acknowledged that he was a master builder of the Church (I Cor. 3:10). Now if we do not infer from that fact that we are to slavishly follow every approach employed by the great apostle to the Gentiles, we can at least profit from a careful study of his methodology. After all, modern architects study the works of master architects of the past even though they may not design and build identical buildings.

Just so, we can learn from Paul. As Richard Longenecker has written:

> It has often been devotionally said: "The world has yet to see what God can do with a man wholly committed to Him." Paul was such a man, and the world has witnessed the effect. He possessed a firmness of commitment to his Lord, a fervency of spirit, a compassion of heart, a breadth of outlook, a keenness of perception, and a constant openness to the Spirit. *Such an example of a Christian life and ministry stands as both a paradigm and an inspiration to us today* [italics added]."[11]

To What Extent Is Paul's Methodology Normative?

It is clear from the New Testament Scriptures that Paul's *message* is normative. To the Galatians—troubled as they were by the Judaizers—he could say, "But even though we, or an angel from heaven, should preach to you a gospel contrary to that which we preach to you, let him be accursed" (Gal. 1:8). To the Corinthians—plagued as they were with church difficulties—he could write, "For I have received of the Lord that which also I delivered to you" (I Cor. 11:23a).

-----

[11]Richard Longenecker, *The Ministry and Message of Paul* (Grand Rapids: Zondervan, 1971), p. 112.

It is also clear from the New Testament that, in a secondary sense, Paul the *man* was a normative example of what a Christian should be and do. To the Corinthians, who desperately needed an example of what a Christian should be, he could make that remarkable statement, "Be imitators of me" (I Cor. 11:1a). But Paul was not perfect. He knew it. And therefore he added those all-important words, "just as I also am of Christ" (I Cor. 11:1b). So Paul's example is normative because it reflects the perfect pattern—that of Jesus Christ Himself.

Then what about Paul's missionary *method*? As we have said, there seems to be little to indicate that the Holy Spirit expects us to slavishly follow every Pauline procedure in our evangelistic outreach. On the other hand, there is explicit teaching in the Epistles which directs us to carry on the same activities in a similar way—namely, to go where people are, preach the gospel, gain converts, gather them into churches, instruct them in the faith, choose leaders, and commend believers to the grace of God. And where would we find a pattern for these activities that is less likely to lead us into blind alleys than is the apostle Paul's missionary work? As A. R. Hay writes, "Paul's ministry and that of his companions is recorded in detail because he and they provide a typical example for the exceedingly important permanent ministry of church-planting."[12]

We conclude, then, that Paul's message was absolutely normative, and that his manner of life and missionary methodology were less normative. It is a matter of degree. There is room for adaptation in each case, but less in the case of his message and more in the cases of his lifestyle and methodology. For those of us who are two thousand years removed from the physical presence of the Master and His apostles, we do well to learn from Paul's preaching, person, and program in dependence on the Word and the Holy Spirit.

---

[12]A. R. Hay, *New Testament Order for Church and Missionary* (Audubon, NJ: New Testament Missionary Union, 1947), p. 220.

The Pauline Cycle

The Logical Elements in Paul's Master Plan of Evangelism

What were the logical elements (steps) in Paul's master plan of evangelism and church development? These elements will be analyzed later. At this point we will simply list them and display them in diagrammatic form (see Figure 5):

    (1) Missionaries Commissioned—Acts 13:1-4; 15:39, 40.
    (2) Audience Contacted—Acts 13:14-16; 14:1; 16:13-15.
    (3) Gospel Communicated—Acts 13:17ff.; 16:31.
    (4) Hearers Converted—Acts 13:48; 16:14, 15.
    (5) Believers Congregated—Acts 13:43.
    (6) Faith Confirmed—Acts 14:21, 22; 15:41.
    (7) Leadership Consecrated—Acts 14:23.
    (8) Believers Commended—Acts 14:23; 16:40.
    (9) Relationships Continued—Acts 15:36; 18:23.
   (10) Sending Churches Convened—Acts 14:26, 27; 15:1-4.

Possible Objections to the Pauline Cycle

To some the steps in the Pauline Cycle may seem to be almost too obvious to be really important. Our response is that for people who are thoroughly acquainted with a given task, the logical elements which go to make it up should be obvious. Chemists would be hampered in working with hydrochloric acid if its molecular structure were not common knowledge in their laboratories. Once the basic elements of anything are discovered, they are more or less obvious. At that point, the only real expertise that is required is in working with them.

To others, the Pauline Cycle may seem somewhat contrived. Ten steps, alliterative phrases—the whole thing seems too tidy to be true, too programmatic to be practical. Our response is that there is nothing sacrosanct about this particular way of breaking the task down into manageable elements. In this sense, the mission of the Church is not analogous with a molecule of hydrochloric acid. Variation

FIGURE 5
"THE PAULINE CYCLE"

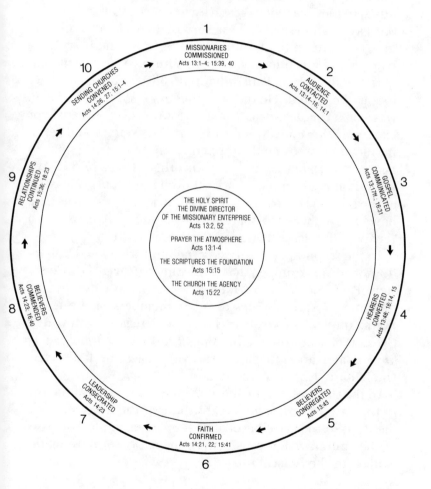

1

MISSIONARIES
COMMISSIONED
Acts 13:1-4; 15:39, 40

10

SENDING CHURCHES
CONVENED
Acts 14:26, 27; 15:1-4

2

AUDIENCE
CONTACTED
Acts 13:14-16; 14:1

9

RELATIONSHIPS
CONTINUED
Acts 15:36; 18:23

3

GOSPEL
COMMUNICATED
Acts 13:17ff.; 16:31

THE HOLY SPIRIT
THE DIVINE DIRECTOR
OF THE MISSIONARY ENTERPRISE
Acts 13:2, 52

PRAYER THE ATMOSPHERE
Acts 13:1-4

THE SCRIPTURES THE FOUNDATION
Acts 15:15

THE CHURCH THE AGENCY
Acts 15:22

8

BELIEVERS
COMMENDED
Acts 14:23; 16:40

4

HEARERS
CONVERTED
Acts 13:48; 16:14, 15

7

LEADERSHIP
CONSECRATED
Acts 14:23

5

BELIEVERS
CONGREGATED
Acts 13:43

FAITH
CONFIRMED
Acts 14:21, 22; 15:41

6

is possible. Nevertheless, we believe that careful analysis of the missionary task will reveal something very similar to the steps in the Pauline Cycle. And it makes little difference to us how those steps are identified.

To still others it may seem that the cycle is not really Pauline. They may grant that Paul engaged in these various activities but not necessarily in every locality. If that is the case, is not the cycle a sort of hybrid or composite inferred from a total ministry rather than the basis for a plan in any given local situation? Our answer is fourfold.

In the first place, Paul did not establish a church in every locality he visited. He did not plan to do so. As far as Paul was concerned (and as far as we know), in Athens, for example, the cycle went through the contact and communication steps and stopped with the conversion of Dionysius, Damaris, and certain others (Acts 17:34). We know that later on there was a church in Athens. But as far as the biblical record and Paul's ministry are concerned, we have no further information concerning it. Athens was a "layover" for Paul. It was not "his kind" of city.

In the second place, by using the phrase *Pauline Cycle* we do not mean to imply that Paul himself carried out each step. Paul led a team of men. The record is clear that he delegated responsibilities to other members of the team. For example, Paul wrote to Titus, "The reason I left you in Crete was that you might *straighten out what was left unfinished* and appoint elders in every town, as I directed you" (Titus 1:5, NIV, italics added).

In the third place, the more complete the biblical record in the case of any given local situation, the more explicit the steps in the cycle become. Take, for example, the case of the church at Ephesus. There the basic steps are made explicit in the biblical record:

Audience contacted—Acts 18:19; 19:1, 8, 9
Gospel communicated—Acts 19:4, 9, 10
Hearers converted—Acts 19:5, 18
Believers congregated—Acts 19:9, 10

Faith confirmed—Acts 20:20, 27
Leadership consecrated—Acts 20:17, 28; I Tim. 1:3, 4; 2:2
Believers commended—Acts 20:1, 25, 32
Relationships continued—Acts 20:17; Eph. 1:1-3, 15, 16

In the fourth place, while the cycle grows out of Pauline methodology and is not imposed upon it, nevertheless it also grows out of logicality and the larger experience of missions. Given the nature of the task to which we have been commissioned, these steps are practical and reasonable, as we have already said. Look at them again. If any of us as the modern counterparts of Paul, Peter, Thomas, or Timothy, were to go to a designated city to evangelize and establish a church, would we not carry out these very same steps? And would we not carry them out in this order, more or less?

Four Important Aspects of the Pauline Cycle

Before we close this preliminary discussion of the Pauline Cycle, four aspects of it should be especially noted.

First, it has a beginning and an ending. A large number of books in the area of church growth and development have appeared in recent years. Some of them make exceedingly stimulating reading for those concerned about the mission of the Church. Some of the principles discoverable in these books are invaluable. There is a shortcoming in many of them that often proves to be frustrating to the practitioner, however. It is this. The practitioner who is trained in church-growth principles contemplates church-extension evangelism in a new area only to find that he doesn't know how to string these pearls of wisdom on one strand! He doesn't know where to begin! And he has not even thought about how to end. By thinking in terms of a cycle with a beginning and an end and logical steps in between, it may be possible to overcome this weakness.

Second, though we speak of a beginning and an ending

to the cycle, there is a sense in which it does not admit of either. When Paul was recommissioned in Antioch before his second missionary journey (Acts 15:39, 40), he reestablished contact with and continued his ministry to fledgling groups of believers, confirming them in the faith (Acts 15:41). At the same time, he pressed the frontiers of the gospel a little farther from the home bases in Jerusalem and Antioch. To legitimately think of a beginning and an ending, therefore, one must think of the task in relation to one church or one limited area.

Third, the cycle must be viewed synchronically as well as diachronically. That is, while we can think of progressing from the contact stage to communication, to conversion, to congregating believers, and so on, we must also remember that as we proceed through time to the more advanced stages of development, we must still carry on the activities of the initial stages (or see to it that they are carried on). For example, we must always be making new contacts and working for new conversions from the world even as we are confirming the first believers in the faith. Not to do so is to displease the Head of the Church. Therefore, bold lines should not be drawn between the major elements of the cycle. In one sense they are distinct and sequential. In another sense they impinge upon, and flow into, one another.

Fourth, it is of vital importance that the Pauline Cycle strategy be applied to existing churches as well as to pioneer situations. By evaluating existing churches step by step from "audience contacted" right on through "relationships continued," the pastor and responsible believers in a church can actually analyze where their church is successful and where it is falling down on the job! Then they can make necessary changes in their overall plan, decide on standards, gather the resources, and put promising innovations into operation. In addition, they will constantly gain new insights into the mission of the Church at home and abroad.

Effective missionizing and evangelizing requires careful, prayerful planning and strategy. When God was preparing to lead His people out of Egypt and into the Promised Land, He called Moses and communicated a plan: "Go and gather the elders of Israel together, and say to them. ... And you with the elders of Israel will come to the king of Egypt, and you will say to him. ... But I know that the king of Egypt will not permit you to go. ... So I will stretch out My hand, and strike Egypt with all My miracles" (Exod. 3:16–20). When God was ready to bring believing Jews and Gentiles into a new community of faith, He arrested Saul and said, "But arise, and stand on your feet; for this purpose I have appeared to you, to appoint you a minister and a witness" (Acts 26:16). And when Saul—now Paul—had ministered, witnessed, and established groups of believers from Syria in the East to Macedonia and Achaia in the West, he wrote to one church,

> I planted, Apollos watered, but God was causing the growth. ... We are God's fellow-workers; you are God's field, God's building. According to the grace of God which was given to me, as a wise masterbuilder I laid a foundation, and another is building upon it. But let each man be careful how he builds upon it. (I Cor. 3:6, 9, 10).

Above all, the accomplishment of God's plans and purpose requires divine wisdom, intervention, and grace. But it also requires that a Moses and the elders, or a Paul and his companions, dedicate themselves—body, heart, and mind—to the task.

three

Education for Mission

Several years ago, while one of the authors was teaching at Evangel Theological College in Hong Kong, he had occasion to spend some time with Dr. Philip Teng, who pastors a flourishing Christian and Missionary Alliance church in that city. In discussing the work of the churches Teng indicated that in recent years his church had initiated a program to establish five daughter churches. Finances for workers and facilities had been supplied, and much encouragement given. One or two of the daughter churches were progressing well but one major problem had become apparent. There seemed to be no Christian workers who knew how to enter a new area and lay the foundation for a new church! Workers had been trained to build on someone else's foundation, but not to lay their own. Dr. Teng wondered why this was so.

The explanation was and is simple. Systematic and practical theology as we know it has been produced largely in Western nations where thousands of churches dot our countryside and thousands more send their spires towering above the surrounding roof-tops of our cities. The existence of these churches has been taken for granted. Consequently systematic theologians have been preoccupied with the "inner concerns" of the Church and have given comparatively little consideration to the theology of its mission. Practical theologians have prepared pastors to serve existing congregations but have done little or nothing to prepare workers for the development of new ones.

What has been generally true of institutions for theological training has been almost universally true of other types of institutions of Christian education. They have multiplied degree programs and courses in the arts and sciences while neglecting courses in ecclesiology and church-extension evangelism. Yet, when their public-relations departments lay out plans for recruitment and fund-raising, they assume both the existence and the cooperation of local churches!

But we must go still another step. The most important center of Christian education is the local church itself. After all, only a small percentage of its members are privileged to go on to Christian institutions of higher learning. And education in the believing home will seldom improve upon that received in the local church. Nevertheless, in spite of its importance as a training center and its well-oiled organizational machinery and crowded schedule, the average local church is woefully deficient when it comes to educating, training, and deploying its membership in a really viable program of church-extension evangelism.

Meanwhile, every Kingdom Hall is a training station for the Jehovah's Witnesses. Witnesses are called "publishers," and all are assigned territories which become their missionary responsibility. They are to make at least two calls a year on every household in their assigned areas. Not only that, they are carefully trained for their task, not simply or primarily by listening but also by doing. Newer members "perform" in simulated house calls before local congregations and their leaders, and are publicly evaluated on their "performance." Finally, the whole program of propagation—local forums, home Bible studies, publications, headquarter's involvement—is coordinated by the leaders and explained to the members. No wonder that the movement increased from 3,868 believers in one nation in 1918 to 2,091,432 members located in 210 nations in 1973 (a fifty-five-year period).[1]

Meanwhile, the Mormon missionary program also proceeds apace. As is well known, Mormon young men are expected to serve in the mission for a period of two years at the expense of their own families (the church pays the return fare from their assignments). They are prepared for their assignments in training programs offered at various educational levels. The high-school level "Seminary" program offers four years of off-campus classes in Old Testament, New Testament, the Book of Mormon, and L.D.S. church history. At the college level there is a similar program called the "Institute of Religion." In addition, missionaries are given special preassignment training which includes memorizing the general concepts of a 200-page handbook of instruction and sample dialogues. Those going to areas where foreign languages are spoken receive special language training. Once on the assigned field, the new missionary fits into a daily routine, every part of which dovetails with an existing program for bringing new converts into the church and adding new churches. In 1974, 170,000 were enrolled in the "Seminary" program and 62,000 in the "Institute of Religion." There were 17,564 missionaries. And somewhere in the world, a new member joined the church every six minutes.[2]

---

[1]Wilton M. Nelson and Richard K. Smith, "Jehovah's Witnesses," in *Dynamic Religious Movements,* ed. David J. Hesselgrave (Grand Rapids: Baker, 1978), pp. 173–99.

[2]Jerald and Sandra Tanner, "Mormonism," in *Dynamic Religious Movements,* pp. 201–20.

Meanwhile, Soka Gakkai Buddhism with headquarters in Japan has devised a program designed to win first the Orient and then the entire world. It claims the largest temple in the world at the foot of historic Mount Fuji. It features gigantic spectacles including parades, speeches, and athletic demonstrations. But all of that is for believers. At the heart of Soka Gakkai outreach is a program of coordinated lay involvement. All members are expected to master a manual which explains Soka Gakkai doctrine and prepares them to propagate it. All meet regularly in designated homes where they participate in disciplined interaction devoted to strengthening the faith of members and introducing new prospects to the movement. Home groups divide as they exceed the small-group limits. Each year thousands of lay members of both sexes and all ages voluntarily submit to examinations which will qualify them for larger spheres of responsibility in the organization. No wonder that, within twenty-five years, the Soka Gakkai grew from an almost insignificant number of adherents to some 16,000,000 members in Japan and an additional 300,000 in more than thirty countries of the world.[3]

Meanwhile, every local congregation of the *Iglesia ni Cristo* in the Philippines, whether it consists of fifty or a thousand members, is organized into committees of about seven members each. Each committee has its own officers and concerns itself with discipline and propagation. When one member of the committee makes a new contact for the church, he notifies the president of the committee and all members are mobilized for follow-up. No wonder that this church which was not even in existence prior to World War I has grown to about one-half million adherents and over 2,500 congregations![4]

[3]David J. Hesselgrave, "Nichiren Shoshu Soka Gakkai—The Lotus Blossoms in Japan," in *Dynamic Religious Movements,* pp. 129–48.

[4]A. Leonard Tuggy, "Iglesia ni Cristo: An Angel and His Church," in *Dynamic Religious Movements,* pp. 85–101.

What is desperately needed in evangelicalism today is a complete reevaluation and overhaul of Christian education and programs of outreach in the light of the Scriptures and the new missionary situation that exists in both Western and non-Western worlds. That reevaluation and overhaul should occur at three levels: in the local churches, in Christian schools of the arts and sciences, and in theological schools for the training of Christian workers.

Education for Mission and Evangelism in the Local Church

The place to begin education—or reeducation—in mission and evangelism is the local church. And it should not be merely for the spiritual elite who already have a profound interest in world outreach (many of whom are connected with the Women's Missionary Society!), but for everyone who belongs to Christ. All children of the King should be interested in, and knowledgeable about, the King's business!

But this has been said over and over *ad nauseum*. So what is new? What will be new to many congregations is the kind of education advocated in the following paragraphs!

To most concerned believers, this business of evangelism seems as simple as a witness to an unconverted acquaintance and this business of mission seems as complicated as international diplomacy. And evangelism *can be* that simple, and mission *can be* that complex. But the larger implications of New Testament evangelism and the heart of mission need to be understood, and understood by all. Evangelism should lead converts to active participation in the local church; whatever else world mission may entail, it must give first priority to that kind of evangelism. This requires understanding. And understanding requires careful, prayerful study.

It is no credit to Christ when His work must go forward

on the basis of misinformation, inadequate information, or no information at all. It brings no glory to Him when personal preferences take priority over divine principles in spiritual endeavors.

Pastors, leaders, and mission-evangelism committee members at the local level need to spend more time with the Scriptures and literature on evangelism, missions, and church growth—and also with missionary-evangelists who have experience and expertise in the basic task of planting growing churches. Thus instructed (woe to the leader that refuses to be led!) they can teach the membership and encourage participation in evangelism and support for workers who have developed viable strategies and long-range goals.

How, then, might we proceed with this process of missionary education? It seems that the very best way is to start with the local church itself—to see what God says about it in His Word and to conform the local church as much as possible to that model. The local church, then, becomes a microcosm of what needs to be duplicated and reduplicated around the world. Evangelism is not something different "out there." Mission isn't something totally incomprehensible which is "somewhere else in the world." Essentially, both are what every local church should be doing in the here and now!

"Well and good," someone says, "that's idealism for you. Leave it to the educators to come up with solutions that are 'out of this world.' "

But wait a minute. Stop to calculate the hours spent by the faithful in committee meetings, Bible studies, prayer meetings, evangelistic enterprises, and missionary conferences, to say nothing of worship services, special film showings and fellowship suppers, and home meetings connected to and separate from the church. Do believers know how all of these activities fit together and contribute to the primary reason for the Church's very existence? For that matter, does the pastor himself know?

Have you ever put a jigsaw puzzle together? Of course.

What saves the day if you are working with the pieces of a really complicated puzzle? *The larger picture.* When you have the larger picture in mind, you can examine the shadings and lines of the smallest piece and know that it will be a part of the lawn or the wooded area or the sunset.

So it is with the Church. When we see God's plan and purpose, and when believers get a picture of what the local church aims to be and do by the grace of God, then the pieces will come together: "I see now. This is why we need *corporate* prayer"; "Oh, this is how our home Bible study contributes to church growth"; "Now I understand how a gymnasium could be God's will for us in this situation"— these and similar remarks will be heard in the gatherings of believers.

More, when church members see that what they are doing in their church in Centerville is what God wants duplicated (with cultural accommodations) around the world, then responsible dialogue, prayer, and stewardship for cross-cultural missions and evangelism will result. And God knows how much we need this.

Where do we begin? We suggest that pastors and their people take the Bible and this manual and do the following:

(1) Set aside one hour a week, whether during Sunday school, Sunday evening, or the midweek prayer service for systematic, step-by-step study, discussion, and prayer.

(2) Describe for themselves in biblical terms what the Church is designed to be and do in the plan of God.

(3) Gradually piece together a picture of the life and program of their local church, showing how each part contributes to the basic purposes for the church's existence.

(4) Evaluate and modify the existing program in terms of its conformance to the biblical pattern and actual results.

(5) Practice prayer for, and participation in, the various programs of the church in accordance with the plan and resources God has provided.

(6) Promote mission-evangelistic outreach in other

communities at home and abroad in accordance with the understandings gained from this study.

If this kind of exercise were to be substituted for some of the good but often disconnected and general studies taking place in the average church, and if its implications were faithfully carried through, we would be able to plant growing churches everywhere.

Education for Mission and Evangelism in Church-Related Colleges

A dear and trusted friend who has had long years of experience in the pastorate and in teaching in various church-related schools once said, relative to a certain well-known Christian college, "I think the world of that place. But the last church I would want to pastor would be a church composed primarily of its graduates." He then went on to explain that the students of that institution were well instructed in personal faith and private devotion. Some of them would do great things for God. But in the local church most of them could be counted on to support the Sunday morning worship service and that's about all. He feared that he would be rather lonely at the weekly prayer service and other important corporate activities of the church. And he produced solid evidence for his contention!

At the time we understood what he was saying. But several months later his words came back with renewed force. One of the prominent faculty members of that same institution remarked in conversation, "Church? Why wherever Christians meet, there you have a church. As a matter of fact, the parish as we have known it is a thing of the past. The churches of tomorrow will be coffee klatches, dorm bull sessions, and ad hoc Bible study groups."

To say that we disagree with that faculty member is to put it mildly. Of course, Christ is present where two or three meet in His name. Of course, such gatherings can be spiritually meaningful and God-honoring. But such an ecclesiology is hardly worth the name.

Churches need to take a long, hard look at the educational (and other) institutions which they support. Do they stand for Christ? If so, that is praiseworthy. But it is not enough. Do they stand for the Word of God? If so, we should be grateful. But that is not enough. There is a third and crucial question. Do they stand for the Church and the churches, and do they support them in every possible way? That is not too much to expect. Christ loved the Church and gave Himself for it. Much of the Bible is devoted to descriptions of, and directions to, the churches. Moreover—and at a very pragmatic level—the churches are asked to support the schools in very specific, tangible ways. Why shouldn't the schools support the churches similarly?

Let's be clear. We are not talking about a tip of the hat in the direction of the churches, or even the circulating of choirs and gospel teams among the churches. We are talking about curricula that include solid, biblical instruction on the Church—its meaning, make-up, and mission. And we are talking about counseling and other practical programs that encourage students to put roots down in local churches and faithfully work for their strengthening and outreach. The time has come to ask whether or not it is Christian for schools to solicit and accept support from the churches if they do not help supporting churches to grow and multiply.

Education for Mission and Evangelism in Schools of Bible and Theology

Recently one of the authors had the privilege of giving a series of lectures in a Bible school located on the outskirts of a metropolis in another country. It was a fine school with excellent facilities, dedicated faculty, bright students, and a typical Bible School curriculum. But with respect to church growth, it had a basic problem despite all of those fine assets. Students were studying the Bible, taking voice lessons, practicing preaching, learning to teach, and discussing personal evangelism. On Sundays most of them would go to some Christian service assignment—singing, teaching a Sunday school class, or leading a youth meeting in some church in the city. However, in two or three directions from that school one could have traveled twenty or thirty miles without discovering more than two or three struggling evangelical churches. And still the curriculum of that school did not offer one course in church-planting evangelism, and only one such effort was engaging the attention of any of the school personnel.

It would certainly seem that, if it is to be found anywhere, practical training for winning people to Christ, establishing them in local churches, and planting churches in churchless areas around the world would be found in Bible institutes and seminaries. But, as we have indicated, one can't count on that being the case. The average curriculum contains a course in personal evangelism, a section of a course in systematic theology given over to ecclesiology, a few lessons of a course in practical theology devoted to evangelistic campaigns, and a general course in missions.

Very likely these courses will be taught by dedicated and competent instructors. Students who apply themselves will benefit greatly from them. It is likely that a large percentage of those who graduate from these institutions will have a desire to faithfully serve Christ and lead men and women to put their faith in Him. Many will be prepared to serve in some local church at home, or in some area of missions overseas. But, as Dr. Teng discovered in the Far East, very few graduates will have the vision or the know-how to establish new churches in churchless communities. Very few Pauls will graduate from these schools unless some significant changes are made.

There are two reasons for this. First, missionary and evangelistic vision has not been clearly spelled out in terms of planting growing churches.

Second, there are no courses that concentrate on devising strategies for church-extension evangelism in designated areas. And until courses in mission and evangelism have that kind of concreteness and specificity, they will always lack practicality.

Few schools, if any, have really solved these problems. Happily, the number of schools offering courses in church growth has increased dramatically in recent years. What remains to be done is to enroll students in courses—and engage them in ministries—which afford the opportunity to translate all that they have been able to learn about the Church and its mission into definite plans and programs for specified target areas.

In a limited way we have attempted this at Trinity's School of World Mission and Evangelism. Advanced students are encouraged to enroll in a ten-week seminar on church-extension evangelism. The class is divided into small units ranging from two to four members each. Each unit decides on a specific target area and people within a larger geographical interest area. Target areas have included such culturally divergent and geographically separated targets as a tribe in the "Bird's Head" region of Indonesia, a "bedroom community" in Japan, a town in Guatemala, a tribal village in Kenya, and a community within walking distance of Trinity! At the introductory stage, students talk about planning procedure, and are introduced to the Pauline Cycle. They also make demographic surveys of their target areas and peoples. (These are only as complete as available data and time will allow.)

Then, taking one phase of the cycle each week (beginning with "audience contact"), the members of each unit collaborate on developing a master plan for their target area. Each member of a unit concentrates on one or two important aspects of each phase. All are encouraged to bring the best insights from the Scriptures, research, and experience to bear upon each issue involved.

Students and instructors meet three times each week. Beginning with the second week, the three class periods are spent as follows:

Session One: A lecture and discussion designed to introduce the phase of the Pauline Cycle to be dealt with that particular week ("audience contact," "gospel communication," etc.). At the close of the session the units meet separately in order to determine points of concentration for each member.

Session Two: Students meet in units but in a common location. They share problems and ideas related to their individual and collective concerns, and make the adjustments required to settle on a larger strategy for the phase of the cycle under consideration. Instructors circulate among the units in order to ask and answer pertinent questions and help keep the discussions moving along fruitful lines.

Session Three: Each unit circulates rough drafts and reports the main outlines of its strategy for that phase of the cycle. Class members offer criticisms and suggestions to be considered in the finalization of the various master plans.

At the close of the ten-week seminar, units circulate completed master plans. In this way, participants have the added satisfaction that comes from sharing master plans with colleagues in the ministry at home and abroad. But for instructors and students alike, the most important part of the whole enterprise is to increase effectiveness in church-planting and growth at home and abroad.

A by-product of the course has been a significant upswing in student and faculty interest and participation in the establishment of evangelical churches in churchless communities.

The Trinity effort is a humble, beginning one. Our plan is to involve more students in actually planting churches in surrounding communities in the future. Despite its weaknesses, the Trinity approach points to new possibilities for schools, churches, and missions. Only the Lord of the Church knows how rapidly growing churches would multiply if all His followers were bending every effort to cooperate with Him in building His Church!

Education for Mission and Evangelism in the Missions

Is it presumptuous to suggest that the constituency of missions needs education in mission and evangelism? Many will think so. "If missions' personnel need this kind of education perhaps they have missed their calling," someone will protest. In a very few cases that may be true, and in those cases, education will not help. But education—or reeducation—will help those who are called, are sure of their calling, and want to be true to their calling!

Reliable statistics on evangelism in North America are readily available. According to a recent study the total number of missionaries abroad affiliated with the Division of Overseas Missions (National Council of Christian Churches), the Evangelical Foreign Mission Association, and the Interdenominational Foreign Mission Association is 19,786. Of this number, 28 percent are involved in establishing churches, 25 percent are involved in "church support," and 47 percent are assigned to other ministries.[5] In

---

[5] *Mission Handbook: North American Protestant Ministries Overseas,* ed. Edward R. Dayton, 11th ed. (Monrovia, CA: Missions Advanced Research and Communication Center, 1976), p. 43.

round figures, about one-fourth are primarily engaged in winning people to Christ and planting churches, one-fourth assist existing churches, and almost one-half are engaged in a wide variety of other ministries. The following survey of the general activities of various missionary agencies is illuminating:[6]

General Activity	Agencies Reporting	Percentage
Education	510	19%
Evangelization	398	15%
Literature	352	13%
Relief and Development	317	12%
Service and Support	248	9%
Church Growth	209	8%
National Support	183	7%
Media	163	6%
Medical	152	5%
Other	173	6%
Total	2,705	100%

Statistics reveal, then, that more missionaries in the reporting agencies are involved in education than are engaged in evangelism. Half again as many missionaries have relief and development as their basic task as devote themselves to church growth.

This leads us to conclude that there are at least four good reasons why education in evangelism and planting growing churches is vital within missions today.

First, those who establish churches need to avail themselves of fresh insights from the Scriptures and sciences as to ways and means of effectively carrying out their task. True, the Word does not change. But our understanding grows. And the world changes. Reeducation is essential.

Second, those who assist existing churches abroad will make the greatest possible contribution if they are prepared to help those churches reach out to new people and communities in evangelistic and church-extension minis-

---

[6]Ibid., p. 45.

tries. To do this, they too must keep current with the best thinking in missions and evangelism.

Third, we must give much greater consideration to the needs of that large group of missionaries who are engaged in ministries that have been variously termed "enabling," "support," and "secondary." Several years ago we visited two missionary medical centers in adjacent areas. The personnel in both institutions had a burden for evangelism. People were being introduced to Christ in both centers. But one institution had but a tenuous association with existing churches. The other had a healthy relationship with surrounding churches, and was credited as being directly responsible for the establishment of over one hundred new churches over the years! The basic difference between these two institutions was not to be found in the dedication of their staffs. Commitment was apparent in both places. The difference was that one staff had a planned strategy for church development. The other did not.

Fourth, as missionary—and evangelistic—efforts become more and more varied and complex, it is apparent that we need to give increased attention to biblical priorities. Not only local churches and schools, but missions themselves must "win their spurs" by producing believers and churches. To do this, and do it effectively, continuing education must focus on specific strategies, lest the gap between precept and performance become ever wider.

Perhaps one of the most difficult things for all of us is to get out of old ruts and chart new paths. The time has come, however, to give serious consideration to our future course of action in the Church's mission.

Depletion of resources, the population explosion, changing political climates, social stress, and a host of other realities of the new world now emerging challenge individuals and families to lop off the nonessentials, determine what is really basic, and simplify their lifestyle.

The Church must do the same. It cannot undertake *all* good and worthwhile endeavors. It may not be able to continue all the praiseworthy efforts that have been initiated in more normal times. The world's needs are on the increase. Many churches and missions have seen their budgets double in recent years without any significant increase in personnel or services. For many churches and missions the time has already arrived when, faced with new needs and opportunities, they are forced to respond, "Silver and gold have we none."

Will we also say, "Such as we have we give unto you"? We in the Church can always share our most precious Possession—Jesus Christ. And when we do so—and do so in a scriptural, disciplined way—God will multiply those growing churches without which resources for all other endeavors will gradually be exhausted.

PART TWO

The Christian Leader and the Christian Mission

four

Leading the Mission

The Leaderless Army

Imagine an army without generals or a resident commander-in-chief. It has tens of thousands of troops. It has corporals, sergeants, lieutenants, and captains. It has airplanes, trucks, tanks, and the latest weaponry. It has administrative buildings, schools, and barracks. It has mess sergeants, kitchens, dining halls, and an almost limitless supply of food. It has specialists in military strategy, logistics, communications, and physical fitness. And it has bands complete with drum and bugle corps. But it has no generals and no resident commander-in-chief.

Everyone in our imaginary army is busy. In fact, wherever one goes throughout the length and breadth of the encampment one is amazed at the activity. Classes are in session. Units are marching. Bands are playing. Traffic is moving. In fact, quite regularly special units take it upon themselves to go out and harass the enemy in territory he invaded and occupied long ago. Periodically there are special maneuvers in which some entrepreneuring individuals rally everyone together just long enough to put on a full display of men and machines—and within sight of the enemy! Remember, however, our imaginary army has no generals and no resident commander-in-chief.

"Stop right there," some loyal member of the Christian army protests. "I see what you are saying. But our Christian army *does* have a Commander-in-Chief, and generals too. We are pressing the battle on many fronts. And we are taking 'captives' and winning back some ground too!"

Granted. The analogy may be overdrawn. But if you were to travel the length and breadth of our land and spend months and even years inspecting the "battlefields" in every part of the world, you would probably agree that the analogy has some validity.

Oh, there are many Christians in our army. And there is no small amount of expertise. We have some sophisticated equipment too. And activity on every side.

But all too often the units of the Christian army are out of touch with one another. Generals there are, but not a few of them give the appearance of being self-appointed. Those who are not, often seem to be so preoccupied with logistics that they have precious little time or inclination to map out an overall strategy or direct an assault on the enemy. Finally, there is the disconcerting fact that many members of the army claim to be getting directives that are contradictory and self-defeating. One wonders. Are they setting themselves to obedience, or to do their own thing in the hope that somehow the larger cause will be aided?

How unlike the campaign of Paul and his apostolic band—the campaign that won a foothold in city after city and province after province right up to and including the palace of the pagan emperor! One can understand why. Under God, Paul was at the forefront of that campaign. If there were defections and disagreement, there was also direction. Read the record: "Now those who conducted Paul brought him as far as Athens; and receiving a command for Silas and Timothy to come to him as soon as possible, they departed" (Acts 17:15); "For this reason I left you [Titus] in Crete, that you might set in order what remains, and appoint elders in every city as I directed you" (Titus 1:5). It seems obvious that the early missionary enterprise was characterized by discipline and direction. No wonder the leader of that apostolic band could humbly write in terms of accomplished tasks and occupied territory: "For I will not presume to speak of anything except what Christ has accomplished through me . . . so that from Jerusalem and round about as far as Illyricum I have fully preached the gospel of Christ" (Rom. 15:18, 19); "I have fought the good fight, I have finished the course, I have kept the faith" (II Tim. 4:7).

We of the twentieth century will never return to apostolic authority (in this personal sense) and first-century simplicity. But there must be much more strategic thinking and serious direction on the part of those who have been duly appointed as leaders of the Church and its missions—and much more disciplined involvement on the part of the soldiers of the cross—if we are ever to accomplish what should be accomplished in the time that remains to us to obey our commission and complete our mission.

Leadership and Strategy for Home Missions

Our understanding of the task can never be complete until it is defined in terms of specific target areas. But who decides what areas should be entered with a view to establishing new churches? Who determines the master plan for actually doing so? And who gathers the resources that make it possible? The answer should be obvious. Church and mission leaders.

Home-mission leaders must resist the temptation to become only, or primarily, caretakers of the churches already established. Some of their most important functions should be to encourage an overall plan for church extension, to suggest ways and means of carrying out the plan, and to provide leadership in implementation. Obviously there are alternative ways of going about the task. But acceptable ways should be agreed upon and elaborated into master plans, and those plans should be studied in the churches and missions. Laymen and pastors often stand ready to devote themselves to the task. What is lacking is the leadership and organization required for their recruitment and deployment.

Granted an understanding of our missionary task and the elements that go to make it up, the next requirement is a basic organization that will provide for direction and cooperation in a plan to retake ground occupied by the enemy and extend the frontiers of the Church of Christ. In the suggested model (see Figure 6), this requirement is met by organizing leaders in such a way that they can take responsibility for planning strategy, and gathering and deploying human and financial resources for the task. Of course, organizational and procedural details must be worked out in accordance with the governing rules of the denomination or mission involved.

Leadership and Strategy for Overseas Missions

Missions overseas are the arms of the churches. Their executives must see that missionaries and evangelists are not simply deployed and busy—but are deployed in a way advantageous to the communication of the gospel and the building of churches. In fact, of the many services that missionary executives perform for the field missionary, perhaps the most important is that they insure that the men and women on the field are informed and situated so that they can work in harmony with their colleagues in

FIGURE 6

Basic Model for Cooperation in Church Extension— Home Missions

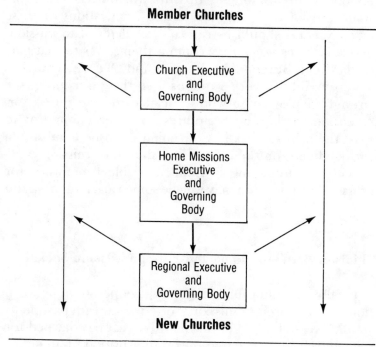

Member Churches

Church Executive
and
Governing Body

Home Missions
Executive
and
Governing
Body

Regional Executive
and
Governing Body

New Churches

accordance with a meaningful strategy and clearly defined goals.

This is no small order, as those experienced in foreign missions will recognize. Field organizations tend to be characterized by egalitarianism and rotating leadership. Endless hours can be spent in keeping the field organization functioning, in the decision-making process, and in secondary activities. The national churches have prerogatives which are divinely ordained but which greatly complicate the field situation and may frustrate the missionaries. Proper organization and planning at home and on the field, however, will assure missionaries with great church-planting potential that they will not be lost in the crowd at home or frustrated in the ministry abroad.

In those cases where administrative arrangements with national churches might jeopardize the outreach of expatriate missionaries, the nature and implications of these arrangements should be carefully spelled out to missionary candidates *before* they commit themselves to that particular field. But sending churches and receiving churches alike should be very cautious lest they discourage or wrongly deploy those who are called to, and gifted for, extension work. The Scriptures are clear enough as to what the primary task is. Convenience is a poor substitute for obedience on the part of any church or mission.

With the foregoing in mind, a viable framework for cross-cultural mission may well be some variation of Figure 7.

Liaison Between Home and Foreign Mission Societies

Finally, meaningful liaison and cooperation between home and foreign mission societies and departments should be established in this new day that has dawned for the Church. It is true that the administration of an enterprise involving the regulations of foreign governments and cooperation with Third World churches entails unique problems and expertise. And obstacles will almost always increase as we move out from ME-1 to ME-2 and ME-3 mission-evangelism. Nevertheless, we are (or should be) carrying on the same basic ministry at home and abroad. It follows that there should be a high degree of correlation between strategies employed by home and foreign missions. No longer can we afford the luxury of missions going their separate ways. Planning should be the result of united prayer and corporate consultation. The

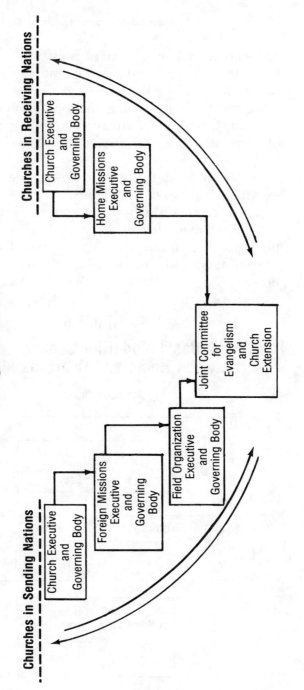

FIGURE 7

**Basic Model for
Cooperation in Church Extension—
Foreign Missions**

Churches in Receiving Nations

Church Executive and Governing Body

Home Missions Executive and Governing Body

Joint Committee for Evangelism and Church Extension

Field Organization Executive and Governing Body

Foreign Missions Executive and Governing Body

Church Executive and Governing Body

Churches in Sending Nations

elaboration and execution of master plans for specific intra- and cross-cultural areas are quite enough to occupy the attention of the separate departments.

Figure 8 presents a suggested organizational model for mutually beneficial consultation and planning on the part of home and foreign missions.

Before we leave this section on the "decision makers," we must flash two caution lights.

(1) Representatives from congregations participating in any church-extension effort should be involved in planning as well as in carrying out the plans. This is especially true in democratic societies, but it has universal application.

FIGURE 8

Basic Model for Cooperation Between Home and Overseas Missions

Member Churches

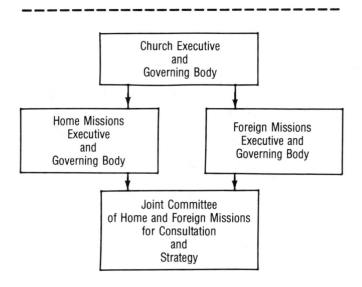

A seminar on church-planting was held in the Far East some years ago. After several hours were spent discussing the raw materials of a master plan, one leader volunteered, "But we already *have* a master plan upon which all have agreed."

He was correct. The plan was available. It was relatively sound. And all *had* agreed to it—formally. But when inquiry was made as to why the plan had not actually been put in operation, a problem became apparent. The leader had drawn up the plan and presented it to the church and mission. For reasons that were largely cultural they had voted to accept it. But their attitude was, "That is not our plan. It is yours. You carry it out."

(2) The second caution light follows closely upon the first. Though there is great wisdom in including representatives of cooperating churches in the planning stages of church extension, there is always the danger of exhausting cooperative input in decision-making and planning. The lion's share of energy should be conserved for the far tougher tasks connected with actually getting the job done. Planning for witness in a new area is important. But actually contacting the people and bringing them under the sound of the gospel are the imperative.

five

Selecting Target Areas

Often we are too vague when it comes to the mission of the Church. When we see our primary task as winning people to Christ and establishing them in the faith and in local churches, we will have come a long way in our understanding. But even that is just a beginning. Before we can get on with the task, we must decide on definite areas and peoples that will become the foci of our immediate attention and labors. One of the fundamental problems with much of our study of church growth is that principles are studied without incorporating them into a plan for reaching a specific target area. In a very real sense the task does not become clear until we decide the questions of "whom" and "where."

Priorities in Selecting Target Areas and Peoples

In foreign missions especially, the twin questions of target areas and peoples have precipitated some rather heated debates that are relevant to both home and foreign missions.

Priority to Home Missions?

Shall we do all that we can at home before devoting our efforts to needy areas abroad? Many earnest Christians insist upon this and for seemingly good reasons. They cite Acts 1:8 and say that this Scripture indicates that we are to witness first in our Jerusalems, then in our Samarias, and, finally, to the ends of the earth. They also insist that unless we have a strong home base we cannot hope to evangelize the rest of the world.

These arguments are not without some validity, but more must be said. First, the grammatical construction in Acts 1:8 ties the target areas together: "You shall be My witnesses both in Jerusalem, and in all Judea and Samaria, and even to the remotest part of the earth." The field is the world, and its parts are tied together here in a way that will not allow us to think of one part to the exclusion of another—not even to do so temporarily. Second, the growing, dynamic religious movements of our day have a vision for the whole world even when, for logistic or economic reasons, they are confined to one part of it. It seems that, in most cases, a world vision is required to win our Jerusalems!

Certainly we need a strong work at the home base. A strong foreign-mission program cannot long survive a weak home-missions program. As we said previously, it is both/and, not either/or!

Priority to Responsive People?

Shall we grant priority in our planning to tribes, classes, cities, and nations that are particularly receptive at any given time? Or should priority be given to maintaining a witness among all groups irrespective of receptivity or resistance to the gospel?

A major contention of the Church Growth movement is that great growth can occur only when we concentrate our efforts on those areas and peoples where responsiveness assures us that large numbers of people will embrace Christ and join the churches. Resistant areas should have a missionary witness, but it should be more of a "holding action" until the people become more responsive to the gospel.

Understandably, those who work among difficult populations in North Africa, Europe, and Asia, and in the inner cities of North America, are disturbed about this ordering of priorities. They do not dispute the need to reach responsive peoples. But they are greatly concerned that concentration upon receptive areas will diminish interest in resistant areas where, they feel, we have little more than a holding action at present.

Balance is needed. Our Lord did tell His disciples to shake the dust of unresponsive houses and cities off their feet and go on to others (Matt. 10:11–15). And when Paul's message was rejected by the Jews he said, "This salvation of God has been sent to the Gentiles; they will also listen" (Acts 28:28). But we should not lose sight of the fact that in these cases the preparation afforded by previous revelation should have assured a response. These cases are hardly parallel to some resistant areas today. Years of patient preevangelistic endeavor may be the price of responsiveness. In faithfulness to Christ, most missions should give consideration to maintaining a witness in some difficult area(s) even as they send reapers into the whitened harvest fields of receptive populations.

Priority to the Unreached?

Still another argument has to do with whether we should give priority to those who are unreached—those who have never had a chance to hear and believe the gospel. Subsidiary questions here have to do with the advisability of devoting vast resources to reaching tribal groups whose population is actually decreasing, and what it means to "hear" the gospel.

A great deal of mental effort has been devoted to these questions. The number of linguistic communities without any portion of the Word of God in the language of the people has been the subject of continued inquiry. Ways of reaching the unreached have been explored in conferences and seminars. Prodigious efforts to communicate the gospel by means of radio and literature to people who are sealed off from a missionary presence have been undertaken. Strategies for reaching populations behind closed doors which are now opening up again, are being researched.

The true Christian can only rejoice at these efforts. The Word of God does single out for special attention those who have never heard about Christ. Missionaries *are* to be sent so that such people might hear and be saved (Rom. 10:11–15).

Once again, however, balance is needed. The question of priorities should never be settled on the basis of simple slogans like, "Why should anyone hear the gospel twice before everyone has heard it once?" How many Christians would there be in the world if the number were reduced to include only those who believed after one hearing? And how will the gospel continue to go to remote tribes and "hidden peoples" unless we plant growing churches elsewhere—churches which provide the resources for those operations?

Priority to Urban or Rural Areas?

Still another debate has to do with the relative importance of urban as opposed to rural areas. At an earlier period in missions history, it was quite usual for missionaries to "head for the hills" where people were perishing not only without Christ but also without culture. More recently, increased attention has been given to the large cities which are centers not only of population, but also of ideas and economic potential.

Proponents of an urban-oriented strategy usually emphasize two points: Paul's strategy, and the sociological significance of cities. Both points are important and merit some elaboration.

Paul's Strategy

In the Book of Acts, when Paul's extensive missionary endeavors are related to a specific area, the reference is usually to a city. He considered an area evangelized when a church was planted in its major city.

In church-extension evangelism there is much to be said for giving a certain priority to cities. But that does not end the matter. Roland Allen notes that "all the cities, or towns, in which he [Paul] planted churches were centres of Roman administration, of Greek civilization, of Jewish influence, or of some commercial importance."[1] Walter Liefeld adds that they were located on major trade routes oriented towards Rome.[2] Each of these characteristics should be pondered, for each has its significance. When Paul chose a target city for missionary endeavor he looked beyond the city to the surrounding region. That is why these characteristics were important. In this regard, Liefeld's further words are instructive: "Paul's abortive attempt to evangelize northern Asia Minor should probably not be seen as a change in strategy, i.e., to visit sparsely settled areas, but rather as a determination to preach in several cities which lay on the northern trade route."[3]

---

[1]Roland Allen, *Missionary Methods: St. Paul's or Ours?* (Grand Rapids: Eerdmans, 1962), p. 13.

[2]Walter L. Liefeld, "The Wandering Preacher as a Social Figure in the Roman Empire" (Ph.D. dissertation, Columbia University, 1967), p. 150—quoted in Liefeld, "Theology of Church Growth," in *Theology and Mission,* ed. David J. Hesselgrave (Grand Rapids: Baker, 1978), p. 179.

[3]Liefeld, "Theology of Church Growth," p. 179.

Allen's conclusion to the matter merits careful consideration on the part of proponents of urban or rural strategies. He insists that more than the natural advantages for outreach which characterized certain cities of Paul's day should be considered when analyzing Paul's strategy. "To seize a strategic centre we need not only a man capable of recognizing it, but a man capable of seizing it."[4] In other words, one significant reason that cities became important in Paul's ministry was that he was the kind of man who was capable of seizing them for Christ.

The Sociological Significance of Cities

To the unreflective observer the city is different from the countryside simply because it has crowds of people, tall buildings, lots of excitement, and increased economic opportunity. But there are differences which are much deeper and more important. Cities and villages may represent entirely different sets of problems and potentialities to the missionary (as well as to any other advocate of change).

Cities are focal points of change. Anthropologist George Foster writes that most changes first occur in the city among the upper classes and spread downward to the lower classes and outward to the countryside.[5] He is referring specifically to social and economic changes; but even in the case of religious change, a visit to Bombay, Bangkok, Tokyo, Manila, Nairobi, Kinshasa, or Ibadan will convince one that there is a tremendous concentration of potential for Christian evangelism and growth in the cities, and from the cities to the surrounding countryside. Of course, all cities are not centers of change to the same degree. Such factors as the presence or absence of educational institutions and whether or not the city is located on main

---

[4] Allen, *Missionary Methods,* p. 16.
[5] George Foster, *Traditional Cultures and the Impact of Technological Change* (New York: Harper and Row, 1962), p. 29.

lines of commercial traffic will determine the degree of openness and innovativeness.

It is important in this regard to note an important difference between Western and non-Western urban areas. Especially in the inner core of most Western cities, Christianity with its stately but often cavernous cathedrals and churches may be identified with a past and passing period of history. Therefore, the closer one comes to that inner core, the more difficult it may be to win a hearing for the gospel and establish, or renew, churches. In the non-Western world this usually is not true. Christianity is new and represents a viable option to many.

It is also important to distinguish two fundamentally different types of rural societies. One type is tied to the city in the sense that the city is the source of much of the community's resources, whether of finance, material goods, or new ideas and values. The other type is isolated and self-contained. It views the city from afar, if at all. The first type of rural society is variously designated as a folk, village, traditional, or peasant society. The words *primitive* and *tribal* are usually applied to the second type. Social scientists view these two types of rural society very differently and for good and obvious reasons (see Figure 9).

FIGURE 9
The City-Peasant-Primitive Continuum

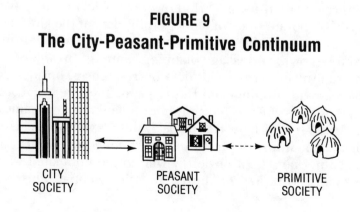

CITY
SOCIETY

PEASANT
SOCIETY

PRIMITIVE
SOCIETY

Contemporary research helps us understand the urban strategy of Paul and why he chose certain types of cities for initial contact in an area. His cities were such that when he evangelized them, he could speak of the surrounding area as being evangelized. All cities are by no means the same, but, generally speaking, they do present the greatest potential and possibilities for planting churches. This is due to: (1) openness to change, (2) the concentration of resources, and (3) the potential for significant contact with surrounding communities.

It is incumbent upon leaders of home and foreign missions to prayerfully think through these issues and then to settle upon definite target areas as a part of an overall plan.

Analysis of Target Areas and Peoples

The target area itself requires analysis. As was suggested previously, we cannot completely understand our task until we are able to define it in relation to the particular area to be entered. That will require continued study. But analysis should begin before workers actually enter the area. No area should be entered with a church-planting effort simply because some believer, however saintly, has a desire or vision for a work, however noble and lofty. We need corporate study of demographic data of the kind that is readily available in many areas of the world. City, county, town, and village planning commissions will often make available maps with data on residences, businesses, parks, roads, zoning, and future plans. In some instances, studies of businesses, corporations, telephone companies, and power and light companies will be available. This is invaluable information. If an area is zoned for industrial use, for example, it obviously will not be populated with people who represent church-growth potential. Further,

FIGURE 10

Overall Profile
of
Potential Target Community

I. Map

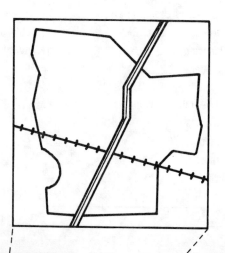

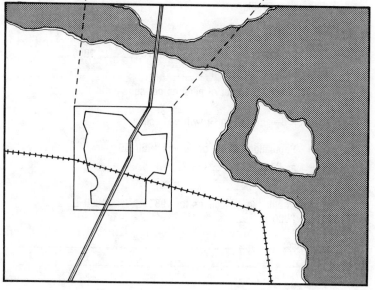

II. Geographical Profile

Section A—Description of the Land
1. Rolling Hills_____%
2. Plains _____%
3. Rivers & Streams _____%
4. Mountains _____%
5. Forests _____%

Section B—Land Use
1. Farming _____%
2. Ranching _____%
3. Lumber _____%
4. Commercial_____%
5. Unused _____%
6. Other _____%

Section C—Transportation
1. Railroads
2. Roads
3. Airport
4. Rivers

Analysis: _____

_____

III. Population Profile

Section A—Population
1. Population in 1960 _____, 1970 _____, 1980 _____
2. Present population _____
3. Density (number of persons per square mile) _____

Section B—Population Growth or Decline

1. Population growth or decline 1960–80:
   a. Growth _____ (_____%)
   b. Decline _____ (_____%)
2. Population projections for 1985 _____ 1990 _____
   2000 _____

Analysis: _____

_____

IV. Economic Profile

Section A—Occupation
1. Farming or ranching _____%
2. Business and clerical _____%
3. Education _____%
4. Government or military _____%
5. Other_____ _____%

Section B—Income
1. Less than X _____%
2. Between X and Y _____%
3. More than Y _____%

Analysis: _____

_____

V. Sociological Profile

Table A—Ethnic Groupings
1. _____ (%)
2. _____ (%)
3. _____ (%)
Etc.

Table B—Classes, Castes, Clans
1. _____ (%)
2. _____ (%)
3. _____ (%)
Etc.

Table C—Age
1. Under 18 _____ (%)
2. Between 19 and 35 _____ (%)
3. Between 36 and 50 _____ (%)
4. Over 51 _____ (%)

Analysis: _____

_____

VI. Religious Profile

Table A—Christian Population

1. Roman Catholic _____%   4. Conservative
2. Eastern Orthodox _____%   Protestant _____%
3. Liberal Protestant _____%   5. Other _____%

Table B—Non-Christian

1. Muslim _____%   4. Jewish _____%
2. Hindu _____%   5. Unaffiliated _____%
3. Buddhist _____%   6. Other _____%

Analysis: _____

_____

VII. Overall Evaluation

_____

_____

_____

_____

industrialization will determine the kind of people who eventually will live in the adjacent communities. The choice of specific target areas, then, should be preceded by the gathering of data essential to the carrying out of the church-development task. These data will include:

(1) The need for an evangelical church and the potential the new church will have for growth and the planting of still other churches.

(2) A map of the area showing zoning as well as the location of buildings and places where people often congregate.

(3) A demographic projection to ascertain the ethnic, socio-economic, educational, and religious background of the target-area population, the districts where various homogeneous groupings are located, areas of future

FIGURE 11

Rating Sheet for Church-Planting Priority

COMMUNITIES ITEM	Community A	Community B	Community C	Community D	Etc.
Geographical profile					
Population profile					
Economic profile					
Sociological profile					
Religious profile					
Total score					
Priority					

1. Compare the overall profiles of potential target communities.
2. Rate each on scale of 1 to 10 (1 = lowest rating; 10 = highest rating). Rating is relative and communities must be compared to each other.
3. Priority: the highest total score is #1, next highest #2, etc.

growth, and the types of people who will be located in those areas.[6]

Figure 10 will be of help in this analysis.

Once such an analysis of potential target communities has been carried out, a priority for church-planting efforts should be set. This can be done by making a prayerful evaluation on the basis of a rating system such as is found in Figure 11.

---

[6]Various publications designed to assist in making such a survey are available. One such is Paul Benjamin, *Analyzing the Community* (Cincinnati: Standard Publishing, 1973).

It is imperative that church leaders give prayerful consideration to the selection of areas for evangelism and church-planting. The difference between selecting an area where, on the one hand, there is real potential and the Holy Spirit has a prepared people, and an area lacking these characteristics, on the other, can mean years of unrewarding and frustrating service. That difference is too great to leave the matter of selecting fields of labor to individual or ad hoc decisions.

six

Deploying the Resources

The Holy Spirit has His ways of deploying all of the human, material, and spiritual resources that God has made available to the Church. There is little to indicate that apostolic Christianity would have spread very far or fast from its Jerusalem and Judean home apart from the intervention of the Holy Spirit. To assure that the churches would grow and multiply, the Holy Spirit gave visions that communicated the divine provision for people of other nationalities and areas (e.g., Acts 10 and 16:6–10); He sent awakenings and revivals which alerted the Jerusalem leaders to distant lands (e.g., Acts 11:25–30); and He even allowed persecution to scatter the believers as seed for a greater harvest (e.g., Acts 8:1). Assuredly, the Holy Spirit is the Missionary Spirit who prods the Church to move onward. But His primary method is to work in the hearts of God's people so that in loving obedience they will—without waiting for painful prods—purposively move out to claim new peoples and places for the kingdom.

It is good stewardship as well as good planning to determine what a task will cost in terms of people, time, talent, and money, and then to assess our resources. Our Lord had rather critical words about the man who began to build a tower but did not have resources to finish it (Luke 14:28–30). As we proceed with the building of a church in any location, our prayer will be that new resources become available as people turn to Christ. But as we begin (or begin anew with a plan), we do so primarily with that which we have and are by His grace—not so much with what we hope to have and be. Faith we must have. Presumption we can do without.

When looking ahead to a new work, therefore, let the planners make a realistic appraisal of the resources available from the following sources: (1) headquarters (the offices of the denomination or mission); (2) churches surrounding the target area; and (3) existing resources in the target area.

Missionaries and Evangelists

The New Testament makes it clear that the ascended Christ gave "person gifts" to the Church in order that it might grow (Eph. 4:1–13). Usually, four such "person gifts" are enumerated (or five, depending on whether or not "pastor" and "teacher" constitute a single category): apostles, prophets, evangelists, pastors, and teachers (or pastor-teachers). Of special concern to us are the apostles and evangelists.

In the present context it is especially significant to notice that the first of the "person gifts" mentioned in both I Corinthians 12 and Ephesians 4 is the apostle. In fact, in the former passage Paul writes, "And God has appointed in the church, first apostles . . ." (v. 28). The apostle is the missionary. We will take a closer look at this "gift" in Chapter 8.

The word *evangelist* is not emphasized in many passages in the New Testament. Philip is called an evangelist (Acts 21:8). II Timothy 4:5 indicates that Timothy was to "do the work of an evangelist." But the New Testament does make much of the work of evangelizing or heralding the Good News of Christ. Some fifty-five passages bear upon this ministry. In fact, Paul writes, "Woe is me if I do not preach the gospel [evangelize]" (I Cor. 9:16).

The Role of Laymen

The fact that in the case of Timothy, for example, the roles of missionary-evangelist and pastor-teacher were combined indicates that we should not press these distinctions too far. One person can—and often does—carry on the various ministries simultaneously or successively as the case may be. Neither should we press too far the distinction between these special "person gifts" and the "saints" who make up the great part of the spiritual body of Christ. All are given the privilege and responsibility of building up one another and the body (Eph. 4:16). The apostles or missionaries, prophets, evangelists, and pastor-teachers are to take the lead and "perfect the saints" so that the saints can minister also. In that sense we are justified in concluding that in a very real sense every member of the Church is a "person gift" to all the others.

Without question, the fact that New Testament churches were established and grew as rapidly as they did was due in significant measure to the contribution of dedicated lay persons. Though the origin of the church at Rome, for example, is obscure, it seems likely that it was founded by Jews and proselytes who had been present at Pentecost (cf. Acts 2:10) and that some of the people mentioned in Romans 16 were people who had been converted in the Eastern churches and who had taken the message of Christ to Rome. In his *Life of Claudius,* Suetonius mentions that

Claudius "expelled the Jews from Rome because they kept rioting at the instigation of Christus." This may indicate that when the message was preached, unbelieving Jews in Rome rebelled as was the case with their counterparts in Thessalonica, Berea, and other places.[1]

At any rate, as victims of Claudius's edict, Aquila and Priscilla moved to Corinth where they continued their occupation as tentmakers (Acts 18:2, 3). From a human perspective the founding and growth of the Corinthian church (to say nothing of the success of Apollos—Acts 18:24-26) were due in large part to the ministry of these well-informed and dedicated lay people.

These humble believers—and a host of others like them, named and unnamed as far as the record goes—had a vital part in the planting of growing churches in the apostolic era. And this was as it was supposed to be. It was entirely in keeping with the teaching of Peter himself who wrote that believing people constitute a "chosen race" and a "royal priesthood" (I Peter 2:9).

History reveals that one of the most successful missionary movements of the modern era was that of the Moravians. Within twenty years (1732-52) they started more missions than all Protestants had started in the two preceding centuries. Why? Because they saw evangelization as essential and made it a "common affair" of the Moravian community. How? By sending small groups of ordinary believers to establish themselves in new areas and raise up testimonies for Christ. In the case of the Moravians, they sent nuclei of believers to even the remote areas of the world! The proportion of missionaries to communicant members over a two-hundred-year period was one in twelve![2]

---

[1] *Harper's Bible Dictionary*, ed. Madeleine Miller and J. Lane Miller, 7th ed. (New York: Harper and Row, 1962), p. 622.

[2] J. Herbert Kane, *A Global View of Christian Missions* (Grand Rapids: Baker, 1971), pp. 79-80.

The Use of Teams in Church-Planting

Teams in missions and evangelism are popularly associated with the gospel teams used in campaign and crusade evangelistic efforts. Christians who are acquainted with the world missionary enterprise will be aware of the use of international teams that are assembled and sent out in the hope that they will be able to identify with audiences of various ethnic and social backgrounds. At times this hope has been realized. At other times it has not. American-born Blacks and American-born Orientals may actually be at a disadvantage in the lands of their roots because they do not know the language or culture of nationals even though their physical features indicate that they *should* know the language and culture!

A more successful "team strategy"—one that seems to be reflected in the Scriptures—is the deployment of teams whose members complement one another in their gifts and ministries. Paul made strategic use of such a team. Included, at various times, were Luke, Silas (the Silvanus of the Epistles), Timothy, Sopater, Aristarchus, Secundus, Gaius, Tychicus, Trophimus, and others (cf. Acts 20:4). These team members were of varying ages and backgrounds and possessed complementary gifts. Paul often left team members behind, or sent them to places visited previously in order to complete the cycle and help develop mature, responsible local churches.

Talents and Spiritual Gifts

In taking stock of its available resources the world speaks of talent, abilities, "know-how," competency, and so forth. Talents and abilities are often referred to as "*natural* talents" or "*native* abilities." The Christian, of course, recognizes that they are really God-given and that they must be developed and used for God's purposes and glory. Such diverse abilities as those of the surgeon, mechanic, pilot, musician, radio technician, writer, artist, and linguist can be and should be utilized in evangelism and church extension. Those responsible for directing the mission of the Church must exercise caution in this regard, however.

In the first place, talent, ability, and expertise are not to be confused with the spiritual gifts enumerated in Romans 12 and I Corinthians 12. We will speak more of the spiritual gifts later, but it must be stressed here that talents are neither the same as, nor are they substitutes for, spiritual gifts.

In the second place, there is the very real danger of recruiting missionary-evangelists primarily on the basis of their abilities and expertise. "Whatever your special interest is, we can use it in our mission"—this is an all-too-common approach to recruitment. As a result, many workers become frustrated when their special ability is not fully utilized; they react by simply "doing their thing" and contributing only indirectly to the task of planting growing churches. Consequently, the so-called secondary or supporting ministries have a way of becoming primary and actually eclipsing the central task!

Finances and Material Resources

It was not difficult for Roland Allen to make a case for three rules which guided the practice of the apostle Paul in regard to finances: (1) he did not seek financial help for himself; (2) he took no financial help to those to whom he preached; and (3) he did not administer local church funds.[3] But by the same token Allen was not hard pressed to find certain exceptions to these rules. In any case, perhaps his sagest advice in this regard is contained in the following words: "What is of supreme importance is how

---

[3]Roland Allen, *Missionary Methods: St. Paul's or Ours?* (Grand Rapids: Eerdmans, 1962), pp. 49–61.

FIGURE 12

Nucleus Church-Planting

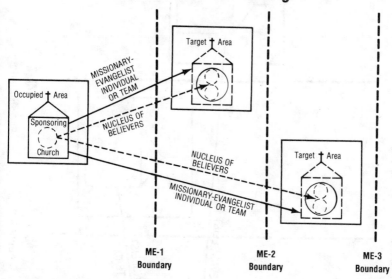

these arrangements, whatever they may be, affect the minds of the people, and so promote, or hinder, the spread of the Gospel."[4] On the one hand, it is imperative that we do not enter a new area with so much manpower, talent, and money as to create the impression that local initiative is not needed. On the other hand, those undertaking the task of developing churches must not discourage local participation by saddling local people with responsibilities that neither we nor our fathers could have borne!

Nucleus and Pioneer Church-Planting

Depending on circumstances, the geographical and cultural boundaries to be crossed in establishing new

---

[4]Ibid., p. 49.

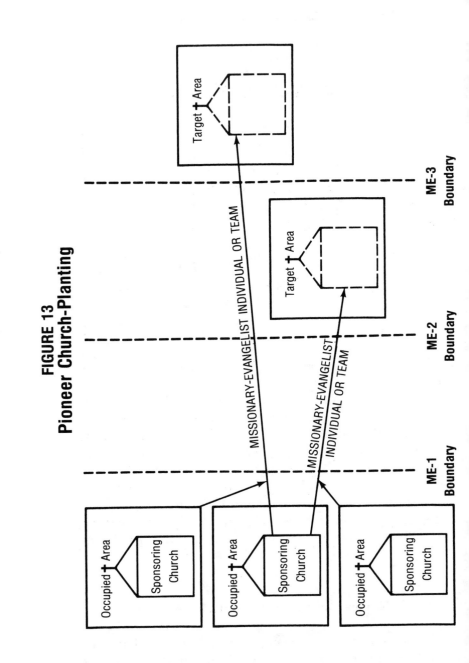

FIGURE 13
Pioneer Church-Planting

churches will require various personnel and variant approaches. Basically, the existing church (and its leadership) has two possible courses of action. First, guided by the Holy Spirit, it can plan to start another church on its own. Second, it can cooperate with other like-minded churches (which belong, for example, to the same denomination or mission association) in such an enterprise. The first option is most feasible in our "Jerusalems" and "Judeas" where considerable Christian work has been carried on, but where many churchless communities are still to be found. The second option is more viable in the "Samarias" and "uttermost parts" where great populations of relatively unreached and unchurched people are located.

The former option usually involves ME-1 and ME-2 programs. It can be called "Nucleus Church-Planting" because, in most cases, a nucleus of believers (from the sponsoring church or already residing in the target area or both) will be on hand to aid the missionary-evangelists (see Figure 12).

The latter option usually involves ME-2 and ME-3 programs. It can be called "Pioneer Church-Planting" because, in most cases, nuclei of believers with which to start will be small or nonexistent (see Figure 13).

God has provided the Church of Christ with all that is needed for its mission in the world. The challenge to the Church, then, is to dedicate itself to Christ and deploy its resources in accordance with His will.

seven

Measuring Growth

An old adage says, "Aim at nothing and you will probably hit it." Goals are essential, especially in a task as important as that of planting churches cross-culturally. Most will agree with that. But in spite of that agreement we often lack well-understood goals. Why? For four main reasons. First, because measurable goals sometimes seem incompatible with spirituality. Second, because of our lack of discipline. Third, because of confusion as to what the goals should be. Fourth, because even when we establish goals they are often too general and imprecise.

None of the four reasons offers a sufficient excuse for the lack of goals. Goals are necessary if we want to be effective, faithful stewards of the resources God has given to us. Measurement is essential in order to analyze progress and make "in-course" corrections.

In this chapter, then, we will consider some of the primary questions related to growth, the establishment of goals, and ways of measuring progress.

Basic Questions Relating to Church Growth

Quantitative or Qualitative Growth?

Growth can be quantitative or qualitative (Acts 9:31; 16:5). The former has to do primarily with the number of believers being added to the churches and the number of new congregations being established. The latter has to do with the level of understanding, Christian life, and dedication demonstrated by church members.

A rather pedantic and somewhat pointless argument has occurred between proponents of these two types of growth as to their priority and relationship. Advocates of the Church Growth school of thought have put so much emphasis on the number of members and percentages of membership growth that they have been the targets of a great deal of criticism. Church Growth proponents have responded to this criticism by noting that (1) it is evident in Scripture that God is interested in numerical (quantitative) growth, and (2) one of the best measures of qualitative growth is numerical increase.

The first response has validity. The second leaves something to be desired. There is a relationship between these two kinds of growth, to be sure. But there are churches made up of "quality Christians" in such widely separated areas as Morocco, Mindanao, and Montana which are experiencing very limited numerical growth. Moreover, even in receptive areas where there is considerable potential for numerical growth, that growth can actually be deceptive as a measurement of qualitative growth. After all, growth occurs in non-Christian movements as well as Christian ones. Sometimes it occurs in Christian churches when they employ Madison Avenue techniques at the expense of scriptural standards of Christian ethics and spirituality.

There is certainly nothing unspiritual about numerical growth unless one considers the post-Pentecost church at Jerusalem unspiritual! But numerical growth must be accompanied by spiritual growth. Goals for numerical growth should be set. But one can feel an empathy with the North American pastor who said, "My people are so fed up with numbers that the mere mention of a membership goal turns them off completely. What do I do?" (Probable solution: Set goals but do not overemphasize them.)

Can Qualitative Growth Be Measured?

In most situations numerical growth is an indicator of spiritual growth. But it is not the only indicator. It is important to realize that qualitative growth is measurable in ways other than taking a head count (or making up a financial report)! The Jehovah's Witnesses (who are vitally concerned about numerical growth) regularly test members on their ability to present the teachings to others. Soka Gakkai Buddhism has a system of voluntary examinations on their teachings which all believers who want increased responsibilities are expected to pass. And, to think in terms of Christian outreach, one historic mission in Korea required candidates for baptism to first win another to Christ. The church among an illiterate Indian tribe in Mexico required its believers to produce witnesses that they were living out the Bible truths under study before they could go on to study new truths! Where there is discipline there is a way!

How Do Churches Grow Numerically?

Church Growth specialists distinguish between three kinds of growth: *biological growth* (children of Christian parents coming to know the Lord), *conversion growth* (people converted from the world and brought into the fellowship of the church), and *transfer growth* (new members transferring from other churches).

Depending upon birth and death rates in the target

area, biological growth is more or less predictable. Specialists calculate that the average church in North America can anticipate a biological growth rate of about 25 percent per decade. Of course, the vitality of the local church and its Christian homes is an important factor here. We cannot simply assume that children of Christian parents will become believing members of the church.

Conversion growth from the swelling ranks of those multitudes of unbelievers who are unrelated to the church is essential if the church is to grow significantly. In the first place, and again depending on the target area involved, the birth rate among Christians may be lower than among non-Christians. In the second place, the addition to the church of people converted from the world has a salutary effect on the spiritual temperature of the local church. The freshness and devotion of those who have been rescued from spiritual rebellion and despair lend encouragement to the church and strengthen its outreach.

Transfer growth is not to be frowned upon unless it represents "sheep stealing" from other churches that are faithful to the testimony of Jesus Christ. Of course, it is imperative that believers who move into the areas of our churches be brought into the fellowship (and membership) of the churches as soon as possible. At the same time, transfer growth must be seen for what it is: the removal of believers from one church and their addition to another. The gain of one congregation represents the loss of another congregation! Transfer growth can never be a substitute for biological and conversion growth!

How Big Is Too Big?

Recently—particularly in America—a good deal has been said and written about the size of Sunday schools and churches. Bigness is certainly one measure of success—and perhaps the most obvious one. Some of what is said pro and con on the issue tends to be self-serving. But there is a

serious argument for large churches that merits consideration by churchmen in great urban centers around the
world. It is made by Robert Schuller, pastor of the
flourishing Garden Grove Church in California.[1] He
maintains that large churches with multiple staffs can best
meet the expectations and needs of mushrooming areas
and mobile populations. Furthermore, they can have an
influence and ministry that reach far beyond the immediate environs.

There is something to be said for Schuller's argument.
Perhaps the cause of Christ is best served by having some
"super churches" when God gives the appropriate form of
leadership and circumstances are right.

But several additional factors must be considered: (1) A
large church that does not provide for identification with
small groups included within the whole cannot possibly
meet the spiritual and psychological needs of its members;
(2) Large churches generally are not as effective as smaller
churches in terms of the utilization of believer potential;[2]
(3) A large church may be so self-contained that the members do not move outside it to serve the community; (4)
Some societies are better suited to the multiplication of
small churches than they are to the formation of large
churches; and (5) Today's dream of a large, impressive
edifice, once realized, can become tomorrow's nightmare
of large maintenance costs and unimpressive echoes!
Meaningful answers to these disadvantages of large
churches can come only in relation to specific target areas
and leadership.

In conclusion, let it be said that God desires both quantitative and qualitative growth for His churches, but
neither at the expense of the other. Certainly our Lord

---

[1]Robert H. Schuller, *Your Church Has Real Possibilities* (Glendale, CA:
Regal Books, 1974), pp. 7–18.
[2]Cf. Charles L. Chaney, "A New Day for Churches," *Church Growth
Bulletin*, vol. 12, no. 4 (March 1976), pp. 512–16.

desires fruitfulness—and *fruitfulness* is measurable in one way or another (John 15:16). But He also requires *faithfulness*. Measured by human yardsticks there will be many situations in which the two will seem unfriendly to each other. But in the divine economy they usually are closely related.

Measuring and Analyzing Growth in the Church

Unquestionably, God is desirous of spiritual growth in His people. But spiritual life precedes spiritual growth. Unbelievers must be converted and become members of the family of God. Leaving the consideration of spiritual growth for later chapters, let us think now in terms of measuring and analyzing numerical growth in a local church. This is a matter that should be carefully studied by church leadership in anticipation of entering a target area to plant a new church. Otherwise goals will be nebulous, proper records will not be kept, and meaningful analysis of progress will be difficult.

Three tasks are imperative in this connection: (1) the establishment of measurable goals; (2) the keeping of accurate records; and (3) the analysis of past progress.

The Establishment of Measurable Goals

When a target area has been adequately surveyed and studied, it should be possible to make some meaningful projections as to growth potential in the new work. Even when based upon sound data, any such projections will be expressions of *faith* for only God can "grow a church." But just *that kind* of faith is needed. If our survey of the target area reveals, for example, that the area contains only two comparatively static congregations, that the population of 6,000 is increasing at an average of 500 annually, that the residents tend to be of similar class and ethnic background, that a majority of the present residents are not committed to another faith, and that newcomers tend to be responsive (with a significant number of committed Christians among them), then we have good grounds for projecting a certain growth rate.

Such projections will have two primary aspects: the number of people we anticipate will be brought into the local body of believers, and the time required to reach successive stages of growth. By superimposing this information upon the Pauline Cycle in the manner of Figure 14, the workers will see the task in a new light. They can plan and pray according to projections based on faith and knowledge. If the work does not progress on schedule, they will ask what they might be doing wrong, and will change their approach or revise their expectations in accordance with experience. If progress exceeds expectations, they can revise their projections upward!

The Keeping of Accurate Records

One of the most serious problems encountered by specialists who are asked to analyze the growth patterns of local churches and denominations is the lack of adequate records. All too often church records are ambiguous, incomplete, or altogether lacking. When there is a record of the number of church members in a given year with no corresponding records of average attendance, how the members came into the church (transfer or confession of faith, for example), and how many members were removed from the church rolls (whether by discipline, death, or transfer), the membership statistic means little. In fact, unless such records are available over a period of years, it becomes all but impossible to diagnose the health of a church.

Denominational and mission leaders should see to it that accurate and uniform records are kept in new churches

FIGURE 14
"THE PAULINE CYCLE"

THREE MONTHS
Planning and target area analysis

MISSIONARIES
COMMISSIONED
Acts 13:1-4; 15:39, 40

Initial contacts made: surveys undertaken; evangelism initiated

SENDING CHURCHES
CONVENED
Acts 14:26, 27; 15:1-4

AUDIENCE
CONTACTED
Acts 13:14-16; 14:1

THREE MONTHS

GOSPEL
COMMUNICATED
Acts 13:17ff.; 16:31

RELATIONSHIPS
CONTINUED
Acts 15:36; 18:23

THE HOLY SPIRIT
THE DIVINE DIRECTOR
OF THE MISSIONARY ENTERPRISE
Acts 13:2, 52

PRAYER THE ATMOSPHERE
Acts 13:1-4

THE SCRIPTURES THE FOUNDATION
Acts 15:15

THE CHURCH THE AGENCY
Acts 15:22

HEARERS
CONVERTED
Acts 13:48; 16:14, 15

Permanent meeting-place and organization;
Missionary leadership withdrawn
ONE YEAR

BELIEVERS
COMMENDED
Acts 14:23; 16:40

LEADERSHIP
CONSECRATED
Acts 14:23

BELIEVERS
CONGREGATED
Acts 13:43

Temporary meeting-place; worship and instruction initiated
THREE MONTHS

FAITH
CONFIRMED
Acts 14:21, 22; 15:41

Witness and service; emergence of leadership; organization effected
SIX MONTHS

from the very first. The resultant statistics will enable the church-planter to ascertain whether or not the projected goals are being reached as he moves through the first months and years of the church-planting effort. Later on, those statistics will be invaluable in ascertaining the growth patterns of the church on a long-term basis.

At the very least, adequate attendance and membership records should include the following:

(1) The results of initial surveys.

(2) Information concerning successful contacts (i.e., contacts who have responded by an expression of faith and/or coming to church meetings), including how they were contacted, etc.

(3) Attendance at the various meetings of the developing congregation.

(4) Membership statistics (from the time the new church is organized), including data as to how new members were gained (whether by transfer from other churches or by confession of faith—and when children make confession of faith, it should be noted whether their parents are believers or unbelievers), and why former members were lost to the membership.

The Analysis of Past Progress

A prominent preacher recently announced to a Midwestern congregation that the sermon they were about to hear was being preached for the 1,030th time and that it had always brought results! Before criticizing the preacher, we should take stock. A sermon that has been in for 1,030 tune-ups can be expected to be a fairly good sermon! Besides, if it always gets results it certainly bears repeating! One would wish that our plans for extending the Church of Christ were as carefully devised, thoroughly mastered, regularly reviewed, and universally effective as that sermon!

An overall or master plan requires periodic evaluation and modification. We should change our plan, not by scrapping the whole and initiating a new one each time we encounter a problem or some new idea is promulgated, but by modifying the part that is ineffective or rendered obsolete. This we can do by changing conditions or by adding new insights.

In one Asian country, we were devising the major elements of a plan for planting new churches when, suddenly, the face of one of the participants registered shock.

"I believe we have such a plan," she said. "Didn't we appoint a committee to develop a five-year plan for evangelism and church-planting several years ago?"

Another face brightened. "I believe we did. We do have a plan. But where is it?"

A thorough search extricated one copy of the master five-year plan from the secretary's file cabinet! That plan had been carefully devised, prayerfully considered, unanimously passed, and promptly forgotten!

Periodic evaluation and modification are essential. In fact, they are part of the plan!

One of the most widely used small books on church growth (it has been translated into about fifty languages) is primarily a book on the analysis of membership statistics. The author, Vergil Gerber, explains in simple steps how to diagnose the strengths and weaknesses of a church by analyzing its growth patterns over a period of time. Using a ten-year span for the sake of convenience, let us outline the basic steps Gerber recommends for carrying out this kind of analysis.[3]

Step One: Compile membership statistics for the ten-year period.

Step Two: Plot these statistics on a graph. See, for example, the growth rate of Church A as plotted in Figure 15.

---

[3]Vergil Gerber, *How to Keep a Church Going and Growing* (South Pasadena, CA: William Carey Library, 1973), pp. 43–62. See also Bob Waymire and C. Peter Wagner, *The Church Growth Survey Handbook* (Santa Clara, CA: O. C. Ministries, Inc., 1980).

FIGURE 15
CHURCH A
Graph of Growth Rate: 1971–80

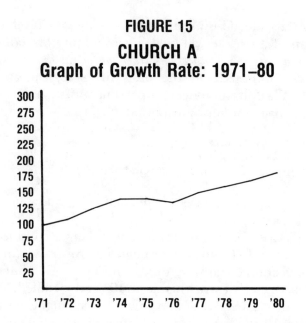

Step Three: Calculate the growth rate of the church for the decade. In the case of Church A:

Current membership	180
Membership ten years ago	− 100
Ten-year increase	80
The growth rate is	80%

This gives the overall picture. Of course if one also calculates the annual growth rates and compares them, it is possible to ascertain whether the rate of growth is increasing or declining. In the case of Church A, after a period of stagnancy, there has been steady growth of ten members for each of the last three years, but since the increase of ten is figured on the base of a larger membership each year, the rate of growth actually has been declining somewhat.

Step Four: Compare the actual growth with the projection of biological growth. Calculate that, as a rule of thumb, biological growth can be projected at about 25 percent per decade. This means that the average church over the span of a decade will have a growth rate of about 25 percent *apart from conversions from the world and transfers from other churches.* On the basis of biological growth Church A will have added 25 percent to its original 100 members over the ten-year period:

Ten-year increase	80
Projected biological increase	−25
Increase from conversion and transfers	55

Obviously, further analysis is needed to see how healthy Church A really is.

Step Five: Refine the data. Some members are lost to the church. They fall into three categories: reversion (or excommunication), transfer, or death. Very few churches keep statistics that are this accurate and detailed, even though such statistics would be highly revealing. Consider, for example, the bar graph in Figure 16, which gives this very kind of information for Church B over a five-year period.

FIGURE 16
CHURCH B
Analysis of Kinds of Growth: 1976–80

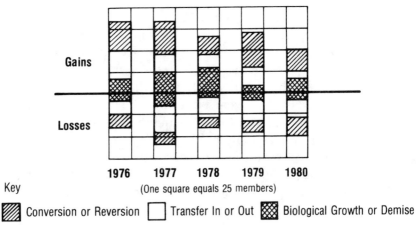

Gains

Losses

1976   1977   1978   1979   1980

Key   (One square equals 25 members)

▨ Conversion or Reversion   ☐ Transfer In or Out   ▩ Biological Growth or Demise

Even a cursory analysis of this graph is revealing. Notice that the number of conversions is consistently higher than the number of reversions. That is as it should be. In the last year, however, the ratio of reversions to conversions has been higher. That certainly needs prayerful consideration.

Notice also that, with the exception of one year, considerably more members have been transferring out of Church B than have been transferring in. Perhaps this indicates that something is wrong in the church. Or perhaps people are just leaving the area. In either case, something must be done or Church B will not continue to exist!

Step Six: Analyze the church's growth patterns. When the kind of study suggested above has been done, one can look back and analyze the results. Every church will be different, but as the lines and bars on these simple graphs rise and fall, they tell the story of successes and failures, of strengths and weaknesses.

Step Seven: Set goals for the future. With a view to starting new churches as well as strengthening existing ones, this is a most important step. In the pioneer situation about the only way to accomplish this is to look at the record of surrounding churches or churches in similar situations. The existing church can project goals on the basis of the past record, expected biological growth (25 percent per year), and faith in what the Lord will do in response to praying, planning, and working. In the case of Church A, the goal might well be something like 225 members at the end of five years (see Figure 17).

In order to carry on the kind of analysis suggested above, church leaders need to understand that they are in business for the King. That being the case, it is wise stewardship of personnel, gifts, money, and time to take an accounting, set measurable goals, and seek ways of attaining them.

The King's business is not like any other business, however. The supreme objective of the churches is to obey and

FIGURE 17

CHURCH A
Projected Growth: 1980–85

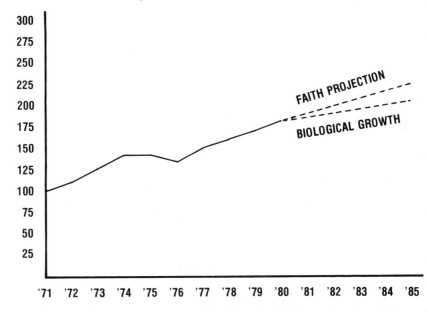

glorify God in all that they do. That being the case, faithful leaders and churches will give of themselves in order that the number of both churches and church members might grow all around the world!

It is not unusual to see a sign in business establishments which says, "Under New Management." The churches and missions do not need new management necessarily, though a periodic infusion of new blood and new ideas is always good. But in view of the importance and immensity of our task, and the challenges of secularism, materialism, mysticism, and the rest, it would be good to hang up a sign in our various home offices, "Management Under Review." Self-examination is good for all of us.

Who will marshal the Christian forces? Who will take the lead in developing sound strategy? Who will help us determine where and when to march forward? Who will direct available resources of men and money, talent and time, gifts and energies, into occupying new territory for Christ? Who, if not the administrators God has given to His Church?

And when they do, all true Christians will rise up and call them blessed. And, more importantly, the Commander-in-Chief will someday raise them up and say, "Well done."

PART THREE

The Sending Church and the Christian Mission

eight

The Missionaries Commissioned

Someone has said that everyone's task is no one's task. There is some truth to that statement. Some people must take the lead if anything is to be accomplished. If local churches are to be truly missionary churches, denominational leaders and local pastors and officers must furnish the required information, inspiration, and example. If the work of planting growing churches at home and abroad is to be advanced, specialists in pioneering (i.e., evangelists and missionaries) must be called out, trained, and sent. Of course, lay participation in the missionary task is absolutely essential, especially in accessible target areas. But someone must take the lead and, moving out into new areas, give direction to the church-planting enterprise. It is the responsibility of existing churches to respond to the Holy Spirit and see that such workers are forthcoming.

Objectives

In this chapter we are concerned with our "Jerusalems" and "Antiochs"—churches that have already been estab-

FIGURE 18
"THE PAULINE CYCLE"

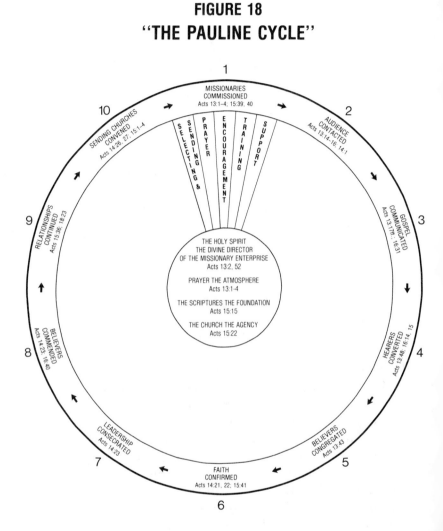

"Then, when they had fasted and prayed and laid their hands on them, they sent them away. So, being sent out by the Holy Spirit . . ." (Acts 13:3, 4a).

lished by the grace of God and the faithfulness of our predecessors, and form the bases for further outreach. Our objectives for these churches are:

(1) To foster the kind of missionary spirit that encourages pastors, officers, and lay believers to participate in the God-given task of planting growing churches in adjacent and more distant unreached communities.

(2) To mobilize believers in a program of missionary outreach.

(3) To recognize, prepare, send, support, and cooperate with those whom Christ has specially appointed to take the leadership in this work.

The Selection and Sending of Church-Planting Missionaries

Biblical Principles and Precedents

(1) The apostles (missionaries) and evangelists were at the forefront of the early effort in church-extension evangelism. There were many ordinary saints, of whom only a few are named, who "went everywhere preaching the Word" and participating in the task of planting churches. But there were also specially gifted apostles and evangelists who "led the troops."

In the New Testament there are two kinds of apostles. First, there is the relatively small group of those who were personally chosen and instructed by the Lord. These men held the *office* of apostle, to which there is no succession. Second, there are those men who had the *gift* of apostleship and were called "apostles of the churches" (II Cor. 8:23). In this group were included such men as Barnabas, Silas, Timothy, Epaphroditus, Andronicus, and Junias.

The term *missionary,* of course, is not a New Testament word. Etymologically, however, it is closely related to "apostle." Both words carry the idea of one who is sent forth to do a task. The emphasis in the New Testament is more on the task to be performed than on the place to which the man is to be sent. The task was that of proclaiming the gospel and planting churches or aiding those who were doing so.

The role of the evangelist was similar to that of the "apostles of the churches." The evangelist was particularly gifted by the Holy Spirit to proclaim the gospel in such a manner that men were persuaded to accept the Savior. There is little evidence that the evangelists actually organized churches. That seemed to be the particular job of the apostles. Take the church on the island of Crete by way of example. Although there were undoubtedly believers who had been present in Jerusalem on the day of Pentecost (Acts 2:11) and then returned to the island, they did not even appoint elders. It was not until Paul visited the island in the early sixties that the process of appointing elders was begun (Titus 1:5). It is apparent that some form of evangelistic work had laid the foundation for the church before Paul came, but no formal organization had been developed.

(2) God calls and sends missionary-evangelists in and through the churches. Michael C. Griffiths writes:

> Not even one missionary call recorded by the Holy Spirit in the Acts of the Apostles was subjective or the result of individual initiative alone. In most cases, the subjective sense of call is not the aspect of the call which is brought to our attention by the Holy Spirit. In every case either the church or another missionary had a considerable part to play in the call. God's call is based primarily on objective external events rather than on subjective, internal experience.
>
> Barnabas went to Antioch because his church sent him there (Acts 11:22). Saul went to Antioch because Barnabas brought him there (Acts 11:26). Both men went out from Antioch, as a result of a decision made jointly with the other Antioch church leaders at a time of prayer and fast-

ing (Acts 13:2). Silas joined Paul at his invitation (Acts 15:40) and so did young Timothy (Acts 16:3).

How do we apply this?

(1) What we find is not wild individualism or sensational guidance, but God's people working, praying, and planning together responsibly for the evangelization of the world. We see not just a selfish concern for an individual calling, but a dovetailing of God's plan for many lives.

(2) A general call for missionary volunteers is not stressed in the New Testament. Missionaries went because their churches sent them, or because older missionaries brought them.

(3) Our willingness to go anywhere is an intensely personal matter between us and our Master. But in order for "anywhere" to become a definite "somewhere," both our home churches and the older missionaries must have a say.[1]

Turn to the record of the sending forth of Paul and Barnabas from the church in Antioch (Acts 13:1–4). Here is a delicate balance of the working of God in the Church, in its leaders, and in the missionary-evangelist candidates. The direction of God is seen in the roles played by those early believers corporately and individually.

First, God spoke to the men who were to be sent. Both Paul and Barnabas had been called by God prior to this event. Paul's call is recorded in Scripture and was dramatic. Barnabas's call is not recorded and may have been less dramatic. In Paul's case, close to nine years had elapsed since his personal call. Nevertheless, he waited until God spoke to the church.

Second, God spoke to the church and its leaders. There is no evidence as to how the Holy Spirit communicated God's will. It may have been as spectacular as Paul's call or the events of the day of Pentecost. But this is not indicated.

---

[1]Michael C. Griffiths, "You and God's Work Overseas" (Chicago: Inter-Varsity Press, 1967), pp. 20–21.

There may have been a crisis in the church, for the group was fasting. Perhaps God placed a special burden for the lost upon the church. It seems probable that the extension of the gospel to other areas was discussed frequently. Undoubtedly the leaders had conferred with one another and with other church members as to how the gospel might be given to other peoples. In any case, the Holy Spirit spoke. He communicated to the church which men He wanted to go to new areas.

So, in God's time, the missionary-evangelists were selected by the Spirit, separated for the work, released by their believing followers, and sent forth by the Spirit with the laying-on of hands. This official commissioning implies both a blessing and a recognition. It was a blessing in that the senders acknowledged that those who were being sent had been called and equipped for the task; they were going forth with the approval of the church. But the ceremony signified more. Just as in the Old Testament the priest laid his hands on the sacrificial victim, thus signifying that the victim was taking the place of the offerer, so in the commissioning of the missionary-evangelists the church recognized that those who were being sent were going in the place of the church.[2]

It is important to note that Paul and Barnabas were men who had demonstrated their abilities before the Spirit spoke to the church. There were five men in the group of prophets and teachers from which Paul and Barnabas were selected. Each one had some special qualification for the missionary task. Simeon was black. Lucius was from Cyrene and thus could have been sent there. Manaen had been brought up with Herod and could have had influ-

---

[2]In interpreting the laying-on of hands, care must be taken not to make the Church a mediating agency. The Church did not mediate Paul's call. His call was direct from God (Gal. 1:1). Therefore, we have used the words *recognition* and *blessing* in connection with the ceremony. Cf. also Gal. 2:7-9.

ence in the government. Evidently none of these qualifications was crucial or sufficient. Barnabas was a proven quantity. He was the first teacher of note in the church. Paul was the second teacher. Under these two men the church had grown. It could be said that the church sent the best of its leadership group. At any rate, men of proven maturity and effectiveness were selected to lead the extension ministry of the Antioch church.

Relevant Research

Successful mass movements generally exhibit a succession of leadership that falls within a rather distinct pattern. Eric Hoffer notes three kinds of leaders of such movements and the order in which they appear: men of words, fanatics, and practical men of action.[3] The men of words articulate the teaching. The fanatics marshal the believers, take the message to the masses, and gain converts. The practical men of action consolidate the movement. According to Hoffer, one man may possess the varied abilities necessary to see a movement through the various stages, but more often than not, a succession of leadership is involved. Hoffer's work qualifies as research only in the broadest sense of that word, but certain subsequent studies do indicate that his analysis has a good deal of validity.[4]

Our concerns are radically different from Hoffer's, to be sure, but there may be some value in differentiating between the theorists, missionary-evangelists, and consolidators in our programs of church extension. Not everyone who can begin a work can sustain it. And on the

---

[3]Eric Hoffer, *The True Believer: Thoughts on the Nature of Mass Movements* (New York: New American Library of World Literature, 1958), p. 120.

[4]*Dynamic Religious Movements,* ed. David J. Hesselgrave (Grand Rapids: Baker, 1978), p. 309.

other hand, not everyone who can shepherd a congregation is effective in finding lost sheep and bringing them into a fold. The implications of the biblical distinction between various types of "person gifts" merit attention.

Practical Reflection

(1) As we have noted previously, in the churches we have tended to let practice determine the definition of some terms that closely relate to church extension. On the one hand we have tended to define the "mission" of the church very loosely. As a consequence, "foreign missionaries" are "those who do missionary work abroad," and "missionary work" is "the good things foreign missionaries do for the needy people among whom they work." It follows that "home missionaries" are "those who do good things for needy people at home." All of this may be true, but it is also vague and misleading. Actually, the central missionary undertaking is to win men to Christ and establish churches in new areas.

On the other hand, we have tended to define "evangelism" very narrowly. As a consequence, the "evangelist" becomes one who "preaches" (usually) the "good news" and "wins men to Christ." Actually, the proclamation of the gospel *is* basic to the evangelist's task, but we cannot afford, and the Scriptures overall do not support, evangelism that is divorced from, or but tenuously related to, the churches.

It is incumbent upon pastor-teachers especially to carefully delineate the terms and tasks related to the growth of the Church. All Christians are witnesses, but not all of them are missionary-evangelists any more than all are pastor-teachers. We need "specialists," but specialists according to biblical definitions and guidelines.

(2) We have built the greater part of our contemporary evangelistic and missionary enterprise upon a vast pro-

gram of volunteerism. New Testament missions were *voluntaristic*—that is, those who participated did so voluntarily and of their own free will. But New Testament missions were not based on *volunteerism*—that is, a general call for, and the sending of, anyone who would offer himself to go.

In overseas missions the result of our approach has been the sending of many relatively untrained missionaries to accomplish a task which is ill-defined and in which they have not had experience. In home missions the result has been that those who are most successful in the ministry of local churches move on to larger churches and higher salaries rather than moving on to challenging unchurched areas where their experience and abilities could be used in starting new congregations. And because home missions is not defined primarily in terms of entering new territories for Christ, because funds are limited, and because partial self-support is not usually considered, even younger persons ready to launch out into the Christian ministry seldom begin new congregations.

Prayerful Concern for Church-Planting Missions

Biblical Principles and Precedents

The New Testament is replete with exhortations to prayer. It carefully teaches the Christian how to pray. The subject of prayer receives extensive doctrinal development in the New Testament. It is not strange, then, that much is said about prayer and missions.

Prayer and the Selection of Missionary-Evangelists

The Church is commanded to pray that missionaries will be sent. When Jesus looked upon the great harvest field, He told His disciples to pray that the Lord would send forth laborers into His field (Matt. 9:38; Luke 10:2). When the church at Antioch was ministering and fasting, the Lord indicated which leaders He wanted to go to the harvest field (Acts 13:2). Both the command and the example make it clear that the selection of missionary-evangelist candidates should be bathed in prayer.

Prayer and the Sending of Missionary-Evangelists

Just as the selection of the candidate is to be the concern of much prayer, so the commissioning of the candidate is to be accompanied by prayer (Acts 13:3). The commissioning of church-planters is no different than the installation of the elder or deacon in this regard. The first deacons were commissioned only after prayer (Acts 6:6) and the elders were commended to the Lord after prayer (Acts 14:23). The normal biblical procedure is to saturate commissioning services with prayer.

Prayer and the Support of Missionary-Evangelists

Prayer for the church-planter, whether at home or abroad, is part of the support which the Church is to give. Paul requested prayer for himself with respect to his many needs. He asked the church at Rome to pray for his protection from enemies and the acceptance of his ministry by the saints (Rom. 15:31). He asked believers at Ephesus to pray that he might be bold in the proclamation of the message (Eph. 6:19). The Colossian Christians were asked to pray for an open door so that he could clearly present the gospel (Col. 4:2, 3). The Thessalonians were requested to pray for the rapid spread of the gospel and protection from perverse men (II Thess. 3:1, 2). If to the above specific requests for prayer, one adds the items mentioned in the general commands relating to prayer for all church leaders, it is all the more obvious that the entire church-planting operation is to be continually bathed in believing prayer.

Relevant Research

Church history reveals that there is an intimate relationship between sincere prayer and successful outreach.

After several abortive attempts on the continent of Europe, a great deal of missionary activity grew out of the Pietist movement and the dedication of men like Philipp Spener (1635–1705) and August Francke (1663–1727). They supplemented their Sunday sermons with cottage meetings for prayer and Bible study. Two centuries after the Protestant Reformation, the movement fathered by these men bore fruit in the form of successful missionary efforts.[5]

In England, in 1723, Robert Millar wrote *A History of the Propagation of Christianity and the Overthrow of Paganism*. In this book he advocated intercession for the conversion of unbelievers all around the world. Within a few years prayer groups were found throughout the British Isles. In 1746 American Christians were invited to participate in a seven-year "Concert of Prayer" for missions. Jonathan Edwards echoed the call in a pamphlet. Forty years later—back in England—John Sutcliff encouraged all Baptist churches and ministers in Northamptonshire to set aside the first Monday of each month to pray for the non-Christian world. Soon, William Carey (1761–1834) joined the Baptists. In 1793 he sailed for India and a new day dawned for Christian missions.[6]

In America, missions and evangelism were likewise the result of prevailing prayer. A burden for world mission grew out of meetings called by Samuel J. Mills for prayer and discussion at Williams College in the first decade of the nineteenth century.[7]

---

[5]J. Herbert Kane, *A Global View of Christian Missions* (Grand Rapids: Baker, 1971), p. 77.
[6]Ibid., pp. 83–85.
[7]Ibid., pp. 86–87.

History speaks unequivocally: The harvest is seen through opened eyes after those eyes have been closed in prayer.

Practical Reflection

Collectively and individually, Christians everywhere should pray: "Lord of the Church, be at work among us and from among your sons and daughters in our fellowship call out those who will proclaim the good tidings of Christ and plant His Church in needy areas of the world. For the glory of God and the good of mankind, hear our prayer offered in Jesus' name. Amen." Prayer is the starting point. God delights to answer this kind of prayer. It is always in His will to do so.

But prayer is more than the starting point. It is the continuing force behind the entire program of outreach. Over and over the apostle Paul exhorted believers in the churches to pray, not just for their personal needs, but for him and for the work of Christ among the lost. And pray they did. And pray we should. After all, they and we are servants who minister to the Lord of the Church. We are sons who should be communicating with the Father about the "family business." We are soldiers—in an army that goes forward only on its knees!

Whatever reasons we may adduce for our all too feeble and poorly attended congregational prayer meetings today, we can rest assured that the members of the churches of the New Testament era would not be impressed! The fact of the matter is that contemporary prayer meetings often do not attract even some of the most likely candidates for leadership in church outreach. And why? Because the average prayer meeting in the average church does not seem to be a vital part of that outreach! This does not excuse the absentees. But it should give pause to pastors, staff members, elders, and deacons in the churches.

It is at the prayer meeting that we transact the business of the King! Whoever began the tradition of separating church business meetings from church prayer meetings and running the former according to *Robert's Rules of Order* and the latter according to the "orders of the day" did the churches a great disservice. Let us plan to bring business and prayer together again—with some degree of regularity. And let us bring the Word of God to bear upon the work committed to us. Let leaders in planning and outreach discuss the local work of Christ in which all should be involved in one way or another, and the more distant work of Christ in which our representatives participate— not just in a general way, but in terms of definite plan, stated programs, and real people. Let us share our thoughts on these matters—and then let us pray that God will burden and bless us, and choose and use us according to His will. And let our goal be that prayer-meeting attendance will at least approximate the number of members who reside within a reasonable distance of the location of the meeting. And let another goal be that periodically the Lord will place a divine claim on some in the congregation and make of them special "person gifts" to the building of His Church and the blessing of all.

The Encouragement of Church-Planting Missionaries

Biblical Principles and Precedents

The Need for Encouragement

When Paul arrived in Corinth, he was a very discouraged man. Having sent Timothy to Thessalonica to ascertain the state of the believers there, he had been left alone at Athens (I Thess. 3:1, 2). He was so worried about the Thessalonians that he wished to visit them but was hindered from doing so by Satan (I Thess. 2:18). He had failed to win many converts in Athens after successful ministries in Philippi, Thessalonica, and Berea. Perhaps this prompted him to examine his ministry. He determined to preach only the message of the crucified Christ (I Cor. 2:2–5). Whatever the reasons, Paul seems to have been a discouraged missionary. If a man as great as Paul could become discouraged, all missionaries can become discouraged. The need for encouragement is apparent.

The Provision for Encouragement

God has provided encouragement. The Holy Spirit is the official "Encourager" (*Parakletos*) (John 14:16). The gift of encouragement has been given to men of the Church (Rom. 12:8a, NIV). An example par excellence has been provided in the person of Barnabas (Acts 4:36). It is noteworthy that Barnabas, the "son of encouragement," is the first missionary named in Acts. It was he who introduced Saul to the skeptical apostles (Acts 9:26, 27). It was he who was sent by the church at Jerusalem to Antioch (Acts 11:22). It was he who enlisted Saul to work in the Antioch church (Acts 11:25, 26). Later, it was he who gave John Mark a second chance and had much to do with Mark's restoration to usefulness (Acts 15:36–39; II Tim. 4:11). In all probability, it was because Barnabas encouraged Paul that Scripture records no periods of depression in the life of Paul while Barnabas accompanied him.

But Barnabas was not alone in the ministry of encouragement.

There are a number of indications of workers whom Paul encouraged or who encouraged him in his labors. In 1 Cor. 16:10 he asks the Corinthians (believers) to "put him (Timothy) at ease among you." Paul's two letters to Timothy were in the nature of encouragements. Paul admits his loneliness in 1 Cor. 16:17–18 and tells how the coming of two friends cheered him up. Again and again he refers to the encouragement which was brought to him by the coming of Epaphroditus and gifts he brought (Phil. 4:18). More important than having his needs supplied was the thought that he was remembered and that this effort on the part of the Macedonian Christians was a sure sign of spiritual growth on their part. In Paul's letter to Philemon, Paul speaks of Philemon as giving him "much joy and comfort" (Philem. 1:7).[8]

In Romans 1 Paul gives an insight as to how the encourager might stimulate a depressed servant of God. He says: "For I long to see you in order that I may impart some spiritual gift to you, that you may be established; that is, that I may be encouraged together with you while among you, each of us by the other's faith, both yours and mine" (Rom. 1:11, 12). The idea is clear. As the missionary-evangelist uses his gift, faith is stimulated in the congregation. This in turn encourages the missionary-evangelist. In other words, the depressed servant in this case is stimulated to use his spiritual gift; this creates faith on the part of the hearers; and the result is that the depressed missionary-evangelist himself is encouraged.

Relevant Research

It is most interesting that Gary Collins begins his book *How to Be a People Helper* with a chapter entitled "People Helping and the Great Commission." In that chapter he shows that the discipling activity of the Great Commission requires that the Christian community be a helping and encouraging community. Though Collins's book is basically a popular treatment, he does refer to studies which reinforce his main contention. Concerning the "effectiveness of group helping," he writes:

> Psychologists discovered the effectiveness of group helping many years ago. Mental patients who had been chained in unsanitary asylums were found to improve dramatically when they were treated with compassion and kindness. As

---

[8]Taken from a paper entitled "A Search for New Models" submitted by Dale W. Bjork on January 19, 1978, in a class in church-extension evangelism at Trinity Evangelical Divinity School.

part of something called "moral treatment," the hospital administrators and staff lived with the patients, ate with them, and showed that the hospital could be a therapeutic community instead of a prison-like dungeon. This idea was extended further after World War Two, when a British psychiatrist named Maxwell Jones published an account of a therapeutic community in which all of the patient's daily activities were directed toward his or her recovery. "Milieu therapy" was a term which applied to this kind of treatment. One-to-one counseling was part of the treatment but equally important was the daily support, help, and encouragement given by the staff and the patients to each other.[9]

In the present context, of course, we are not dealing specifically with therapy as such. But Collins's thesis, and numerous studies, indicate the value of the kind of helping relationships being advocated here.[10]

Practical Reflection

Encouragement is a part of the spiritual ministries of all believers. Barnabas-like spirits should take special note of young people in the Church who demonstrate dedication to Christ, a cooperative spirit, the ability to communicate, dependability in inconspicuous tasks, and other gifts and qualities so vital to the mission of the Church. They should be singled out for counseling. They should have opportunities for discussion with visiting evangelists, preachers, pastors, teachers, and mission leaders. They should be blanketed with prayer.

This approach has application to successful pastors and older church workers as well as to the younger sons and daughters of the Church. The work needs Pauls and Barnabases as well as Marks and Timothys! Might not some

---

[9]Gary Collins, *How to Be a People Helper* (Santa Ana, CA: Vision House Publishers, 1976), pp. 130–31.

[10]Perhaps it is worth noting that the category "Helping Behavior" was added to the listings of the *Social Science Index* (New York: H. Wilson Co.) six years ago.

pastor-teachers be divinely appointed to do the work of an evangelist in a new area? Where are the modern Pauls— divinely motivated to go to churchless vacuums rather than larger churches? And what about lay people who are in a position to provide for their own while still moving out to help claim new territories for Christ?

ME-1 illustration: One of the greatest preachers America ever produced, George Truett, once said that he probably never would have become a preacher at all apart from the encouragement of the saints of God in his church back home. Encouragement is a part of the plan of God. It should be a part of our master plans. It need not be less spontaneous or sincere for being so.

Training Christian Workers for the Missionary Task

Biblical Principles and Precedents

Two types of training can and must be distinguished in Scripture. Otherwise confusion will arise as to what the Bible teaches concerning the training of missionary-evangelists. While it is popular today to obliterate the distinction between laity and clergy, Scripture maintains the distinction. However, the biblical distinction is not the hierarchical one that some churches make today. Rather, it is in regard to the training of the workers that the true distinction is seen. It can be readily seen that Paul, Timothy, and Titus were not trained in the same manner as were the saints at Berea, Thessalonica, or any of the other churches which Paul founded. Likewise, the Twelve were not trained by our Lord in the same way as were the multitudes.

The reasons for this distinction are varied. First, the Lord taught that the disciple is not above his teacher. This indicates that the teacher must know more than the disciple. Second, the gifts given to each type of ministry differ.

Logically, a person is trained according to his gifts. The gifts given to the missionary-evangelist, being different, involve him in a training program distinct from that for a deacon. Third, the role of the missionary-evangelists and pastor-teachers is that of training laity for the work of the ministry. That is, these leaders must be "trained to train others." Their purpose in the Church is not so much to carry out the entire ministry as it is to equip others to minister. The training of the missionary-evangelist, then, must differ from that of the laity in profundity and intensity in accordance with the gifts which God has given.

While Scripture mentions only the school of Tyrannus as a place where disciples were instructed daily, one must not infer from this that the training given first-century workers was less than profound. A cursory reading of the pastoral Epistles shows that the two young missionaries trained by Paul had a profound grasp of the Word of God and could put it into action. Paul taught them both true doctrine and sound practice.

That doctrine was taught can be seen in Paul's command to Titus to make sure that the Cretans adorned the doctrine of God in every respect (Titus 2:1, 10). Timothy was told to pass on that which Paul had taught him (II Tim. 2:2). He knew fully the doctrine of Paul (II Tim. 3:10, KJV). He was to pay attention to doctrine until Paul came (I Tim. 4:13). Clearly the two young missionaries were taught doctrine.

But they were also taught practical theology. Titus had been schooled in financial matters and was entrusted with the mission of carrying the offering for the poor from Corinth to Jerusalem (II Cor. 8:1-6, 16-21). Timothy knew about deacons and their qualifications (I Tim. 3:8-14), and both he and Titus knew the qualifications for the office of elder (I Tim. 3:1-7; Titus 1:5-9). The content of a course in practical Christian living can be seen in Titus 2:1-10. Paul even hints at pedagogical techniques in this passage. Titus was to speak (*laleō*) to the elders, have older women teach the younger women, and be an example to the young men (vv. 1, 3–4, 7).

Not only the substance of doctrine and practice, but also the manner in which they were taught can be seen in the New Testament. It was on-the-job training. For the younger missionary-evangelists this meant accompanying the apostle. John Mark, Timothy, and Titus were all required to leave home to be trained. This is one of the big differences in the training of the elder and the missionary. There is no evidence that the elder had to leave his home environment in order to receive training, but the missionary-evangelists who are described in Scripture did leave home.

Relevant Research

Of course, the approach of the New Testament to the training of Christian workers is of paramount importance to the believer. But it also is of interest that both sound pedagogy and church history confirm the validity of this approach.

It is often assumed that the preparation of the clergy in modern times has been much the same as the pattern with which we are familiar today. Such, however, is not the case. In the past the vast majority of the clergy in the United States, for example, were trained by the apprentice system. Indeed, one of the most important recent trends in theological education in America is to emphasize internship as part and parcel of that education. And one of the most important recent trends overseas is theological education by extension—an approach designed to take at least some of the learning process out of the classroom and put it into the local areas where church leaders live, work, and serve. Educational and historical research upholds the validity of these approaches.

Practical Reflection

The time has come to rethink our programs of preparation for the various Christian ministries. In view of the rapid rise of educational standards all around the world there can be no question that thorough preparation is needed. The question is, "What kind of preparation is needed?"

Negatively, we can no longer afford to take young men and women, send them off to schools which effectively seal them off from both the Church and the world for a longer or shorter period, and then thrust them into the work at home or abroad.

Positively, we must find ways of bringing the church and the school closer together, thus providing training in the existing churches and in the world in which churches are yet to be established.

One of the priceless possessions of the Church of Christ is her present and potential leadership—especially that kind of leadership that labors at the cutting edge where new territory is being claimed for Christ. Contrary to popular Christian opinion, it is this kind of pioneering that makes the greatest demands upon the Christian worker. That being the case, every local church should give special attention to directing and helping those who may be called of God for this task.

PART FOUR

The Emerging Church and the Christian Mission

nine

The Audience Contacted

"God is no respecter of persons" (Acts 10:34, KJV). He loves all men and "desires all men to be saved and to come to the knowledge of the truth" (I Tim. 2:4). Our Lord reached all types of people—including a Matthew, a Zacchaeus, a Mary Magdalene, and an anonymous but disreputable Samaritan woman. The Church knows no barriers. Not only has the distinction between Jew and Gentile been superseded, but the same is true of distinctions of race, sex, and social standing (Gal. 3:28).

We begin this chapter with these understandings. *But they do not militate against selectivity in making contacts for Christ and His churches!*

In the first place, it is manifestly impossible to reach all people simultaneously with the message of Christ. Therefore some must be contacted before others.

In the second place, our Lord was selective in His contacts!

In the third place, the privilege of hearing, believing, and being reconciled to God through Christ entails responsibility. Therefore, fairness is not an issue. Even the

FIGURE 19
"THE PAULINE CYCLE"

"... they arrived at Pisidian Antioch, and on the Sabbath day they went into the synagogue and sat down" (Acts 13:14).

natural descendants of Abraham were chosen—not simply with a view to their own blessing—but with a view to the blessing of all the nations of the earth (Gen. 12:1-3).

In the fourth place, our aim in any strategy of contact should be to reach all men with the gospel. Selectivity in initial contacts can contribute toward that goal.

In the fifth place, Paul had a "strategy of contact" that involved a degree of selectivity.

> Whatever the actual method the principle which we learn from Paul, not only from his time in Athens but from his entire missionary career, is that the way to reach people is not to expect them to come to us, but for us to go to them.
>
> Being a pioneer made . . . demands upon him which are very different from what we expect of an evangelist today. There was no existing church or group of churches in Athens or most of the other cities he visited to invite him to come and conduct a series of meetings. Nor were there any local Christians to whom he could look to prepare for his arrival and invite their friends and neighbours to come and hear him. Rather it was the evangelist himself who was first on the scene and who had to go out and make his own contacts. And it was in the ability to do this, that the gifts of the evangelist largely lay.
>
> Admittedly this is where our present society is not quite as pagan as the situation that faced Paul. . . . Yet . . . the really difficult task for which God's help is especially needed is not to find someone who can come and deliver evangelistic sermons—quite a number can do that—but to find those who can make effective contact with unbelievers wherever they are. If we insist on having meetings addressed by an evangelist, the major task will still be to persuade people to come and hear him.[1]

Objectives

Of course, the objectives of the church-planter will become more concrete and specific as he gains an acquain-

---

[1]Kenneth F. W. Prior, *The Gospel in a Pagan Society* (Downers Grove, IL: Inter-Varsity Press, 1975), p. 33.

tance with his target community. Generally speaking, however, his objectives should be as follows:

(1) To gain the understanding and goodwill of the local citizens (especially their leaders), insofar as possible.

(2) To reach unchurched Christians and invite them into the church fellowship.

(3) To reach "prepared people" (those who might be favorably disposed toward the gospel).

(4) To get as wide a hearing as possible for the gospel.

The Christian worker goes into a new community armed with the information gained through preliminary surveys. He knows whether the people can be expected to be receptive or hostile. He knows the general class and ethnic composition of the community. On the basis of such information and his overall strategy he can make preliminary plans and establish objectives in relation to community contact. Clearly, he cannot assume that people owe him a hearing or that it will make no difference whom he approaches or how he approaches them. He must win a hearing and he should prayerfully determine a strategy of contact.

Perhaps the most difficult decisions facing the missionary-evangelist in this regard are those relating to social structure.

A Preliminary Consideration—Social Structure and Response to the Gospel

Biblical Principles and Precedents

There are two absolutely basic sociological facts which come to the fore as one reads the biblical record of the apostolic age.

First, social distinctions arising out of racial, cultural, economic, and other differences were very much a part of the experience of the early Christians. At first Jesus commanded His disciples to go only to the lost sheep of the house of Israel (Matt. 10:6). Later He commanded them to make disciples of all the nations (Matt. 28:19, 20). The first misunderstanding in the early church was occasioned when the Hellenistic Jews complained that their widows were being discriminated against (Acts 6:1). Peter had to overcome his Jewish prejudice in order to help Cornelius (Acts 10:28). It was news of the conversion of a large number of Gentiles at Antioch that caused the Jerusalem church to send Barnabas to evaluate what was happening there (Acts 11:20–22). The presence of Jew and Gentile, masters and slaves (I Peter 2:18), and rich and poor, is clearly a part of the record of the early church.

Second, just as certain is the fact that social distinctions were to be transcended in the preaching of the gospel and in the fellowship of the saints. As far as God is concerned, He "is not one to show partiality" (Acts 10:34) but is "abounding in riches for all who call upon Him" (Rom. 10:12). In Christ there is no male or female, Jew or Gentile, bond or free (Gal. 3:28). It is clear, therefore, that "whoever will call upon the name of the Lord will be saved" (Rom. 10:13). Accordingly, in the fellowship of the early church, masters were to realize that their servants were also brothers (Philem. 16); moreover, the rich were not to receive preferential treatment (James 2:1–4), but were to be generous (I Tim. 6:17, 18).

The New Testament, therefore, recognizes that certain tensions arising from social differences will exist as long as the Church is in the world. Social distinctions which are so much a part of human intercourse are not erased. But neither are they to be determinative of who will hear the Good News of Christ and how believers will be received into the fellowship of the churches.

Social orientations arising out of race, wealth, and other characteristics were a factor in Paul's strategy and in the way his hearers responded to the gospel which he preached. The synagogue community was usually the first to be contacted, and though some Jews from that community believed in Christ, the majority of the converts were from the Gentile proselytes and God-fearers. Paul did preach and even dispute publicly, but he did not make a practice of preaching on street corners or in other public places to the "idle and curious crowd" or to "the loafers, the porters, the ignorant and degraded, the casual laborer on the street."[2] As William Ramsay says, "The classes where education and work go hand in hand were first to come under the influence of the new religion."[3] Roland Allen says, "The majority of St. Paul's converts were of the lower commercial and working classes, labourers, freedmen, and slaves. . . ."[4] Allen emphasizes that within these groups there were people who had personal qualities and community contacts which lent strength and potential to the fledgling churches. To quote Allen once more: "He [Paul] so taught that no church of his foundation was without a strong-centre of respectable, religious-minded people. These naturally took the lead and preserved the church from rapid decay."[5]

Relevant Research

Think of social structure as referring to "those social relations which seem to be of critical importance for the behavior of members of the society."[6] It includes groupings and segments in society which tend to persist: class, caste, clans, age-sets, secret societies, and kinship groups.[7] When Donald McGavran refers to "homogeneous units" in

[2]Roland Allen, *Missionary Methods: St. Paul's or Ours?* (Grand Rapids: Eerdmans, 1962), p. 22.
[3]Quoted in Allen, *Missionary Methods,* p. 23.
[4]Ibid., p. 24.
[5]Ibid.
[6]Raymond Firth, *Elements of Social Organization* (Boston: Beacon Press, 1963), p. 30.
[7]Ibid., p. 31.

society, his primary reference is to these groupings.[8] (Of course, more is involved than that. Ties of language, ways of thinking, value systems, and cultural preferences also tend to bind groups together.) As McGavran notes, people like to become Christians without having to cross the major boundaries that distinguish these groups from one another.[9]

Years ago, P. E. Kraemer demonstrated that American denominations are basically made up of "class churches."[10] He made the following ranking of denominations according to their class representation (denominational identifications reflect the situation at the time of the study):

Upper class: Episcopalian and Unitarian
Upper middle class: Presbyterian, Congregational, and Reformed
Middle class: Methodist, Lutheran, Baptist, Disciples, Evangelical-United Brethren, Evangelical Reformed, and Christian Reformed
Lower class: "Sects"

Essentially the same phenomenon can be found with respect to other segments and groupings within the United States (e.g., ethnic churches) and around the world. On a particular Sunday during a visit to India several years ago, one of the authors visited three churches in Bombay. Not only were the three churches of different denominations, each one was made up of members of different castes (think of caste as "congealed class"), and the approach to worship in each church was appropriate to both the denominational and caste orientation of the members. There is no getting away from the fact that

---

[8]Donald McGavran, *Understanding Church Growth* (Grand Rapids: Eerdmans, 1970), pp. 85–87.

[9]Ibid., pp. 289–91.

[10]Cf. Joel H. Nederhood, *The Church's Mission to the Educated American* (Grand Rapids: Eerdmans, 1960), p. 31.

though there are numerous instances of multiclass, multi-ethnic, multilingual churches, most churches tend to be class, caste, ethnic, or tribal churches in addition to being Christian churches!

Practical Reflection

Insofar as they are truly Christian most churches today will feel the same tensions that were evident in the apostolic church. But insofar as they are Christian they will also rise above those tensions. That does not mean that in planting a church an approach cannot be made to one homogeneous societal unit. Nor does it mean that churches cannot pattern their corporate life and worship (we will call this "programmatic posture") to fit the preferences of a responsive segment of society within the target area. Indeed, sound strategy might dictate that the initial approach be made to members of one group and that the programmatic posture be such that they will feel at home in the meetings.

On the other hand, sound sociological strategy must not be allowed to supersede spiritual reality. No one should be discriminated against because of color, class, caste, or tribe. And, once established, Bible-believing churches must find ways of demonstrating their essential oneness in Christ.

With this in mind, the following factors should be given preliminary consideration before actually establishing contacts in the target area:

(1) A newcomer to a society may find it easier to relate to people of different classes (i.e., people of classes higher or lower than the class to which he belonged in his home culture) than will the person who is native to that society. In closed-class societies especially, this potential for increased class contact on the part of the newcomer (in comparison with the opportunity of the native) should not be overlooked.

(2) One of the results of undifferentiated initial contacts

in church-extension evangelism in many areas has been
that the new churches have become identified with margin-
als and outcasts who attach themselves to the missionary-
evangelist for purposes of self-aggrandizement. Another
result has been that the churches become identified with
people who are more worthy but who—because of disease,
impairment, age, social standing, and the like—do not
commend the gospel to their fellow citizens. Make no mistake. Every individual is equally precious in the sight of
God. That is not in question here. What needs to be
thought through (but rarely is) are the implications of the
rather widespread "nonstrategy" of making initial contacts
with those who are most easily approached.

(3) It can be of great value if a core of solid citizens can
be won to Christ and to the Church. Not only does their
conversion lend stability to the work, it may well enhance
the possibility of still others coming to Christ. If the first
converts are from the lowest class, the conversion of mid-
dle- and upper-class people will be made more difficult. If
middle- and upper-class people are won to Christ, the conversion of lower-class persons may be made easier. Missionary John Kemp won a Fijian chief by the name of
Elijah Veronti to Christ. Thousands followed him into the
faith. Generally speaking, however, the strategy of a prolonged delay in approaching potentially responsive people
who are lower on the social scale while work continues
among unresponsive higher-class people is questionable
strategy.

(4) As is the case with many Pentecostal and some Baptist groups, perhaps more consideration should be given to
reaching the lower-middle and upper-lower classes where
"education and work often go hand in hand." Biblical precedent and the success of these groups indicate that many
denominations and missions may be missing an opportunity for great growth among a responsive people who obviously make good timber for building churches. This may
necessitate a programmatic posture that would be difficult

for more staid, formal, and intellectually-oriented groups to evolve, however.

Preevangelistic Courtesy Contacts

Biblical Principles and Precedents

In our evangelistic zeal we sometimes have a tendency to forget two very basic biblical principles. The first one has to do with the integrity of mankind, who are all made in the image of God. This integrity is reflected in such commandments as, "Love your neighbor as yourself" (Luke 10:27); "Therefore whatever you want others to do for you, do so for them" (Matt. 7:12); and "Do good to all men" (Gal. 6:10). The second has to do with the divine origin of legitimate human authority. It is reflected in such statements as, "The powers that be are ordained of God" (Rom. 13:1, KJV), and in such commandments as, "Render to Caesar the things that are Caesar's" (Matt. 22:21), and "Render to all what is due them" (Rom. 13:7). These principles are certainly relevant to preevangelistic contacts in a target area. Certainly no case can be made for saying that the Lord Jesus and Paul made a practice of heading for the home or office of the highest available governmental official upon entering a new province, town, or city. Indeed the most important factor in their identification with local citizens seems usually to have been a positive response to their message. More should be said, however.

The mission of Paul was, of course, to the Gentiles (Acts 9:15; 26:16–18). He was commissioned to this task (Acts 13:2) and was recognized by the apostles for his mission to the Gentiles (Gal. 2:7–9). At the same time he had a great concern for his fellow Jews (Rom. 10:1). In the light of this commission and concern, Paul's practice of visiting the synagogues (and the homes of certain citizens) can be seen as courtesy contacts of the highest order.

Relevant Research

Research in the areas of anthropology, sociology, and communication underscores the importance of the roles of formal leaders, sponsors, and mediators in society.[11] Depending upon the particular societal arrangements that appertain, the newcomer may find it all but impossible to gain acceptance apart from a proper approach to such persons. Even in Western societies that emphasize egalitarianism, an initial contact with those who fill these roles will usually enhance the missionary cause.

Practical Reflection

Even if it could be successfully argued that missionary-evangelists have no sacred obligation to conform to local rules or protocol in entering a new community, nothing is to be gained by disregarding them out of hand. Even in the United States, a courtesy call upon certain local Christian leaders, government and school officials, and mass-media representatives may occasion goodwill and open doors for the new work. In other societies, such contacts may be even more important and rewarding than in our own.

ME-3 illustration: Missionary James Luckman of Ethiopia has had outstanding success in opening new doors to the gospel in that land. Why? Because he made it a habit from his early days in that land to visit the highest officials, explaining his business and securing their goodwill upon first entering any new territory.

ME-3 illustration: John Ritchie established some two hundred churches among the Indians of Peru. It was his belief that an unexpected and unsponsored evangelistic effort simply did not fit the Indian culture. He never went

---

[11]Cf. Felix Keesing, *Cultural Anthropology: The Science of Custom* (New York: Holt, Rinehart and Winston, 1966), pp. 403, 421.

to a village unless invited by a sponsor (any outstanding member of the community). Often, he would stay with that sponsor while carrying on his evangelistic effort.

ME-3 illustration: Some missionaries while on furlough at Trinity Evangelical Divinity School worked on a master plan for entering new tribal villages in Kenya. They concluded that although the village elders (sitting as a group) were cordial to the missionary effort, they had been thoughtlessly bypassed in most cases of pioneer evangelism. The missionaries then incorporated a courtesy contact with village elders into their master plan.

ME-3 illustration: A missionary to Japan found that one of her most fruitful contacts in any new area was with the principals of the local schools. She would visit them with an offer of appropriate Christian books for their school libraries.

One of the great failures of Christian evangelism at home and abroad has been in the area of preevangelistic contacts. It has often been true that the greater the concern for the lost and the greater the vision for a lasting work for Christ, the less the attention given to social amenities and the building of bridges of friendship and trust. This failure has been most conspicuous in Jewish evangelism. But it is apparent in almost every country and culture, whether in the United States or abroad. We should remember that there is a very real sense in which those who are not against us are for us. Even unbelievers oftentimes will in friendship open strategic doors for those who engage in such noble work as building the kingdom of God.

The Christian worker, thus, should make a simple list of courtesy contacts to be made as he enters the area of his new ministry. He should not assume too much at this point. Even within North American culture there will be significant differences between the subcultures of, for example, a city on the Eastern seaboard, a small town in the Midwest, and a mountain community in Kentucky.

Preevangelistic Community Contacts

For want of a better term, we will call the wider preevangelistic contacts "community contacts." Getting to know the people in the community and allowing them to know us is one part of the process. Participation in community life is still another aspect of it.

Biblical Principles and Precedents

Unlike present-day missionaries, Paul did not have to deal with the problem of isolation from the community. When he arrived in a town, he lived there. This involved not only residing in the town, but working in the community and staying in the homes of the people. Lydia invited Paul to stay at her home (Acts 16:14, 15), and it is certain that he stayed with Jason (Acts 17:6–9), and with Aquila (Acts 18:2, 3), as well as with Titius Justus (Acts 18:7). No wonder he could ask the Thessalonians to remember his life among them (I Thess. 2:8, 9). He had lived with them. Jesus had taught that the good shepherd knows his sheep. Paul certainly qualified as a good shepherd!

Paul also knew the community from the business viewpoint. He plied his trade and sold his tents. While this was done in order to earn a living so that the young church would not have to support him, it also put Paul in contact with people of the business community. He knew those from whom he purchased supplies and those who purchased tents from him. It could be that these community contacts resulted in certain influential people coming into the fellowship of the young churches (Lydia, Jason, Philemon, Priscilla, Aquila, and Aristobulus, to name a few).

Relevant Research

All societies have certain expectations of newcomers. In some societies (e.g., the United States) it is expected that local people will visit the newcomer to their community. In other societies (e.g., France) it is expected that those taking up residence will visit their neighbors. When these expectations are met, lines of communication are opened and the groundwork is laid for continued relationships. By the same token, when these expectations are not met, communication becomes strained and the possibility of good relationships jeopardized.

The foregoing is perhaps more important in the case of a church worker than in almost any other case. In our own culture the reason for this is obvious. People have so many preconceived ideas (many of them negative) about churches and church workers that the new work and worker stand prejudged unless he does something to dispel those ideas.

In many cultures, a study of social organizations and roles will reveal how the missionary and the church he plans to begin will be understood. For example, previous to the coming of the missionary, the Tila Chol society of Mexico had no religious organization comparable to a church and no one in a religious role comparable to that of a missionary-evangelist. Naturally some significant pre-evangelistic contact was required in that situation in order to insure that the missionary was not regarded as another medicine man (with bad medicine!).

Practical Reflection

It appears that the average church-planting missionary—national *and* expatriate—takes far too much for granted upon entering a new community for Christ. If we put ourselves in the place of the local resident whose community is "invaded" by some outsider who has come to preach to us and start a new religious organization in our area, perhaps we will understand what is involved. Ways should be found to break down prejudices, gain a hearing, and secure understanding. Classes in cooking, childcare, and photography, for example, have been used to advantage in some areas. Of course, there is no substitute for living and working alongside local residents over a period of time.

In the initial stages of a work, a house-to-house survey may help to break the ice and monitor community attitudes. It must be recognized that this will not work everywhere, however. Workers in metropolitan areas like New York will probably object on the grounds that apartments are all but inaccessible and personal questions are not well received in that area. Missionaries and national workers in the Philippines, on the other hand, discovered that surveys are fairly well received in the cities. In many cases, therefore, but not all, the kind of surveys illustrated below will be extremely helpful.

ME-1 illustration: Robert H. Schuller, pastor of the flourishing Garden Grove Community Church in Garden Grove, California, writes about ringing the doorbells of hundreds of homes in the area of his church. He advocates setting aside two weeks in order to call door-to-door in ever-widening concentric circles from the location of the church (or the possible location). Suggesting that we listen to what people have to say, he promises the education of a lifetime.

Allocate these two weeks *full time* toward the following project: begin by calling door-to-door in the immediate vicinity of your church. You have called on some of the homes before, but you are going to call now with a different purpose, a different motive, and a different question.

You are going to ask: "Do you attend our church regularly? Have you ever attended it? Do you attend any other church?"

If they give you a negative answer, you will reply by saying: "I'm delighted to hear this because I'm anxious to find out how I can improve this church and make it such an exciting church that intelligent and wonderful people like you will want to come. You are obviously an intelligent

person, so you undoubtedly have good reasons why you
don't attend the church. Would you please tell me what
they are? And could you tell me what our church could
possibly do to help in any area of your life? Is there any
program that you would be interested in?"

Generally, after you have asked the first one or two questions, the answers will be forthcoming. I did this years ago
and it was an eye-opening experience! I heard criticisms of
"typical sermons." And I heard criticisms about other gaps
in the church program. The criticisms of the unchurched
persons in my community became a major learning experience!

If you will spend two weeks calling door-to-door in an
ever-widening circle, beginning from your church property, and will listen with an open mind, then indeed you
will have the education of a lifetime! Listen to the individuals you talk with—listen to them carefully.

Do not be defensive! In spite of all that you have ever
been taught, assume—for one humble time in your life—
that you may have been wrong about a lot of things! So,
listen to what the unchurched are saying and you will find
out where they are hurting, where they are frightened,
where they are worried. Take careful notes. Keep a diary
detailing your calls.

After two weeks you will know what kind of a church
program you have to design to meet the needs of these
people in your community. You will know what kind of
messages to give in order to bring them into the church.[12]

What Schuller has to say is equally valid in the pioneer
situation and for the existing church.

ME-3 illustration: In the Philippines, Conservative Baptist pastors and missionaries found that a simple house-
to-house survey and invitation can be a significant preparation for a church-planting evangelistic effort. They discovered that the surveys here generally were acceptable
only in the larger urban centers, however. Out in the barrios, people were extremely suspicious of this approach.

---

[12]Robert H. Schuller, *Your Church Has Real Possibilities* (Glendale, CA:
Regal Books, 1974), p. 81.

The difference, of course, grows out of the experiences and values of city-dwellers as opposed to those of the relatively isolated barrios.

Selective Evangelistic Contacts

Entering an area without any plan other than to preach the Word to "whosoever will" is in itself a selection. It really means that those who have the most time, or are the most accessible, or are reachable by the particular media and modes of communication utilized, will constitute our selective contact. This approach may result in initial conversions which in effect close doors of opportunity by identifying the new church with those who, in the eyes of unsaved people, are undesirable. It is not likely that this approach will result in reaching those who are best prepared to understand the message and receive Christ. If, on the other hand, initial evangelistic contacts are prayerfully selected, the first converts may be the occasion for a much wider hearing for the gospel. Societal arrangements should, therefore, be taken in consideration before deciding on initial evangelistic contacts.

Biblical Principles and Precedents

Reaching Prepared People

In regards to selective evangelistic contacts, three principles can be enunciated from Scripture. We have alluded to the first one already. We might call it the "doorway principle." The selective evangelistic contact should be a doorway to a wider audience. This principle can be seen in Paul's visits to the synagogue. His target group, the Gentiles, was represented in the synagogues by the God-fearers, the devout, and the proselytes. The utility of the principle can be seen in Paul's visit to Antioch in Pisidia. At the close of Paul's message the record states that "the Gentiles besought that these words might be preached to them the next sabbath. . . . And the next sabbath day came almost the whole city together to hear the word of God" (Acts 13:42, 44, KJV).

The second principle is the "preparedness principle." A group of people or a single person selected for evangelism should demonstrate a degree of preparedness to accept the gospel. This principle is seen at work in the case of the Ephesians. The record states that Paul found some disciples (Acts 19:1) who had not heard of the Holy Spirit (v. 2), but had been baptized into John's baptism (v. 3). Paul then preached the Savior as the One for whom John had prepared the way. These disciples demonstrated a degree of previous preparation and thus became key targets for evangelistic effort.

The Macedonian call could be considered an example of the same principle. The man in the vision said, "Help us" (Acts 16:9). This is the plea of a man who was either a believer who was unable to effectively evangelize his area and thus was in need of aid, or he was an unbeliever who realized his plight and called for help. Whichever might have been the case, the call for aid indicated that a preparatory work had been accomplished.

The third principle in selective evangelistic contacts can be called the "confirmatory principle." It is seen in the case of the lame man from Lystra. It is said that Paul carefully scrutinized (*atenisas*) him and perceived (*idōn*) that he had faith to be healed (Acts 14:9). Then Paul commanded the man to stand on his feet (Acts 14:10). While the episode could be construed as a case of previous preparation, it can also be seen as a case of confirmation (Heb. 2:3). The message was to be confirmed with certain apostolic signs. Such signs confirmed the message preached.

Although one can make the argument that there are no apostles today and thus the confirmatory signs are not to be expected, the principle of confirmation stands. Paul later wrote to others who were not apostles that they were examples "to all the believers in Macedonia and in Achaia. . . . For they themselves report about us what kind of a reception we had with you, and how you turned to God from idols to serve a living and true God" (I Thess. 1:7, 9). Here there is no evidence of physical miracles but it is clear that the miracle of the transformed life was confirmatory evidence of the validity of the message preached.

Perhaps we should go one step further. Roland Allen states that conversions among the God-fearers were not in sufficient numbers to tip the scales in favor of Christianity.[13] Stephen Hsu, however, argues that Paul was following a strategy that led to an increased number of *evangelists,* not just *converts.* The people in the synagogues—especially the Grecian Jews and proselytes of Gentile origin—had ready access and entrée to the Gentile population that surrounded them. In a short time a whole region such as Asia (Acts 19:10) could therefore hear the message. Hsu thinks that many proponents of Church Growth have overlooked this aspect of Pauline strategy. Paul was not thinking simply in terms of bringing many members of a responsive homogeneous movement into the kingdom.

> He saw any harvesting opportunity as a means to reap a greater harvest. . . . The principle of selective evangelistic contacts is, therefore, to select the group which has the greatest potential of response to the Gospel *and* the greatest potential of becoming effective evangelistic witnesses to the target area.[14]

Reaching Those Related to Believers

A study of the kinships of the disciples of Jesus is informative. It reveals the principle of reaching those re-

---

[13]Allen, *Missionary Methods,* p. 13.

[14]Stephen Hsu, "Selective Evangelistic Contacts." A paper submitted at Trinity Evangelical Divinity School—School of World Mission and Evangelism, Feb. 1978.

lated to believers and the principle of working within the family relationship instead of breaking up the family. Andrew brought his brother, Simon Peter, to hear the One in whom he believed. James and John, the sons of Zebedee, are (together with their mother) an illustration that Jesus worked within family relationships.

The principle of working with the family was so important to the apostle Peter that he gave special instructions to those married to unsaved husbands (I Peter 3:1-6). This seems to be the only case in which Scripture speaks of winning an unsaved person without use of the Word. Here, the transformed life is the factor which the Holy Spirit uses to gain an unsaved person within the family.

Paul, in all probability, has this principle in mind when he writes to the Corinthians, urging the believing spouse to remain with the unbelieving spouse. The expression, "The unbelieving husband is sanctified through his wife, and the unbelieving wife is sanctified through her believing husband" (I Cor. 7:14), whatever else it may mean, indicates that the unbelieving spouse (or any other member of the family) is in a state of "set apartness" and thus is a candidate for salvation.

Again, the promise to the jailer in Philippi, "Believe in the Lord Jesus, and you shall be saved, you and your household" (Acts 16:31), does not mean that one believer can believe for another person. Rather, the promise indicates that within kinship relationships there are favorable circumstances for evangelism.

Donald McGavran argues that Paul approached many individuals and groups who were related in some way to the Christians in Antioch, and that he planned to do so. They constituted people who were "on the bridge," to use McGavran's phrase. McGavran finds evidence of a movement of faith across these bridges, igniting a great "people movement" among Greeks even as "people movements" had started among the Jews and Samaritans after Pentecost.

While Paul worked with that Greek-Hebrew Antioch community for a year, he must have come to know hundreds of
relatives of Christians and to hear of thousands more.
Some of these relatives from Cyprus, Pisidia, Iconium,
Lystra and Derbe had quite possibly come to Antioch during Paul's year there and had joined in his hours of instruction. According to the record some of the Christians who
had first spoken of the faith to Greeks in Antioch had come
from Cyprus. They probably belonged to families who had
connections on both the island and the mainland. Having
won their relatives in Antioch, it was natural for them to
think of winning their unconverted relatives, Jews and
Greeks, in Cyprus. . . .

How then did Paul choose fields of labour? To be accurate we must say that *he did not choose fields. He followed up
groups of people who had living relations in the People Movement
to Christ.*[15]

Relevant Research

Psychological Factors Relating to Preparedness for the Gospel

In addition to the sociological understandings noted earlier in this chapter, certain other factors are important to
the preparation of a people for the gospel.

(1) The concept of "world view" as developed by anthropologists is most relevant here. Put very simply, a
world view is simply the way in which a person "sees" the
world. As Norman Geisler says, people do not see things as
they are, but as they appear to be through glasses tinted by
their world view.[16] A naturalist or materialist, for example,
sees no evidence of God's presence or power in the world.
He will always look for psychological or scientific explanations of observed phenomena. An animist, on the other

---

[15]Donald McGavran, *Bridges of God* (New York: Friendship Press,
1955), pp. 27, 31.

[16]Norman Geisler, "Some Philosophical Perspectives on Missionary
Dialogue," in *Theology and Mission*, ed. David J. Hesselgrave (Grand
Rapids: Baker, 1978), pp. 241–57.

hand, sees gods and spirits everywhere. In his view, even natural phenomena must have spiritual explanations. People who share the monotheistic world view of Christianity may be easier to win to Christ (e.g., nominal Christians) or more difficult to win (Jews and Muslims). But once won they often make good timber for the Church because of the broad areas of commonality and consequent understanding.

(2) Another important factor is that of "timing." For example, if tribal people can be reached before they adopt some other developed religion or ideology, they will likely be much more responsive to the claims of Christ. Again, people who have been uprooted from their old communities, who have broken old ties, and have settled in a new area often constitute a group which is most receptive to new ideas and associations. Sociological barriers to conversion are no longer so high. New friendships are sought. Old patterns tend to break down; new ones are in the process of being established. In such a situation Christ and His Church may well receive a favorable consideration.

(3) A third factor closely related to receptivity is that of "fit." When an innovation more or less matches the cultural values and social forms of a target community, the possibility that members of the community will adopt the innovation is enhanced. George Foster notes that in post-Reformation Europe the desire to read the Bible led to the world's first mass literacy movement. He predicts that in the future, as was the case in ancient Mesopotamia, economic needs will be more important than Bible reading as an incentive to literacy.[17] Perhaps so. But situations will vary. In fact, the situation can be turned around. Whatever the motivation for learning to read might be, in numerous situations literacy has opened the door for

---

[17]George M. Foster, *Traditional Cultures and the Impact of Technological Change* (New York: Harper and Row, 1962), pp. 145–46.

missionary-evangelists. The ability to read, coupled with the lack of reading material and the Protestant emphasis on the message of the Book, has made for a "fit" that has been most significant.

Distinguishing Kindred Kinship and Lineage Kinship Systems

The family (nuclear or extended) is the basic social group in human societies. But as Francis L. K. Hsu has noted, "Though the family as the *first human grouping is universally important,* its importance to the individual varies enormously from society to society."[18] In old China the family was most important, in India it is somewhat less important, and in America the family is of still lesser importance. The difference between various societies becomes pronounced when we examine the patterns in which relatives by blood or marriage interact. Peter Hammond and others make a significant distinction at this point between kindred and lineage.[19]

The term *kindred* is sometimes applied to that group of people with whom an individual (ego) can establish a genealogical bond through his parents and with whom he is reciprocally bound by certain conventions and obligations. Note that the kindred is "ego-focused" and that the composition of the kindred group which is important to ego and with whom relationships are living and vital will vary according to his age, situation, and interests (see Figure 20).

The term *lineage* is applied to a group composed of all blood relatives to whom an individual is related through one or the other of his parents, and with whom he is bound in a system of conventions and obligations. The lineage is "ancestor-focused." All descendants of an ances-

---

[18]Francis L. K. Hsu, *Clan, Caste, and Club* (Princeton, NJ: Van Nostrand Co., 1963), p. 6.

[19]Peter B. Hammond, *An Introduction to Cultural and Social Anthropology* (New York: The Macmillan Company, 1971), pp. 169–72.

FIGURE 20

The Kindred Kinship System

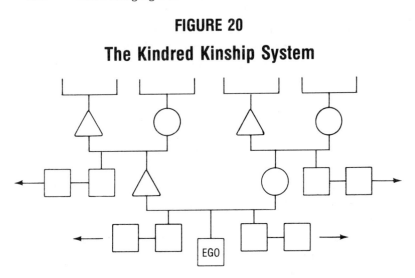

Kindred Kinship is based upon a relationship to "ego" through either parent (squares indicate persons of either sex) (adapted from Peter B. Hammond, *An Introduction to Cultural and Social Anthropology* [New York: The Macmillan Company, 1971], p. 170). Copyright © 1978 by Peter B. Hammond. Used by permission.

tor become members of the lineage upon their birth and grow into a set of relationships with (and responsibilities toward) other members which is predetermined and constant. The composition of the group does not change according to the needs and wishes of ego, but only as new members are born into it and as the older members die. Even in case of death, it is likely that the departed ancestor will continue to occupy an important place in the lineage grouping and will remain bound to the living in a very real sense (see Figure 21).

The social system of the United States is basically of the kindred type. The kinfolk of both parents are included among our relatives. Only rarely, however, do we give consideration to those who are more distant than second cousins. Since the system is ego-focused, every individual will have his own concept of his kindred (a concept he can share only with his full siblings). Moreover, this concept

FIGURE 21

The Lineage Kinship System

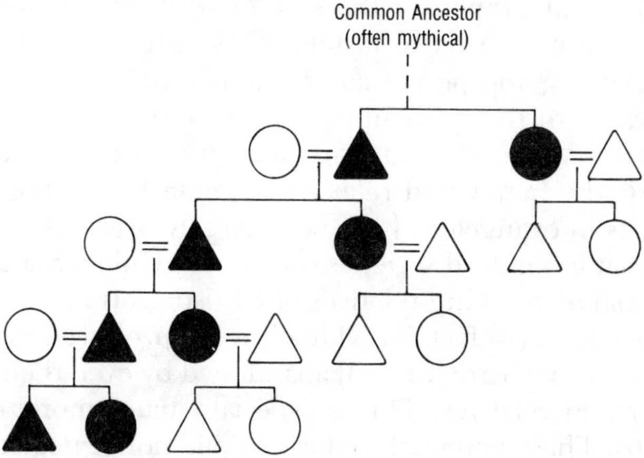

Common Ancestor
(often mythical)

Kinsmen think of themselves as descended from a common ancestor through the male line (adapted from Peter B. Hammond, *An Introduction to Cultural and Social Anthropology* [New York: The Macmillan Company, 1971], p. 177). Copyright © 1978 by Peter B. Hammond. Used by permission.

will change for ego himself according to his age and situation. When he is a child, he relates to his nuclear family and such other kinfolk as are important to his parents (proximity being a key factor). As he grows older, he may become interested in establishing a relationship with various other relatives, especially at times of childbirths, christenings, graduations, weddings, funerals, and so on. When ego grows old, the composition of the kindred grouping may change dramatically due to the death of others of his own generation, the multiplication of descendants, and, in many cases, the rather general disregard for the very old in our society.

The lineage groupings of traditional China, Japan, and literally scores of tribal societies are at the other end of the continuum. In those societies the bloodline (either of the father or the mother, but not both) may well determine an individual's entire life pattern—education, vocation, marriage, the care of elders and younger members of the lineage, religious obligations, and much more. Ego has comparatively little to say. Lineage members are bound together not simply for the sake of convenience and fellowship, but in order to sustain life, secure the good of all the relatives, and perpetuate the ancestral line.

Because of the overemphasis on ego (the individual) in much of Western—and particularly North American— society, the family and relatives of contacts and potential contacts in evangelism have been largely overlooked. It is true that in kindred societies such as the United States the potential of reaching relatives of Christians is not as great as elsewhere. (In fact, individualism has produced numerous people who are [or feel] abandoned by even their own family and relatives. This is especially true among older citizens. These potential contacts should not be neglected.) But even in kindred societies family contacts should not be overlooked.

In societies where lineage patterns prevail (as they do in much of the non-Western world), the missionary-evangelist must view potential prospects in an entirely different light. Contacts will present a whole new set of problems and potentials to the Church. The most important of these can be defined rather easily once one is in the society. Neglect of them will be a great loss to the work of Christ.

Practical Reflection

We have often overlooked the fact that God often *has* prepared people in our target areas, and that He *will* prepare people as we pray. As a consequence, we have neglected many people whom Jesus and His apostles, and Paul and his team, never would have passed by.

Unchurched "Church People"

People who have had an association with churches in other areas may be found to be unchurched. Such people may or may not be genuine Christians, but if they have been in a church in the past we can expect that they will be understanding and appreciative of the Christian world view and faith.

ME-1 illustration: An American denomination has inaugurated a commendable program of church extension in Florida. One key to the success of the program has been that initial contact has been made in each target area with a significant number of retirees who have left denominational churches in the North and have not yet been churched in their new communities.

Newcomers and Other Responsive Segments of the Society

We have singled out newcomers to a target area as being potentially receptive. Of course there may be other responsive segments in any given area. All such should have special attention.

ME-3 illustration: There are some 150,000 Antilleans in France today—many of them in the Paris area. They have come mainly from Martinique and Guadeloupe. They are French citizens, but similarity to their native French neighbors ends at that point. Among the differences is the fact that in many areas they constitute a subgroup that is far more responsive than the French to the gospel. Their responsiveness is occasioned by several factors. No viable plan for church-planting evangelism in that area would be possible without taking these people into consideration.

Classes with Matching Characteristics

The characteristics and interests of some classes in the target area will more closely match the programmatic posture of the projected church than will those of other classes. Let's face it. Churches are largely "class churches" because they appeal to the members of certain classes. In "closed class societies," such as India, churches rarely cut decisively across class (caste) lines. Even in "open class societies," such as the United States, churches usually have a primary appeal to certain class segments. With that in mind it may be wise to match the primary target audience with the programmatic posture. This approach is not calculated to preclude wider contact. It simply acknowledges social realities, especially in the beginning stages. It is true that we have thought of the differences between churches and denominations as being historical and theological. But there can be little doubt that the differences are psychological and sociological as well.

ME-1-2-3 illustration: An outstanding example of a programmatic posture that fits the values and patterns of the target area is that of the Pentecostal churches in Latin America. In general, the Pentecostals have had unusual success in reaching people of the lower-middle and upper-lower classes in a number of areas around the world. Donald Palmer, in his study on the success of the United Pentecostal Church in Colombia, brings out the fact that their program and approach have a special appeal to the mentality of certain segments of that society.[20]

Kinship as a Bridge

Missionaries from highly individualistic, ego-focused, kindred societies have hardly begun to avail themselves of the opportunities that are theirs for reaching the immediate families and other relatives of those who have already decided for Christ. Increasingly—East *and* West—church-planters must think of Christians as links and bridges to the unsaved. It may well be that the relatives of believers constitute the largest single group of prepared people in the world today.

ME-3 illustration: After three terms of planting churches in Japan, a missionary turned the strategy upside down. Instead of making initial evangelistic contacts with chil-

---

[20]Donald Palmer, "Jesus Only: The United Pentecostal Church," in *Dynamic Religious Movements,* ed. David J. Hesselgrave (Grand Rapids: Baker, 1978), pp. 234–35.

dren, young people, and a few interested mothers, and stopping there, the whole strategy was directed toward using these individuals to make contacts with whole families, including fathers whose working hours and misconceptions of Christianity had kept them aloof from the church. The result? Whole families were won and a new church was established in half the time it had required to establish other churches.

Widespread Preaching and Teaching

Biblical Principles and Precedents

The Bible clearly states that God desires all to come to repentance (II Peter 3:9). The principles of selectivity which we have previously discussed do not in any way negate this divine desire. They represent an attempt to accomplish the task in the most efficient manner. But it is clear that if the Church is going to comply with the desire of God for the salvation of all men, it will have to follow the biblical mandate and use biblical methods. It will have to sow abundantly if it is to reap abundantly (II Cor. 9:6).

How did Paul engage in widespread evangelism? First, he used his fellow workers wisely. Seldom was Paul found working alone. He worked in teams. Timothy, Luke, and Titus were often sent on missions of varying types. While the coworkers often carried instructions from the apostle, they were not just messenger boys. Titus was to rectify the problems in the church on Crete (Titus 1:5). Timothy was sent to establish and to comfort the Thessalonian saints (I Thess. 3:2), and upon his return he was to give a report of the work (I Thess. 3:6). All of this freed the apostle Paul for his work and at the same time enlisted others in the task of evangelism.

Second, Paul encouraged and used in the task of evangelism the churches which he had begun. Often it is asked how the Colossian congregation was formed. It is fairly certain that Paul did not visit the area; thus he was not the founding missionary. Donald Guthrie suggests that Epaphrus, a convert of Paul, was the human instrument involved in founding the Colossian church. It is interesting that Paul had a Bible training school in Ephesus (Acts 19:9), and that to the Ephesians he wrote that gifted men are given to the church for edification and increase of the body (Eph. 4:7-16). Paul stressed that the work of the ministry is the responsibility of all the saints and not the work of just a few. The result of this effort is seen in the Book of Revelation—the seven churches singled out include Ephesus and six others in the general area. Again, Paul commended the Thessalonians because from them "sounded out the word of the Lord . . . so that we need not to speak any thing" (I Thess. 1:8, KJV).

Third, Paul withdrew from growing congregations. While in some cases his withdrawal was forced by persecution, in other cases it was not due to either human or satanic opposition. It was in the midst of revival that Paul and Barnabas left Antioch to engage in extension work (Acts 13:1-3), and it was after a tremendous victory that Paul left the island of Cyprus to go to Perga (Acts 13:6-13).

What, then, was the pattern Paul used in order to engage in widespread evangelistic teaching and preaching? He engaged in evangelism himself, he trained others to do the same work, and he left others to do the work for which they had been trained.

Relevant Research

It seems trite to mention the sales principle that the more doorbells the salesman rings and the more contacts he makes, the more success he is going to have. Consumer surveys often determine the sales potential of given products. After the consumer survey has been made, a great part of sales technique is simply to contact as many people as possible in the knowledge that, on an average, one out of seven (or ten or fifteen) contacts represents a sale. Rapidly growing religious movements such as the Mormons and the Jehovah's Witnesses are well aware of this principle.

Practical Reflection

The gospel is for everyone. The invitation is, "Whosoever will, let him come." This has been one of the guiding principles of evangelicalism at home and abroad. Mass meetings, radio, television, tracts, advertising, correspondence courses—all have been used to contact entire populations. In fact, the innovativeness and emphasis on methodologies to reach anyone and everyone (except the next-door neighbor!) prompted Joe Bayly's satirical *The Gospel Blimp.*[21] While that book teaches us an important lesson, we should pray that we not neglect the use of as many means as are honorable to reach as many people as possible.

Churches must find ways of penetrating all classes of society. In North America, Protestantism has traditionally been linked primarily to the middle class. Howard Snyder seems justified, however, in giving special attention to "the gospel to the poor" in his book *The Problem of Wineskins.* He is probably correct in saying that "*renewal in the church has usually meant the church's rebirth among the poor, the masses, the alienated.*"[22] The masses must be reached and won if the churches are to experience unusual growth.

---

[21]Joe Bayly, *The Gospel Blimp* (Grand Rapids: Zondervan, 1960).
[22]Howard A. Snyder, *The Problem of Wineskins: Church Structure in a Technological Age* (Downers Grove, IL: Inter-Varsity Press, 1975), p. 51.

Formation of a Master Plan

There are a number of basic considerations to be kept in mind as we prepare a strategy for entering a target area with a view to making contacts for Christ.

First, the whole church-extension enterprise must be bathed in prayer as we enter a new area. It is not to be forgotten that whenever we enter a churchless community we are, in a real sense, walking on Satan's ground. Therefore, the Christian workers involved, any believers in the community, the public officials, the general populace—all must become the subjects of special prayer.

Second, a basic analysis of the target area and peoples must be carried out. We must know, for example, which classes are represented, their characteristics and distinctives. Ideally, the implications of these findings will have been taken into account in the selection of our target area. Important information that might have been overlooked previously will be taken into consideration at the contact stage.

Third, we will give attention to the selection of our evangelistic team on the bases of the entrée its members will have to the target peoples and their essential qualifications. They must not be chosen simply on the basis of availability.

Fourth, we will take cultural differences into account while working on our plan for making contacts in the target community. Depending upon the cultural context, the ideas and forms that are suggested in the following paragraphs may have to be modified or even abandoned and replaced with culturally appropriate ones.

Fifth, we will keep reviewing and updating the information we have garnered, realizing that it may be incomplete or even incorrect, and remembering that careful discipline will be required if we are to avoid slipping back into old, familiar patterns and routines.

With these basic considerations attended to, we can proceed with a master plan for entering the target community.

Preevangelistic Courtesy Contacts

Review the section in this chapter on courtesy contacts. With that as background, two basic questions must be answered in forming the master plan: (1) What people in the community should be contacted in order to conform to societal expectations? and (2) What additional courtesy contacts can be made with a view to making the proper contacts in a target area? Certain procedures might be helpful:

Compile a List of Courtesy Contacts

(1) What do the people in the target culture expect newcomers in the community to do?

(2) Who are the people in the various social segments of the target area whose understanding and goodwill would be of special importance?

    (a) Governmental community
    (b) Business community
    (c) Educational community
    (d) Religious community
    (e) Others

(3) Are there any persons in this society who would especially benefit (in money, prestige, etc.) by association with the missionary-evangelists and whose influence (at least in the initial stages of the work) might therefore prove detrimental?

(4) Besides understanding and goodwill, what do we desire from the various persons upon whom we will call (for example, introductions to still other people, information on community life and needs, the opening of doors for ministry)?

FIGURE 22

Suggested Letter to Pastors of Churches in the Target Area

Dear Pastor_____

Please allow me to introduce myself. I am (missionary's name) representing the (name of his church organization). In the near future, I and other representatives of our church will be contacting people in this community with a view to establishing a local church of our denomination. In the process of conducting a community-wide survey it is likely that some members of your congregation will be contacted. Be assured that it is not our objective to influence members of other churches to leave their respective churches. Rather, we desire to discover what the needs of the community are and to minister to those needs.

If you have any questions about our church and its place in the community, please feel free to contact me. Our aim is to become better acquainted with you and the members of the larger community, and to be good representatives of our Lord and Savior, Jesus Christ.

Sincerely yours,

Contact Pastors of Existing Churches

Depending upon the circumstances, members of the religious community may merit special consideration. It may be wise to send a letter or, better yet, call on the pastors (and priests) of churches in the target area. If so, the general approach of the sample letter (Figure 22) is suggested.

Preevangelistic Community Contacts

Community contacts can be made in four primary ways: the normal, everyday interaction with individuals in society (free associational contacts); joining certain local groups organized to promote community interests; special surveys; and using the media available in the community.

Free Associational Personal Contacts

(1) With which persons will we normally be in contact in this particular community?

(2) How can their potential as evangelistic contacts be best utilized?

Group Contacts

(1) What groups (civic organizations, special interest groups, etc.) existing in the target area furnish opportunity for community improvement, individual growth, and future evangelistic contacts?

(2) Which of these groups should be contacted and/or joined?

(3) Are there any important functions, services, or ministries that need to be performed in the community and that require the organization of a new group?

Surveys

An area survey should be carefully planned and the participating personnel should be carefully selected, instructed, and prepared. A survey should not be used as a pretense in order to gain admittance to a household. It should represent an honest attempt to gather information, and the survey should be carried out in conjunction with definite plans to utilize that information in a ministry to the community. Anything less than this is unworthy of the kingdom (see Figure 23).

The Use of Media

The availability and effectiveness of media for making contacts will vary greatly with the area of the world and the characteristics of the local community involved. That being the case, it is wise to study the various possibilities and their potential, and then settle on those media that seem to hold the greatest promise in any given situation. (Media should be used in ways that complement personal contacts. Careful records should be kept so that proper follow-up is possible.) (See Figure 24.)

FIGURE 23

Suggested Interview in Area Survey

*
To be filled out in presence of respondent:
Name of Respondent _____
Address _____ Telephone _____
Members of household:
   Husband _____ Wife _____
   Children _____ Sex_____ Age_____ School_____
   _____ Sex_____ Age_____ School_____
   _____ Sex_____ Age_____ School_____
Occupation of husband and/or wife _____
Length of residence in the area _____
Religious affiliation (if any) _____ Active? _____
**
How could our kind of church serve your family? _____
_____

Do you desire a visit from missionary/pastor? _____

Do you need a Bible? _____ Christian literature on any subject?
_____

May we send you information concerning our church periodically? _____
Do you have any friends or relatives who might have a special interest in a church
such as ours? _____
***
_____

Notes: * Church representative introduces himself and explains the reason for the
survey.
   ** Representative introduces the church and its beliefs, objectives, and program, being sensitive to the interests and needs of the respondent.
   *** Representative leaves printed information concerning the church, including an invitation and the name of someone who can be contacted in case of
question or need (as appropriate).

To be filled out by representative after the interview:
What degree of interest was evidenced by the householder? _____
_____

Any item of special interest or concern? _____
Any recommendations? _____

FIGURE 24

A Checklist of Available Media*

MEDIA	COST**	AUDIENCE	RESPONSE
1. Radio or Television			
a. Spot announcement			
b. Identification with existing programing			
c. New program			
d. New coverage			
2. Newspaper			
a. Advertisement			
b. Inserts			
c. News coverage			
3. Public signs			
a. Church signs			
b. Gospel signs			
c. Billboard advertising			
4. Telephone			
a. Directory announcement			
b. Telephone survey			
c. "Dial-a-Message"			
5. Other			

*At the contact stage it is usually sufficient to note the cost per potential individual or household contact, the composition of the audience (age, education, class, etc.), and the actual response received.

**Cost per 1000 = space or time rate × 1000/audience reached

Selective Evangelistic Contacts

From the very outset of a new work, wise stewards of the gospel will want to direct a special witness to individuals and groups who may be unusually receptive to the gospel and who will be bridges to still other people in the target community. At first, efforts to identify and reach those

FIGURE 25

Questionnaire: Prospective Contacts

We would greatly appreciate your assistance in our evangelistic church-planting endeavor here in _____. After prayerful consideration, please fill in the following information concerning any person who you feel would be a likely prospect for contact by representatives of our church.
(Please fill in a separate form for every such prospect.) Thank you.

Name _____ Address _____

Relationship (to the undersigned): Friend _____ Kin _____

  If kindred, specific relationship _____

Other members of household _____

Spiritual condition (as far as you know):

  Unbeliever and unchurched _____

  Unbeliever and churched _____

  Believer and unchurched _____

  Believer and churched _____

Information important in making contact with the above person (who should contact; when contact should be made; cautions in making contact; etc.):

_____

_____

_____

Are you in communication with this person? _____

               Your Name _____

                   Date _____

people who might serve as bridges will be the responsibility of the individual or team that is pioneering the new work. Wise use of the data gathered through community surveys and other means will serve to augment and correct initial information.

In identifying responsive and potentially responsive people, effective church-planters will solicit a continuous inflow of information in addition to the survey already suggested.

(1) The preliminary and community surveys should be analyzed with a view to identifying responsive individuals, families, and segments of the community.

(2) Some denominations and fellowships of churches provide missionaries and pastors in an unchurched area with the names and addresses of newcomers who have in the past been associated with member churches in other areas. Denominations which do not provide this service are indeed shortsighted, and missionary-evangelists who do not take advantage of such a service are even more so.

(3) Obviously, a primary method will be to ask resident believers if they have any relatives or friends in the area who might be interested. This will tend to be a haphazard investigation unless some specific instrument is developed. Figure 25 gives an example of a simple questionnaire to be filled out by resident believers (and persons who become believers) in the target community.

(4) As soon as meetings for the general public are scheduled (whether for Bible study, evangelism, worship, or whatever), missionary-evangelists should make sure that a permanent record of attendees is kept. People who evidence enough interest in the gospel and the new church to attend such meetings should have priority in the program of evangelistic follow-up. Normally, such people should be contacted in their homes within a few days of their visit (see Figure 26).

Widespread Evangelistic Contact

Ultimately, faithful Christian workers in church-planting evangelism will want to contact just as many citizens of the target community as possible with the message of Christ. The timing and type(s) of such large endeavors will be matters for prayer and determination in each locality. Plans (at least tentative ones) should be made at the

FIGURE 26

Registration Card for Visitors

We welcome you to the _____ Church today. We are grateful for your presence and want to do everything possible to make you feel at home in our church. We also want to serve you and your family in any way we can. In order to make this possible, would you be so kind as to supply us with the following information and place this card in the offering plate as it is passed?

Thank you very much.

Name _____

Address _____Telephone _____

Home church (if any) _____ Location _____

How did you become acquainted with our church?

_____ Family member (Name: _____)

_____ Church friend   (Name: _____)

_____ Advertisement   (_____)

_____ Other   (_____)

How can we serve you or your family?

_____Information concerning the biblical teaching on salvation

_____Information concerning the biblical teaching on the Christian life

_____Information concerning the program of the church

_____Information concerning church membership

_____Other

initial contact stage. For example, the involvement of future believers in a program of visitation evangelism, the utilization of mass media in gospel outreach, the scheduling of special evangelistic campaigns, and so on, should be considered very early in the planning process.

In this chapter we have addressed ourselves to another of the great challenges confronting Christian churches.

Peter says Christians constitute a "holy nation." Paul likens Christian workers to soldiers. But all too often the nation is "too holy" to contact the world. All too often the soldiers train and periodically go on parade but never really engage the enemy. Meanwhile, non-Christian and sub-Christian sects are out in the front lines in hand-to-hand combat. Or, to come back to the terminology of this chapter, they are making living, vital contacts. Think! Who rings our doorbells to invite us into their faith? Who sells the religious magazines in our cities? Who engages us in the airports? *Make contact*—this is another of the contemporary challenges to the Church of Christ.

ten

The Gospel Communicated

Probably no subject has been the focus of more attention, discussion, and inquiry in the evangelical wing of the Church in recent days than has the subject of evangelism. Rightly so. The Good News must be proclaimed. The question presents itself: Need any more be said here? We think so. Here is the place for the missionary-evangelist to ask himself, first, "What more can be learned about effective communication of the gospel?" and, second, "What shall we do to effectively communicate the gospel in the target area?"

Objectives

The ultimate objective in evangelistic communication is clear and persuasive presentation of the gospel to every person we can possibly reach within the area of our responsibility—to those whose hearts have been specially prepared by the Holy Spirit; to those to whom there are inbuilt channels of communication; but also, to *all* who will hear us. We want them to respond in repentance of sin, faith in Christ, and commitment to His cause.

FIGURE 27
"THE PAULINE CYCLE"

"Men of Israel, and you who fear God, listen" (Acts 13:16b).

Notice that, although our ultimate objective is clear and persuasive presentation of the gospel to all the unsaved in the target area, the practical problems that stand between us and the achievement of that objective often may be great. That being the case, it is better to draw up a short list of more humble and immediate objectives that, once achieved, will contribute to the overall objective. These immediate objectives may well include the following:

(1) To mobilize as many believers as may be available and can be effectively deployed in evangelizing the target area.

(2) To relate the Good News of Christ to the audience(s) in a way that will be clear, convincing, and compelling.

(3) To employ the most appropriate methods of evangelism.

(4) To utilize the potential of various communication media within the target area.

(5) To reach the unevangelized in the target area in accordance with an order of priority established for the contact phase of the Pauline Cycle.

The biblical message is normative for all people in all places. Some naively believe that nothing more need be said. Perhaps nothing more would be required if God had decided upon some vehicle other than words, and some agents other than men, to communicate His message. But such is not the case. So gospel communication—perhaps above all other steps in the Pauline Cycle—will require thoughtful investigation and planning.

Preliminary Consideration: The Content of the Gospel Message

Biblical Principles and Precedents

New Testament evangelism was full-orbed. It reflected the emphasis of the Great Commission: "Teach them to observe all things, whatsoever I have commanded you." This does not mean that the whole of the revelation was delivered in each instance of evangelism. That would be manifestly impossible. There was, and is, a "gospel" or "salvific" core (I Cor. 15:1–4). This gospel core was determined by the Spirit and not by the evangelists; it was built upon and pointed to the whole counsel of God (Acts 20:27).

Roland Allen stresses that Paul's missionary message contained a great deal of what we would call theology or doctrine:[1]

    (1) God—His nature, plan, wrath, and promises.
    (2) Man—his problem (sin, unbelief, idolatry) and position before God.
    (3) Christ—the facts concerning His person, coming, and work.
    (4) Judgment—its meaning, the certainty of it, and a warning concerning it.
    (5) Salvation—the mercy of God and the kingdom of God.
    (6) Response—the necessity of repentance and faith.

Unaided human understanding is inadequate when it comes to comprehending divine truth. The natural mind could never have conceived that truth (I Cor. 2:9), and the natural mind is not a sufficient instrument for understanding it (I Cor. 2:14). Paul did not want the faith of his converts to rest primarily on human logic and wisdom. Therefore he did his best to communicate God's Word.

Relevant Research

Even when reduced to its most simple dimensions, communication is a complicated process. Its basic objective is the transfer of ideas. It is difficult if not impossible to

---

[1]Roland Allen, *Missionary Methods: St. Paul's or Ours?* (Grand Rapids: Eerdmans, 1962), pp. 68–69.

divorce ideas from words. Still, the ideas which are transferred and the words which transfer them are not the
same. The semanticist's way of expressing this is, "The
word is not the thing"; or, "Words do not have
meaning—only people do." Of course, that is not the
whole truth. Words do not have *inherent* meaning. But
they do convey the meanings invested in them. At the
same time, simply to speak certain words is not necessarily
the same as communicating a message, even though we
choose and articulate those words carefully and speak
them forcefully! Someone has pointed out that the five
hundred most used words in the English language have an
average of twenty-three meanings each! Experts judge
that communication is only about 80 percent effective in
the most ideal circumstances.[2] What is communicated is
not necessarily that which a person says. It is that which
another person (the "respondent") hears! Count on your
respondent to put his meaning into your words!

If all of this is true concerning the communication of
natural messages (and it is!), think of how fragile the gospel message must be. Should it not then be handled with
care and prayer?

Practical Reflection

Perhaps our most common failing as Christian believers,
preachers, and teachers is the failure to realize that the
words most intimately related to the gospel of Jesus Christ
("God," "Christ," "sin," "cross," "blood," "redemption,"
"salvation," and "eternal life"—to say nothing of "atone-
ment" and "propitiation"!) communicate little or nothing
of the gospel to an ever-increasing percentage of the
world's population. Biblical meanings must be put into

---

[2]Martin Joos, "Semology: A Linguistic Theory of Meaning," *Studies in
Linguistics* 13 (1958), pp. 53–72.

these words, or other words must be used! Otherwise true communication will not occur.

Preliminary Consideration: Elenctics

Biblical Principles and Precedents

For some strange reason the subject of elenctics is neglected in contemporary theological studies, although some aspects of it are dealt with in the study of apologetics. The word comes from the Greek word *elengchein*, which originally meant "to bring to a sense of shame," but later came to mean "to bring to a sense of guilt." The latter meaning is found in the New Testament. For example, in promising the Holy Spirit, our Lord said, "And He, when He comes, will convict [*elengxei*] the world concerning sin, and righteousness, and judgment" (John 16:8).

This verse, in fact, relates to a basic question in evangelistic communication. That the Holy Spirit is the subject in John 16:8 is without doubt. Only He can convince the world of sin, righteousness, and judgment. And therein lies our problem. What role, then, does the Christian communicator play? What about *his* arguments? What about *his* pleas? What about *his* strategies? In short, what implications does elenctics hold for evangelism?

While the answers to these problems are far too complex to adequately probe here, there are some facts that require emphasis. First, note that the areas of conviction are given in John 16:8. The Holy Spirit convicts men of sin, righteousness, and judgment. It is as if our Lord is saying to the evangelist, "Preach along these lines because the Holy Spirit will deal with men in these three areas."

Second, sin, righteousness, and judgment are defined. There can be little doubt as to the meaning of these words in the context. The "sin" our Lord is talking about is the sin of not believing on the Lord Jesus Christ (v. 9). "Righteousness" is the sufficient righteousness which the Lord demonstrated—the righteousness with which the Father was well pleased and which Christ alone can give to man (v. 10). "Judgment" is that of Satan, the head of the world system under whose authority every human being is born and from whom Christ saves (v. 11).

We conclude that only the Holy Spirit can bring the sinner to the place of repentance and faith; that human instruments are, nevertheless, used of the Holy Spirit (II Cor. 5:11); that the great themes to be specially emphasized are sin, righteousness, and judgment; and that this Good News of God's provision for sinners is to flow out of, and lead into, the whole counsel of God.

Relevant Research

Classical rhetoricians maintained that there are three kinds of communication. Some modern theorists have added other types, but all communication can basically be reduced to three or, perhaps, four types (corresponding to four purposes):

(1) Entertaining communication
(2) Instructive communication
(3) Persuasive communication
(4) Expressive communication

These are self-explanatory except for the last one. Expressive communication is communication which is primarily designed to meet the (psychological) needs of the *source* rather than to accomplish something for the *respondents*.

Some experts maintain that pure instances of these types of communication are impossible to achieve. For example, they would argue that it is impossible to instruct without persuading. They insist that all communication is in some sense persuasive. Even the common greeting, "How are you?" they say, is not motivated so much by the desire to gain information as by the desire to communicate the idea that the speaker is a tolerably cordial and jolly fellow. When it comes right down to it, persuasion does seem to be what communication is all about. As early as 1957 Vance Packard concluded that approximately 1300 "selling messages" reach the average American home every day.[3] Something approaching this is happening all around the world. Since human intent is involved, perhaps the debate as to whether all communication is persuasive will never be resolved. But that debate is instructive, nonetheless.

Practical Reflection

As we review our past record in evangelism, and the instruction we receive from revelation and research, some soul-searching is in order in at least two areas:

(1) Could it be true that, as Eugene Nida believes,[4] a considerable proportion of Christian preaching is "expressive," designed and carried out to fulfill the need of the preacher to erase his guilt, feel his worth, fulfill his duty, or increase his prestige? Gospel communicators should practice introspection periodically. God tries the hearts of His servants (II Cor. 5:11).

(2) Do we sometimes tend to manipulate men rather than persuade them in the power of the Spirit? It would almost seem so. Some approaches in personal and mass evangelism seem perilously similar to the selling techniques elucidated in manuals for supersalesmen, and designed to get people to accept Christ before they realize what has happened. This analysis may seem unfair, and it may be untrue. But it is worth pondering.

---

[3]Vance Packard, *The Hidden Persuaders* (New York: Pocket Books, 1957).

[4]Eugene A. Nida, *Message and Mission: The Communication of the Christian Faith* (New York: Harper and Row, 1960), p. 4.

The Christian faith is a reasonable faith though it is not the product of human reason. There are compelling reasons for becoming a believing member of the body of Christ. Let these reasons be articulated fervently and forcefully, but always humbly in the realization that we stand on holy ground where divine fire will reveal the deepest motives of speaker and hearer alike.

The Contextualization of the Gospel Message

Biblical Principles and Precedents

Obviously, the whole of God's revelation to man cannot be delivered on any one occasion. Nor need it be. Indeed, not only does Scripture reveal a salvific core, it also reveals that the salvific core was adapted to various audiences— not to their prejudice and taste in order to make the message *palatable,* but to their world view and knowledge in order to make it *understandable.* The New Testament is replete with illustrations. The Lord Jesus approached Nicodemus and the Samaritan woman very differently (cf. John 3 and 4), and the emphasis of the Gospel of Matthew differs markedly from that of the Gospels of Mark and Luke although they present many of the same events. But perhaps the clearest examples are found in the communication of the apostle Paul, who was commissioned to preach the gospel to various Gentile audiences. Notice the difference in his approach in the following instances:

(1) In the case of the monotheists in the synagogues of Damascus (Acts 9:20–22), Pisidian Antioch (Acts 13:16, 17), and Thessalonica (Acts 17:2, 3), Paul assumed a knowledge of God and special revelation and proceeded from there.

(2) In the case of the polytheists at Lystra (Acts 14:15–17), Paul emphasized the fact that the healing of the lame

man did not mean that he and Barnabas were gods. Rather, they were just as human as the Lystrans themselves.

(3) In the case of the pantheistically inclined Athenian philosophers (Acts 17:22–33), Paul began his message with references to the "unknown God," a Greek poet, and nature and man as the creation of God.

Notice in the above cases how the gospel messengers built upon the previous understanding of their various audiences. "Apostolic adaptation" must be kept in perspective, however. First of all, remember that the apostles did not change the gospel (Gal. 1:6–9). Second, though they used common concepts such as *logos* ("word," John 1:1–4) and *plērōma* ("fullness," Eph. 3:19), they invested them with distinctly Christian meanings. Third, cultural misunderstandings were countered and corrected (Acts 14:15–17; 17:31, 32; Rom. 3:28–30).

Relevant Research

It has long been realized that meaning is a function of context. However, in the twentieth century, with its great increase in intercultural contacts and the rise of the science of anthropology, more attention than ever before has been focused on the importance of culture and context. This heightened awareness comes at a most propitious time because it aids us in communicating the Christian message, not only to the non-Western world, but also in the rapidly changing post-Christian Western world.

The word most frequently used nowadays to refer to this process of message adaptation is the word *contextualization*. The extent of adaptation necessary is often reflected in the definitions given to the word. But for our purpose, the definition given by Bruce Nicholls is quite adequate: "the translation of the unchanging content of the Gospel of the kingdom into verbal forms *meaningful* to the peoples in their separate cultures and within their particular existential situations."[5]

Notice that contextualization has to do with making the gospel *meaningful*. Others would add such words and phrases as "making the gospel relevant" and "discovering the implications of the gospel in a given situation." But the point to be stressed here is that the gospel becomes meaningful (relevancy, etc., is dependent, first of all, on meaning) only as it is contextualized.[6]

Practical Reflection

Study of the Scriptures and of people (in their cultural contexts) must go hand in hand. Is it possible that evangelical outreach has suffered because there are some missionary-evangelists who know theology but not people, others who know people but not theology, and still others who know neither? Unquestionably, this area of communication is one in which missionary-evangelists of the future will be most seriously tested.

All effective communicators give attention to contextualization. Folk religion and the great ethnic religions are alive and well all over planet Earth. The West has entered the post-Christian era. The world view of many Westerners is materialist, but false religious systems are gaining ground as well. If the Christian missionary going to other cultures does not adapt his message, he will find himself preaching in Tokyo as he would in Toledo. If the Chris-

---

[5]Bruce Nicholls, "Theological Education and Evangelization," in *Let the Earth Hear His Voice*, ed. J. D. Douglas (Minneapolis: World Wide Publications, 1975), p. 647.

[6]For a more thorough discussion of what is involved in communicating the gospel across cultural barriers, see David J. Hesselgrave, *Communicating Christ Cross-Culturally: An Introduction to Missionary Communication* (Grand Rapids: Zondervan, 1978).

tian evangelist at home does not keep current with cultural change, he will find himself speaking to a past generation!

ME-1-2 illustration: Francis Schaeffer may be taken as an eminent example of one who has "modified" the gospel message in order to communicate it to a new and different generation within his own cultural context. Schaeffer is speaking and writing to a post-Christian audience that has been taught that the world (including man) is the product of a chance collocation of atoms in a vast sea of time; an audience that is poorly equipped to understand the content of words like "God," "blood," "redemption," and so on; an audience that thinks of faith as a leap in the dark. No wonder Schaeffer chooses a different starting point.

Many will argue that very few are able to make a Schaeffer-like adaptation of the Christian message. Granted. But ability is a relative thing. Effort is required, to be sure. And all will not be equally successful. But unless more evangelists make the attempt, fewer and fewer people will "hear" what they are saying.

ME-3 illustration: We will select but one example of contextualization in a non-Western culture from the myriads that present themselves for consideration.

Pastor Baldemore, formerly a Conservative Baptist pastor in the Philippines, has been used of the Lord as one of the most effective missionary-evangelists in that land. One of the factors in his fruitfulness has been his unique approach to church-extension evangelism. Baldemore and his team began by studying target areas in which there was no evangelical church. Prior to opening a three-week tent campaign, contacts were made, homes were visited, and special invitations to the meetings were extended. During the campaign itself, Baldemore preached (with the aid of simple diagrams) on such subjects as "What Is the True Church?" "To Whom Should We Confess Our Sins?" and "Why Do Christians Tithe?" From a Western point of view, these subjects may not seem suitable for an evangelistic campaign. But upon reflection it will be apparent that they have special relevance in the Philippines. Baldemore's topics entailed answers to precisely those questions which Filipinos entertain concerning a Christianity which is based upon the Bible. Baldemore's style also allowed for questions from his audience. By the end of the extended campaign, many of those who had faithfully attended the meetings understood the true gospel. Only then were they encouraged to receive the Savior. Those who did so became the nucleus of a new church.

The Varied Methods of Gospel Communication

Biblical Principles and Precedents

In the New Testament the gospel message is given in a variety of ways and with a variety of approaches:[7]

(1) *Privately* to individuals (John 3; 4; Acts 8) and to family or household groups (Acts 10; 16; 20:20); *publicly* to gathered groups (Acts 13:14–41; 19:8, 9) and to crowds in public places (Acts 17:17, 22–33).

(2) By means of *preaching* (Acts 2:14–40), *teaching* (Acts 10:34–43), and *witnessing* (Acts 26:1–23).

(3) Sometimes in the form of a *monologue* (Acts 2:14–36), but often in the form of a *dialogue* (Acts 17:16, 17).

(4) In a manner that sometimes entailed simple *proclamation* and *exhortation* (Acts 13:14–41), but often was *apologetical* and *polemical* (disputational) (Acts 17:16–31; 19:8, 9).

Note that all of the methods above involve interpersonal (face-to-face) communication. Our Lord and the apostles did not have recourse to the vast resources of communications media that we have today. However, the relative lack

---

[7]For an informative statement on the diversity and depth revealed in the evangelistic approach of the early church, see Michael Green, *Evangelism in the Early Church* (Grand Rapids: Eerdmans, 1970), p. 160.

of mass media in Bible times had its advantages because, in some ways, interpersonal communication is superior to mass-media communication.

Notice also that New Testament methods of communication seem to have allowed for a significant degree of interaction between the speakers and their respondents. Over and over again, we read that listeners asked questions, raised objections, or verbally reinforced the message. This is to say that much of New Testament gospel communication was *dialogical* even though that precise word may not be used. The word *dialegomai,* which literally means to "discuss" or "conduct a discussion," was used "of lectures which were likely to end in disputation"[8] (e.g., Acts 17:2, 17; 18:4, 19; 19:9; 20:7, 9; and 24:12). There is little room to question that the gospel communication of the apostolic age was characterized by much more personal interaction than is generally the case today.

Relevant Research

(1) Reason and research indicate that, as compared to mass communication, interpersonal communication has some very real advantages as well as limitations (see Figure 28).[9]

(2) Some very interesting research carried on by psychologists Albert Dabba and James Dabba, Jr., at the University of Michigan yielded some rather surprising results. In an experiment designed to test the extent to which a speaker's distance from the listener affects his ability to persuade, the psychologists varied the distance between

---

[8]Gottlob Schrenk, in *Theological Dictionary of the New Testament,* ed. Gerhard Kittel, trans. and ed. Geoffrey W. Bromiley, 9 vols. (Grand Rapids: Eerdmans, 1964), vol. 2, p. 94.

[9]James F. Engel, Hugh G. Wales, and Martin R. Warshaw, *Promotional Strategy,* rev. ed. (Homewood, IL: Richard D. Irwin, Inc., 1971), p. 27. © 1971 by Richard D. Irwin, Inc. Used by permission.

FIGURE 28

The Comparative Advantages and Limitations of Interpersonal Versus Mass Communication

	Interpersonal Communication	Mass Communication
Reaching a Large Audience		
Speed......................	Slow	Fast
Cost per individual reached..	High	Low
Influence on the Individual		
Ability to attract attention ...	High	Low
Accuracy of message communicated	Low	High
Probability of selective screening	Relatively Low	High
Clarity of content	High	Moderate to Low
Feedback		
Direction of message flow...	Two-way	One-way
Speed of feedback	High	Low
Accuracy of feedback .:......	High	Low

sources and respondents from one or two feet, to five or six feet, and up to about fifteen feet. They hypothesized that the speakers would be most persuasive at the middle distance because they would not be invading the personal space of the respondents and thus causing discomfort on the one hand, or losing the respondents' attention due to being placed too far apart, on the other. To the experimenters' surprise, the speakers proved to be most persuasive at the greatest distance.[10]

It may not be too far-fetched to say that this experiment gives some support to the biblical practice of preaching to

---

[10]Cf. "Behavior," *Time*, 7 September 1970, p. 27.

an audience with a view to their conversion. From the word *preach* we cannot infer that it is necessary that there be a distance between the preacher and his audience. But in a day when preaching—and perhaps evangelistic preaching especially—is under attack in some quarters, it is well to remind ourselves that much preaching in Bible times (as today) of necessity involved an appropriate spacing of the preacher and his audience. There is a time for the more personalized witnessing, counseling, and small-group teaching with which we are so familiar today. But there is also a time for the more public proclamation of the Word of God.

(3) The limitations of preaching of the more formal, one-way kind are indicated by research such as was carried on by Kurt Lewin. In an assignment which has received considerable attention since it was carried out, Lewin was asked to assist the Red Cross during World War II in an effort to overcome negative attitudes toward eating meats such as hearts and other internal organs. When lectures on the subject produced no significant effect, he substituted group discussions, with the result that 32 percent responded favorably.[11]

Practical Reflection

Innovation is needed in communicating the gospel today, but of first priority (methodologically) is the need to get back to basic New Testament evangelistic methods. If our abilities to innovate are not exhausted in exploiting the potential of biblical models, we can go on to attempt new methods for communicating Christ. But why not give

---

[11]Kurt Lewin, "Group Decision and Social Change," in *Readings in Social Psychology*, ed. Theodore M. Newcomb and Eugene L. Hartley (New York: Henry Holt and Co., 1947), pp. 330–44.

special consideration to didactic, apologetic, and visitation methods (which are quite often overlooked today), especially in the dialogical pattern? Experience seems to indicate that they are still effective.

ME-3 illustration: An arresting example of sound strategy that actually combines a number of principles (didactic evangelism, extended-family evangelism in a lineage society, group communication, the use of a team) comes from the Sevav area of Nigeria and the evangelistic outreach of the Fellowship of Churches of Christ in the Sudan. Missionaries Eugene Rubingh and Ralph Baker took note of the fact that not one person from that area had been baptized into the Tiv (tribe) Church in thirteen years. A special strategy was devised:

(1) In the social structure of the Tiv the smallest unit or segment is called the "ipaven u ken iyou." This normally consists of from nine to twelve extended family compounds. The segment head lives in the central compound. Mr. Rubingh determined as a pilot project to evangelize one segment and to obtain catechumens and eventually baptize believers who were all members of the same segment.

(2) This plan was explained to the leaders of the local church and a team of men enlisted who would give one day a week for fourteen weeks to work in the chosen segment. Mr. Baker prepared a syllabus of fourteen lessons that explained the way of salvation.

(3) The team on the first of the fourteen days went to the segment and there divided so that in each compound one man taught the assigned lesson, preached the assigned sermon, and told the assigned story.

(4) At the close of the fourteen weeks, a three-day conference was held in the compound of the clan head. Decisions for Christ were called for.

(5) Those who responded were organized into a catechumen class and began regular weekly worship. They continued working for the enlistment of other catechumens. While not an organized church they carried out many functions of a church congregation.

(6) Definite plans for another visit were made previous to the team's leaving.[12]

The results of the very first attempt of this type of "segment evangelism" (1962) were most gratifying. Three teams had worked among three segments with a total of 350 people. The total number of catechumens enrolled as an outgrowth of the effort was 60! Remember, this was in an area that had not had one baptism in thirteen years.

Selecting the Appropriate Media for Gospel Communication

Biblical Principles and Precedents

When approaching the target area the modern church-planter must make the decision as to what media he will use to reach the community. In Bible times the task was not as complicated as today because, of course, modern techniques of reaching the masses had not been developed. Nevertheless, there were choices to be made and at least two primary media were used to reach people.

Luke states that when persecution had scattered the Jerusalem congregation, "they . . . went every where preaching the word" (Acts 8:4, KJV). This was person-to-person, face-to-face activity. This was the usual approach to communication, but it was not the only approach. Letters and books were also used, and thus the Scriptures which we have today came into existence. Written materials were widely used to communicate the gospel to unbelievers and also to give assurance and instruction to believers (cf. John 20:31).

---

[12]John B. Grimley and Gordon E. Robinson, *Church Growth in Central and Southern Nigeria* (Grand Rapids: Eerdmans, 1966), pp. 213-21.

Relevant Research

Research indicates that there are good, solid reasons for carefully evaluating the media by which we communicate the gospel:
(1) The various media have differing degrees of effectiveness as channels of suasive communication.[13] Research indicates that at all social, economic, and educational levels (in the United States at least) people are more inclined to believe news reports received by television than those received through the newspaper.[14] A study made in isolated towns in the Andean mountains of Ecuador revealed that while both radio and audio-visual media were effective, they served different functions as far as their influence on the audience was concerned.[15]
(2) Despite the unchallenged potential of the mass media for reaching large audiences rapidly and efficiently, their persuasive potential is more limited than some suppose. *"The mass media can help only indirectly to change strongly held attitudes or valued practices.* Mass communication has never proved very effective in attacking attitudes, values, or social customs that are deep-set or strongly held."[16] G. Ralph Milton concludes:

Enough research has been done . . . to enable us to be certain that a person's communication with family and friends is more significant in terms of attitude change and forma-

---

[13]Cf. Joseph T. Klapper, *The Effects of Mass Communication* (Glencoe, IL: Free Press, 1960), pp. 129–32.

[14]A Roper study cited in a talk by Louis Hausman entitled "Measured View: The Public's Attitude Toward Television" to the Advertising Club of Philadelphia, 8 February 1962.

[15]Cited by J. B. Haskins, "How to Evaluate Mass Communication," a monograph published by the Advertising Research Foundation, 1968, pp. 56–57; and by G. Ralph Milton, "Media Integration—a Fad and a Fact: The Church and the Media," *Asia Focus* 6 (third quarter, 1971), p. 37.

[16]Wilbur Schramm, *Mass Media in National Development* (Stanford, CA: Stanford University Press, 1969), p. 132.

tion than any or all of the media. In fact, this result is reported with almost monotonous regularity. This is especially true of deep rooted attitudes and beliefs such as religious conviction.[17]

(3) Research seems to support the concept of "two-step flow," which was formulated by Paul Lazarsfeld, Bernard Berelson, and Hazel Gaudet. The basic idea is that when local people, especially opinion leaders, relay and reinforce mass-media messages, those messages become especially effective. Studies made in connection with the 1940 presidential election in the United States revealed that these human links in the communication flow were more effective than the media messages themselves when it came to influencing the decisions of voters.[18]

(4) Studies indicate that the various media should be used to complement one another.

As early as 1955, the United States Department of Agriculture made a study of more than 1,100 homemakers in five states. These homemakers had been exposed to messages carried over a variety of media and calculated to influence them to change their homemaking practices. The results were most revealing. Of those who had been exposed to the information through one or two media, about 46 per cent were influenced to make appropriate changes. However, of those homemakers who had been exposed to the information through two or three media, 68 per cent were motivated to change. And of those who had been exposed to eight or more media over 97 per cent were influenced to change!

The implications of the above are clear. While in any given cultural situation there may be a certain medium which will prove to be superior to others when properly employed, overall the Church will greatly enhance the effectiveness of its communication if the various mass media

---

[17]"Media Integration," p. 41.

[18]Merrill Abbey, *Man, Media and the Message* (New York: Friendship Press, 1960), p. 79.

are used in such a way that they complement each other. Generally speaking, no one medium should stand alone.[19]

Practical Reflection

There is certainly much cause for encouragement when it comes to the use of the various media in communicating the Christian message to our contemporary world. The Bible, in whole or in part, has been translated into over 1,300 languages and dialects. Christian radio stations beam the message of Christ to peoples in every area of the globe. Films, filmstrips, cassettes, and audio-visual equipment of varied types are available to gospel communicators. Never before in history has the Church enjoyed the wealth of expertise and technology that is available to Christian spokesmen today.

Unfortunately, some of the most strategic uses of the media in widespread propagation of religious faith come, not from the evangelical Christian sector, but from non-Christian movements such as Mormonism, the Jehovah's Witnesses, Armstrong's Plain Truth movement, and (in Japan) the Soka Gakkai. Evangelicals desperately need to study these examples of the complementary utilization of radio, television, printed materials, local leaders, and small groups. We should note how the messages of the media are taken up at the local level and repeated and reinforced there in face-to-face, dialogical, small-group communication.

Within the Church two areas of concern merit special consideration. First, evangelistic programs and efforts tend to be disjoined and even competitive rather than coordinated and complementary. In large measure this is a result of the fragmentation of the Church and the unprec-

---

[19]Hesselgrave, *Communicating Christ Cross-Culturally*, pp. 396–97; the study cited is by Wilson and Gallup, Extension Service Circular 495, U.S. Department of Agriculture, Washington, DC, 1955.

edented increase in specialist organizations. And to the extent that it is, the problem admits of a solution only to the degree that Christian leaders with a biblical evangel give priority to the larger cause.

Second, it seems that a disproportionate emphasis is given to the mass media in contemporary evangelism. Especially in dealing with such a basic consideration as religious faith, there is no substitute for face-to-face communication. It is not so much our utilization of the media, but our negligence in complementing media messages with local church-related follow-up that is of concern. Every effort should be made to link mass-media evangelism with local, personal witness and instruction. Only by so doing do we prove ourselves to be responsible and faithful stewards of the message of Christ.

ME-3 illustration: For years the well-known Moody Institute of Science films have been used throughout the world in great evangelistic rallies. But recently in a number of areas in the Orient at least, the films are being put to a new and perhaps more effective use. Christians are finding "sponsors" (heads of households for the most part) who are willing to invite their neighbors to their homes one night a week (for four weeks) to see a Christian scientific film. Small evangelistic teams made up of local area Christian leaders show the films and encourage dialogue after each showing. Viewers are invited to the church. At the last showing, opportunity for a meaningful response is extended. This method is especially good in areas where there are educated people who would appreciate (and question!) the message of these films.

ME-3 illustration: In one country in South America a well-known Bible-teaching radio program originating in North America was broadcast in Spanish for a number of years. From the beginning, response in the form of letters from listeners was good, but evangelical churches in the area made comparatively few meaningful contacts as a result of the broadcasts. Local church leaders were concerned. Representatives from the broadcast and local churches met together to see what could be done. As a result, area churches and their programs were mentioned on the broadcast. Local church leaders related some of their preaching and teaching to themes used on the radio broadcasts. As a consequence, the broadcast became identified with local churches and their pastors. Many churches reported a significant upswing in the number of contacts who came to saving faith and fruitful service.

Measuring Audience Understanding and Response

Biblical Principles and Precedents

There is a reluctance on the part of some church-planters and other Christian workers to measure results because to do so is thought to be unspiritual. On the part of others there may be an overemphasis on measuring results, or at least an imbalanced emphasis. In view of this state of affairs it is important to see how the apostles measured response to their message.

First, the apostles measured response numerically. On the day of Pentecost 3,000 souls were added to the 120 (Acts 2:41). Later, it is reported that 5,000 believed (Acts 4:4). Afterwards, it is said that "churches [were] established ... and increased in number daily" (Acts 16:5, KJV).

Second, the apostles measured response qualitatively. For example, Paul knew of the election of the Thessalonians. This knowledge came from his awareness that the Holy Spirit was present in his preaching to them and that they first became imitators of him and then examples to others (I Thess. 1:4–8). After this initial measurement, Paul sent Timothy to Thessalonica. When Timothy returned, he reported that the Thessalonian believers had faith and love but that they did not understand the second coming of the Lord (I Thess. 3:1-7; 4:13—5:10).

Epaphras apparently took the same kind of reading in respect to the spiritual state of the Colossians because Paul in response expressed a desire that they "might be filled with the knowledge of his will" (Col. 1:7-10).

Again, it was news from the house of Chloe about the spiritual state of the Corinthian church that prompted Paul to write a corrective letter (I Cor. 1:11).

We conclude that the apostolic preachers took a rather careful measurement of how many people were becoming believers and how well believers were doing spiritually. They wanted to know if the message had been accepted, and by how many, and whether or not believers were progressing from the elementary to the exemplary stage of Christian understanding and conduct.

Relevant Research

Recent research in the area of Christian communication is most revealing. Consider the following examples:

A church of 650 members seems to be successful from all external measures. But a survey of the congregation revealed that only 20 percent attempted to share their faith in the past month; 21 percent had family devotions; 70 percent confined their church involvement to Sunday services; 10 percent knew their spiritual gift; and 50 percent claimed they are not being fed spiritually in this church.

A Christian-owned radio station offers both secular and Christian programming. It was discovered that programs designed to evangelize the non-Christian are listened to almost entirely by Christians.

Bibles were given to every inmate in a large United States prison. A few days later it was discovered that 90 percent of these found their way into the trash cans, thus causing the unnecessary expenditure of more than $250,000 when this program was prematurely spread to other prisons.

Fewer than 8 percent of the Christians in the seven largest cities of Brazil ever bother to tune in to the many hours of teaching programs directed at them weekly by two major shortwave missionary broadcasters.

The plan of salvation was prominently displayed in a magazine directed toward non-Christians on the college campus. It was largely ignored, whereas several articles focusing on a Christian perspective on pertinent issues were both read and positively evaluated.[20]

Citing these examples, James Engel comments:

This list of examples could be extended for many more pages. Notice the common denominator in each: a reliance on one-way communication. Messages are sent from the pulpit, door-to-door, over the airwaves, or in print. But what is the response? Real communication does not occur until the message is both comprehended and acted upon by the recipient as intended. Communication, in reality, is a two-way process. All too often we ignore the audience.[21]

Practical Reflection

It is imperative that we determine the interest, understanding, and commitment of the audience vis-à-vis the gospel message. In the secular sector there are organizations whose sole purpose is to measure public opinion and audience reaction. Such reports as Gallup polls and Nielsen ratings are the result. Gospel radio broadcasters often use such devices as "letter week" and mail pulls to determine the size of the listening audience and (to a certain extent) audience reaction. At the local level, few efforts are made to secure this type of feedback until the respondents reach the conversion stage, which is often accompanied by the raising of hands, coming forward to the

---

[20]James Engel, *How Can I Get Them to Listen? A Handbook on Communication Strategy and Research* (Grand Rapids: Zondervan, 1977), pp. 14–15.

[21]Ibid.

altar, or the signing of a decision card. The advantage of such methods as visitation-evangelism, family-centered evangelism, and small-group Bible-study evangelism is that they allow for true dialogue in which the respondents have the opportunity to state their opinions and ask questions, and the missionary-evangelist has a chance to relate the gospel to the specific needs of the respondents.

It is important that we think of new ways to measure the attitudes and understanding of those to whom we direct the gospel message. Evangelistic methods that move quickly to the decision stage without taking stock of whether or not the respondents understand the gospel run the risk of measuring response only by ascertaining how many "follow through." Wise stewardship dictates that gospel communicators at every level give more consideration to determining actual listener understanding and response. Especially in a day in which methods for making these measurements are widely known and readily accepted, it is irresponsible to disregard them.

Master Plan Formation

A knowledge of the audience (respondents) is absolutely essential in planning for effective communication. Fortunately, the pioneer worker will have a store of information concerning his audience(s) that has been gathered previously. In particular, he will analyze the data included in Figure 10 (p. 101), which were collected with a view to selecting the target area. He will likely find that those data need to be augmented and refined. This task accomplished, they will serve well in devising a communication strategy.

Contextualizing the Christian Message

Elsewhere we have dealt with the gigantic chasms that separate people of the various religious traditions. If our audience is composed largely of Hindus, for example, that study should be consulted for suggestions as to contextualizing the Christian message.[22] Even when religious loyalties are not so diverse, however, it will be most helpful to take time to characterize the dominant beliefs of target audiences. (Most target areas have people with various religious orientations. Hence the use of the plural.) To activists this exercise may seem too time-consuming and, perhaps, "ivory tower." If, however, the activist will reflect on the prevailing attitudes of his various audiences toward the basic content of the gospel, and attempt to tailor his message accordingly, he will come to recognize the importance of the exercise.

With the information in Figure 29 in mind, the gospel communicator will be aided in contextualizing his message, putting biblical doctrines into language the audience will understand. In the process he should pay attention to questions such as the following:

(1) At what points are the hearers most likely to misunderstand the message?

(2) Which of the religious beliefs held by the respondents are similar to Christian doctrine and can be expected to provide conceptual bridges for communication? Which are decidedly different? (Care must be exercised here. What we view as similarities may be only *seeming* similarities and may occasion significant misunderstanding unless treated carefully.)

(3) To what concerns of the target audience does Christ speak with authority and clarity?

(4) What adaptations have successful Christian communicators used in addressing this or similar audiences?

Determining the Methods of Communication

Once we have identified and characterized target audiences, it is natural to ask how we will communicate the

---

[22]Cf. David J. Hesselgrave, *Communicating Christ Cross-Culturally: An Introduction to Missionary Communication* (Grand Rapids: Zondervan, 1978), pp. 161–71.

FIGURE 29

Audience Orientations Vis-à-vis the Christian Message

A. Religious Orientation: _____ (naturalist, nominal Christian, Hindu, etc.)

B. Percentage of Target Community: _____

C. Basic Beliefs

Biblical Doctrines of Central Importance	Predominant Beliefs of the Target Audience
1. **God:** Creator, Sustainer of universe; a personal being who has will, is moral and holy, reveals Himself to man, demands worship, condemns idolatry. . . .	**God:**
2. **Man:** Created by God in His image; a fallen creature; the object of God's redeeming love. . . .	**Man:**
3. **Jesus Christ:** Preexistent; fully God and fully man; incarnation; Lamb of God; substitutionary death. . . .	**Jesus Christ:**
4. **Sin:** Rebellion against God's will; true moral guilt entailing judgment and resulting in estrangement and death. . . .	**Sin:**

(contextualized) message to them. In this chapter we have used the word *method* as an umbrella term for the varieties of nonmedia communication. The key to successful gospel

FIGURE 30

Methods of Gospel Communication

Target Audience: _____

How?	To Whom?	When?	Where?
1. Privately Publicly 2. Preaching Teaching Witnessing 3. Monological Dialogical 4. Proclamational and Exhortational 5. Apologetical and Polemical			

communication is that we utilize as much variety as possible, with special attention to biblical principles, the gifts of the evangelists, and the preferences of the audiences. The chief danger is that we may get into ruts and unnecessarily restrict our methods.

Much Christian communication is, and should be, spontaneous. But there is much communication that should be carefully planned. Insofar as it is planned, completing the form in Figure 30 should prove helpful.

Selection of Communication Media

What media do the respondents use in communicating with each other? This is an important question. Missionary-evangelists may import new media and introduce innovations in media use, but they will be wise to give attention to indigenous media first. These may range from

FIGURE 31

Evaluation of Media for Use in Gospel Communication

Type	Local Use Overall (high, medium, low)	Subgroup Preference (high or low appeal to the following groups)	Suitability for Church Use (taboos, etc.)	Special Considerations

1. Printed media
  a. Newspaper
  b. Magazines
  c. Journals
  d. Books
  e. Pamphlets and tracts
  f. Mailings
  g. Billboards
  h. Others
  _____				

2. Electronic Media
  a. Radio
  b. Television
  c. Movies
  d. Slides
  e. Records
  f. Cassette tapes
  g. Others
  _____				

3. Other Media
  a. Drama
  b. Puppets
  c. Chalk talks
  d. Others
  _____				

simple chalkboards to television sets. Local availability and usage should be carefully studied. Then the process of media selection can begin. (A small group of two or three informed residents can provide the needed advice for an initial projection—see Figure 31.)

Measurement Implementation

Three questions are paramount: (1) Is the message actually getting through to the intended audience? (2) Is the message we intend the same message that is actually being received? (3) Are the methods and media serving their intended ends, and not becoming ends in themselves? Measurements designed to answer these questions may be taken by means ranging from personal conversation and observation to thorough community surveys employing advanced statistical methods. The means should fit the size and nature of the audience. Proper stewardship demands that we take positive steps to determine whether the five or ten talents entrusted to us are earning five or ten more, or are simply being buried in those messages, methods, and media which are most familiar to us as communicators. Evaluation requires serious effort, but is well worth the information it can provide to guide us as we consider ways to improve our communication to a lost world.

Increasingly, the messengers of Christ are becoming concerned with the *quality* of Christian communication. But quality means far more than employing the best talent and the most up-to-date technology. It also has reference to the content of the message, the method of its presentation, and the kind of media chosen to convey it.

eleven

The Hearers Converted

Concerning conversion Michael Green says:

> We normally use the word, in a religious context, in one of two ways, either to indicate that a man has left one religious position (or, indeed, none) for exclusive attachment to another. Alternatively, we speak of conversion in a man who up till a certain period had been a mere nominal adherent of his faith, but had then awoken to its significance and importance with enthusiasm and insight.[1]

Quite probably this represents what most church people regard as conversion. And it is correct as far as it goes. Much more must be said, however, if church-planters are to mitigate problems such as the lack of conversions and the frequency of reversions in evangelism today.

---

[1]Michael Green, *Evangelism in the Early Church* (Grand Rapids: Eerdmans, 1970), p. 144.

FIGURE 32
"THE PAULINE CYCLE"

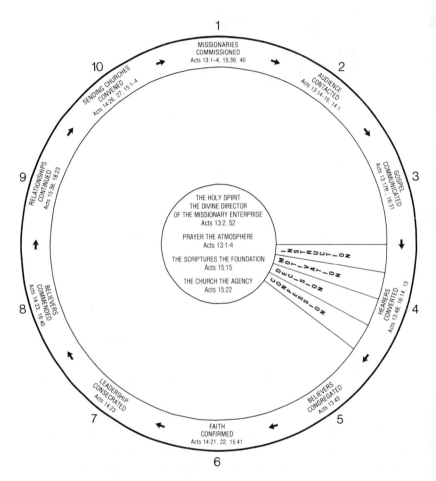

"Therefore, being sent on their way by the church, they were passing through both Phoenicia and Samaria, describing in detail the conversion of the Gentiles, and were bringing great joy to all the brethren" (Acts 15:3).

Objectives

Our objectives in relation to conversion should be:

(1) To secure a response to the gospel that grows out of understanding.

(2) To secure a response to the gospel which takes into account culturally appropriate patterns of decision-making.

(3) To secure a response to the gospel which will be genuine and lasting, and result in spiritual fruitfulness.

(4) To secure a response to Christ which will heighten the possibility of others becoming Christian.

Instruction as to the Meaning and Importance of Conversion

Biblical Principles and Precedents

The Definition of "Conversion"

It is popular in contemporary theology to use the term *conversion* in a loose sense to describe salvation. However, the Bible usually does not use the word in this fashion. A study of *epistrephō* and its related noun forms will sustain this affirmation.

The New Testament uses *epistrephō* in a physical sense to describe a "turning around" (Matt. 9:22; Mark 5:30) or a "turning back" or "returning" (Matt. 10:13; 12:44; John 21:20). Its metaphorical uses are similar. The Septuagint uses the term to describe a "return to" the worship of Jehovah (Jer. 3:14) or, conversely, to describe a "turning away from" the worship of Jehovah (Jer. 2:21).

There are several passages in the New Testament that can be considered central to the doctrine of conversion. Writing to the Thessalonians, Paul states that they had "turned to God from idols to serve a living and true God"

(I Thess. 1:9). Here conversion is both a "turning to God" and a "turning from idols." This is important because the phrase "turning from idols" by itself could mean a "turning to" atheism, materialism, emperor worship, or some other form of religion. It is also important because Christian conversion is seen as a break with former religious practices and beliefs. Conversion excludes syncretism.

In another key passage Paul tells King Agrippa that he had been commissioned to go to the Gentiles "to open their eyes so that they may turn from darkness to light and from the dominion of Satan to God" (Acts 26:18). Here, too, conversion is seen as both a "turning from" and a "turning to." But notice that spiritual blindness had to be lifted before conversion could occur. It is important to distinguish spiritual blindness from spiritual darkness. Darkness is the absence of light while blindness is the lack of capacity to perceive light. A blind man in a lighted room is still blind. Similarly, a spiritually blind person must receive the capacity to comprehend the truth before conversion can occur. This blindness, according to Paul, is imposed by Satan upon the minds of all unbelievers (II Cor. 4:4). Jesus, using another figure, said that the strong man, Satan, had to be bound before his house could be robbed (Matt. 12:29). What we are suggesting is that before an unsaved man can be converted, satanic blindness must be removed.

In a third key passage, repentance and conversion are linked. Peter said, "Repent therefore and return, that your sins may be wiped away, in order that times of refreshing may come from the presence of the Lord" (Acts 3:19). Repentance (*metanoia*) is literally a change of mind. It has to do with the intellect. In the context, Peter is speaking to those who in ignorance had crucified the Lord. They were asked to change their way of thinking about Him. He was to be thought of as the servant of God (v. 13) and the One who had worked the miracle of healing they had just observed (v. 16). Now unless Peter is being redundant, conversion is something in addition to the repentance just described. It is more than something intellectual. It is the forsaking of the entire system that crucified Christ and the embracing of Jesus Christ as Messiah. It is the practice that should follow a change of opinion. Thus repentance and conversion are similar, but conversion is the larger term.

In Scripture belief and conversion are also presented as related concepts. Luke, in describing the revival in Antioch, states, "And a large number who believed turned to the Lord.... Then when he [Barnabas] had come and witnessed the grace of God, he rejoiced and began to encourage them all with resolute heart to remain true to the Lord" (Acts 11:21–23). In this passage, belief precedes conversion. It is the believer who turns to the Lord. But again, conversion is something more than belief. It can be seen. It is the observable phenomenon of the grace of God in action in the believer's life.

One final remark must be made before a full definition of biblical conversion can be attempted. Common to all the passages cited is the fact that the verb forms denoting the process of conversion are always in the active voice. While the King James Version may suggest a passive sense in some places, the Greek text uses the word in the active voice. *It is the believer who turns.* The idea is not, "Repent and let some outside force turn you to the Lord." The idea is, "You repent and you turn." Conversion is an act which is commanded.

Now, based on the preceding exegetical remarks, a more complete and biblical definition of conversion can be made. *Conversion is an act of the believer which follows repentance in which he turns to God in such a fashion that the beliefs and practices of the old religion are completely forsaken and the grace of God becomes observable in his life.*

The Importance of Conversion

Those passages which are central to the definition of conversion also reveal the *importance* of conversion.

First, conversion is important because it is a prerequisite to blessing (Acts 3:19).

Second, conversion is important because it naturally precedes service to God (I Thess. 1:9, 10).

Third, in that conversion is outward and observable, it is important to the Christian witness.

Fourth, conversion is important because it is related to forgiveness of sins (Acts 3:19; 26:18). Peter comments on the relationship between conversion and forgiveness in his first epistle. He states that his readers had returned to the Shepherd and Bishop of their souls—Jesus Christ who bore their sins on the tree (I Peter 2:24, 25). Thus conversion is a return to the Forgiver and is related to forgiveness. Paul argues in the same vein in the letter to the Colossians. Forgiveness of sin is more or less synonymous with redemption. Redemption is in the beloved Son of God, into whose kingdom the believer has been transferred (Col. 1:12–15).

Fifth, conversion is important because it is related to understanding the law. Paul states that the Israelites had a veil over their heart when the law was read. "But whenever a man turns to the Lord, the veil is taken away" (II Cor. 3:16). Charles Ryrie explains that the veil is over the heart "as long as they consider the law as permanent and do not turn to Christ, who takes away the veil."[2] In other words, the law cannot be understood apart from a turning to Christ. Conversion is important to understanding the Old Testament.

Relevant Research

History reveals that conversion of the New Testament variety was utterly foreign to the Hellenistic world of the first century. Michael Green adduces several reasons for

---

[2]Charles Caldwell Ryrie, *Ryrie Study Bible—NAS: New Testament* (Chicago: Moody Press, 1976), p. 318.

this. In the first place, Hellenistic man did not consider belief as a requirement for belonging to a cult. In the second place, ethics was not regarded as part of religion. In the third place, Christian conversion made an exclusivistic claim upon adherents that was startling to Hellenistic man.[3]

Conversion, therefore, should not be looked upon as something that was quite acceptable (or even fashionable) in the first century but is outmoded in the twentieth. Christian conversion was, and is, made necessary by divine requirement in the face of society's antipathy to it. This is part of the believer's cross.

Practical Reflection

Evangelical Christians are quick to point an accusing finger at liberals, many of whom by some strange theological alchemy have produced a salvation that does not require the radical change implicit in conversion. But like the preacher who points his thumb at himself while extending his finger in the direction of others, evangelicals should consider their own failures and foibles in this regard. They also tend to err. Often contemporary evangelism leads to a hurried "decision for Christ" or "receiving the Savior" with but scant attention to repentance and (sometimes) inadequate explanations of faith and conversion itself.

It is important that potential converts be instructed in the gospel and concerning the meaning and significance of conversion. To ask anyone to make such an important decision on the basis of no understanding or misunderstanding is ethically indefensible.

ME-3 illustration: John L. Nevius, the great missionary statesman of China and Korea, writes that the majority of

---

[3]Cf. Green, *Evangelism,* pp. 144ff.

missionaries in the China of his day gave "chief attention" to evangelizing the "middle or more illiterate class."[4] This they did by going to relatively unreached areas and by visiting the fairs that were a striking feature of country life in China. Curiosity assured great crowds and, when an appeal was made, good response. But Nevius warns against assuming that in such cases the people understand what is being preached. He advises missionaries that the important objective in such cases should be to leave an impression of goodwill and to create a sense of expectancy for future visits. That is good advice. The world has an overabundance of "converts" whose curiosity has been satisfied but whose hearts have not been transformed!

Motivation and Conversion

Biblical Principles and Precedents

In the previous chapter the subject of elenctics was treated briefly. That subject is intimately related to motivation. It is abundantly clear that no one comes *to* the Son unless he is drawn *by* the Father (John 6:44). The Holy Spirit was sent into the world precisely for the purpose of convicting the world of sin, righteousness, and judgment (John 16:8). Our Lord's explanation makes it clear that in this context sin is unbelief in Christ, righteousness is Christ's righteousness, and judgment is the judgment of Satan in Christ's triumph over sin and death. Indeed, the Holy Spirit alone can convince the world of these things. That unbelief in Jesus is heinous sin is not easy to accept. With Christ in heaven instead of on earth men tend to compare themselves with their neighbors rather than with

---

[4]John L. Nevius, *The Planting and Development of Missionary Churches* (Philadelphia: Presbyterian and Reformed, 1958), pp. 81–82.

the righteous Christ. And to natural man the idea that the struggle against evil is already a "lost cause" seems preposterous. The "motivation" to accept and act upon these truths must come from the Holy Spirit. However, this does not mean there can be no other motivational factors connected with conversion. Within the potential convert himself there may be at least three types of motivation.

First, there is a self-oriented set of motivational factors. There are several illustrations of this in the New Testament. A leper went to Jesus and asked to be cleansed. His motive was personal—"Thou canst make *me* clean" (Mark 1:40, KJV, italics added). Then there was blind Bartimaeus, who requested, "Lord, that *I* might receive *my* sight" (Mark 10:51, KJV, italics added). Both men were motivated by the desire for a better life in the here and now. The rich young man also evidenced a personal motive by asking, "What shall *I* do to inherit eternal life?" (Luke 18:18, KJV, italics added). Notice that Bartimaeus and the leper were concerned about the present while the rich young man was concerned about the future. But even more interesting and important is the reaction of the Savior. He did not declare the motives of any of these men to be unworthy. He recognized self-oriented motives as having a certain legitimacy.

A second set of motivational factors can be described as being God-oriented. There are some people who already comprehend something of the majesty or holiness of God. Paul was in this category. He saw the light, heard the voice, and was blinded. Only upon inquiring, "Who art Thou, Lord?" (Acts 9:5), did he come to recognize the lordship of Christ. Paul's conversion was instantaneous. It came as a result of his being God-oriented.

A third type of motivational factor can be termed society-oriented. This is evident when an individual does not seek something for himself but seeks the good of another person or his own social group. In the New Testament, society-oriented motivation was apparent when the people brought the sick and afflicted to the Lord and the apostles for healing. It was also apparent in Zacchaeus, who, at the time of his conversion, evidenced a new concern for the poor and for anyone whom he might have wronged (Luke 19:8–10).

There is a crucial question related to these motivations. It is this: Is the preacher justified in appealing to self-oriented and society-oriented motivations? Perhaps our Lord resolved the problem when He said, "Seek ye first the kingdom of God, and his righteousness; and all these things shall be added unto you" (Matt. 6:33, KJV). He was speaking to a nation that was actively seeking a better life. The words "these things" definitely referred to food and raiment (v. 25). But the Lord did not demean His hearers by telling them their motives were unworthy. Rather, He told them that by seeking for the kingdom and the justice of God they could have these things. In other words, Jesus appealed to the "nonspiritual" self- and society-oriented motivational factors. *But in doing so, our Lord did not pass over the conditions necessary to their fulfillment.*

Paul and the other apostles emulated the Lord in this respect. They did not cease to preach the kingdom because inherent in this subject was an appeal to self- and society-oriented motivations. They preached the kingdom (Acts 8:12; 28:31) and they explained the necessary conditions (Acts 8:22; 14:22).

Our discussion has brought us to another question. Can we today preach the kingdom in the same way that Christ and the apostles preached it? Can today's missionary-evangelist promise fulfillment of personal and social desires on the basis of changing allegiance from Satan to God? The answer to these questions seems obvious. A converted sinner is not exempt from social injustice. Suffering is the lot of the believer (II Tim. 1:8, 12; 2:11–13; 3:12). No one has the authority to promise the absence of suffering. Nevertheless, the kingdom is to be proclaimed. It is part of the "all things" of the Great Commission. All believers will participate in it when the Lord establishes His reign on earth. Believers will reign with Christ (II Tim. 2:12).

Moreover, salvation is not for the future alone. The personal blessings of peace with God, true freedom in Christ, absence of guilt, and victory over vices can be promised to those in any age who make Christ Lord.

We conclude that the benefits which accrue to the believer from conversion to the Lord Christ should be preached. Men's desires for these benefits do constitute a legitimate basis for appealing to them to convert.

Relevant Research

Obviously, conversion is closely related to motivation—a subject that has proved difficult for researchers and theorists. Out of the vast literature on the subject, several items are of special importance in the present context:

(1) Real needs and felt needs should be distinguished. Felt needs are not always real or basic, though they may be. Real needs arise out of what man is by virtue of creation. Created a biological organism, man needs food, rest, sleep, exercise, and so forth. Created a sentient being, man, whenever he makes choices, requires reasons which are grounded in his intelligence or feeling of well-being. Created a social being, man needs fellowship with, and the approval of, other men. Created a spiritual being, man needs fellowship with God. Understanding this, missionary-evangelists, in the very nature of their calling, must give attention to the real needs of the whole man, and especially to essential spiritual needs.

Those needs which are merely felt may well serve as points of contact, but they should not be confused with real needs, nor should they be allowed to divert the missionary from ministering to real needs or delivering the whole counsel of God.

(2) A study carried out by the Lutheran World Federa-

tion in Japan in 1973–74 is germane to our discussion.[5] Of 1,428 believers baptized during the two years in four Lutheran denominations, 438 replied to a questionnaire. Several questions were asked relating to motives for conversion to Christ. The answers to these questions (and perhaps the questions themselves) need careful analysis. But, taken at face value, they are instructive.

Question: What were you seeking at the beginning of your search?
Answers: The meaning of life 40%
The way to live rightly 40%
True love 37%
Meaning of death 20%
Release from loneliness 15%
Understanding of fate 15%

Question: At the beginning of your quest what in the church interested you?
Answers: Warm fellowship 48%
Love 44%
Forgiveness of sin 43%
Peace for the soul 39%
Meaning and purpose of life 31%
Encounter with people 30%

Question: What kind of burdens did you feel?
Answers: Powerlessness 32%
Reproach of sin 20%
Breaking of trustful relations ...17%
Dark past life 11%
Sickness 11%
Disharmony in the home 10%

Granted that both the questions and answers (especially an answer such as powerlessness) must be interpreted in context, it seems evident that the majority of these con-

---

[5]"How Japanese Become Christians: Second Report of the Baptism Motivation Survey of 1973–1974" (Tokyo: Lutheran World Federation, Office of Communication, n.d.).

verts evidenced motives that can be broadly categorized as group-oriented (e.g., seeking warm fellowship and love in the church), though some of them fall quite clearly within either the God-oriented or self-oriented categories (e.g., seeking the meaning of life, the way to live rightly, forgiveness of sin, peace for the soul).

(3) Research conducted in India by Waskom Pickett indicates that "purity of motive" may not be as great a factor in multiplying the church as we would like to think.[6] A careful, scientific study of Indian converts of a previous generation revealed that their primary motives for becoming Christians could be categorized as follows:

(a) Spiritual motives (34.8%)
(b) Secular motives; e.g., a better job, a better life (8.1%)
(c) Social reasons; e.g., others were becoming Christians (22.4%)
(d) Natal influences (34.7%)

The study concluded that there was a much higher degree of "follow-through" or "spiritual attainment" among those who became believers for other than strictly "spiritual reasons" than we would ordinarily anticipate. Seventy percent of those who became Christians for other than spiritual motives, and seventy-five percent of those who became Christians because others of their family or caste did so, went on to attend church regularly.[7] What we might ordinarily term "purity of motive" in conversion, then, is not necessarily decisive in determining whether or not converts will go on to become fruitful believers.

(4) A careful examination of the effects of upbringing in societies where non-Judeo-Christian faiths form the basic orientation has led Robert Oliver to the conclusion that a direct appeal to self-interest is not appropriate in

---

[6]J. Waskom Pickett, *Christian Mass Movements in India* (New York: Abingdon Press, 1933), p. 165.
[7]Ibid., p. 168.

many societies.[8] In areas where the Buddhist concept of non-ego or no-self predominates (and, by implication, all areas where the emphasis is upon subordination to group interests), it would be better not to appeal directly to self-interest. Oliver acknowledges, however, that people everywhere do evidence some measure of self-interest and that this can be appealed to indirectly.

The validity of Oliver's conclusions is borne out by a study of incentives offered to the salesmen of a Tokyo branch of an American company.[9] Incentives offered to individual salesmen did not lead to sales increases. But when "rewards" were divided equally among all salesmen irrespective of individual performance, sales increased significantly. The explanation? Salesmen valued the goodwill of their fellows (equals) more than higher pay for themselves as individuals.

Translated into Christian terms, this research would lead one to believe that the appeal to the prospective convert to "be true to himself" (i.e., his own convictions) should be balanced (preceded?) by an appeal to help his family, friends, tribe, or nation by embracing the only One who can meet their deepest needs.

Practical Reflection

(1) Two facts must be borne in mind when urging conversion to Christ. First, all motives that are not strictly spiritual are not thereby unworthy. There is nothing wrong with the desire to become a Christian in order to have warm fellowship with the people of God, for example. Second, though Sir Galahad professed, "My strength

---

[8]Robert Oliver, *Culture and Communication* (Springfield, IL: Charles C. Thomas, 1962), pp. 148–49.

[9]W. S. Howell, "A Survey of Problems in Face-to-Face Communication Encountered by American Corporations Overseas" (a paper delivered at the Central States Speech Association Conference in Chicago, Illinois, on April 15, 1966).

is as the strength of ten because my heart is pure," it is doubtful that in real life anyone can make such a claim. We must not limit the ministry of the Holy Spirit. The fact that great Christians still wrestle with ulterior motives should be enough to indicate that God accepts something less than "pure converts" and takes considerable time (a lifetime plan?) and trouble to make them into "pure saints." This does not mean that our Lord lowers the standard. He *did not* keep the believer's cross a secret in order to gain disciples. He *did* say that those who are "pure in heart" will see God (Matt. 5:8). Ultimately, we can bear our crosses only because He walks with us, and we can be pure in heart only because in His grace He makes us so.

(2) As an outgrowth of Western individualism, missionary-evangelists are liable to overlook the high value which many cultures place upon group identity. The new emphasis being given to family life, communal living, and group dynamics in our society is a reaction against individualism which has been carried too far. One can only imagine the loyalties that were involved in the conversion of the household of Cornelius, the jailer's family in Philippi, and other groups in the New Testament. These examples are not to be confused with the large numbers responding to the invitation at a Billy Graham crusade. The latter are still individualistic, almost to the core. We need to consider approaches to conversion that encourage homogeneous units to become "one in Christ" and individual members of unbelieving units to be true to Christ, not only with a view to their own salvation, but also with a view to the salvation of their fellows. Notice again what a high percentage in the Pickett study were motivated to receive Christ by social and natal influences, and went on to become productive Christians.

(3) Finally let us remember that the missionary-evangelist is always called upon to be faithful. It is not promised that he will always be successful. Jesus wept over Jerusalem. Great hosts were not converted on Mars' Hill.

But Jerusalem had heard words from the lips of the Son of God. And those Athenian inquirers had listened to the greatest apostle of them all.

The Decision to Convert

Biblical Principles and Precedents

(1) The biblical record is clear that both privilege and responsibility are involved in hearing God's Word. It is not the "hearer" but the "doer" that is justified (James 1:22). The gospel is not only a message to be proclaimed, it is also an invitation to be received (John 1:12) and a commandment to be obeyed (II Thess. 1:8). A. R. Tippett calls this "verdict theology."[10] By whatever name, it is biblical.

(2) Conversion in the New Testament sometimes involved only one individual, but often it involved groups of people. There are cases in the New Testament where individuals came to accept Christ without apparent relationship to anyone other than the evangelist. The Ethiopian eunuch is a case in point (Acts 8:30). Sometimes individuals were called upon to decide for Christ in the face of opposition from friends and even family. When sending out His disciples, Christ warned that faith would sometimes bring a sword between members of the same family (Matt. 10:34–36).

It is also true that whole households were converted in Bible times (Acts 10:24, 47; 16:30–33). And on at least one occasion, so many came to Christ simultaneously that the historian could write, "All who lived at Lydda and Sharon saw him, and they turned to the Lord" (Acts 9:35).

(3) The call to repentance and faith was addressed to

---

[10]Cf. A. R. Tippett, *Verdict Theology in Missionary Theory* (Lincoln, IL: Lincoln Christian College Press, 1969).

those capable of making the decision. Fully responsible people especially were called upon to convert to Christ. Care must be taken not to place too much weight on an argument from silence. Children were undoubtedly present on many occasions when the gospel was preached and its claims were presented. That children followed Christ is clear from narratives such as that of the loaves and fishes (John 6:9–13). And Christ made it clear that children have a special place in His kingdom (Mark 10:14). But the record is clear and specific as to the identity of those who were primarily invited and commanded to repent and believe the gospel: it is basically adults (including young adults) who are in view.

Relevant Research

(1) Societies differ in their attitude toward decision-making. Some societies are decision-oriented (e.g., the United States). Any decision is considered to be better than no decision. Other cultures avoid decisions as often and as long as possible (e.g., traditional China). When decisions do become necessary, one does not "burn the bridges behind himself," but leaves the door to reconsideration as wide open as possible. The Chinese (and people of similar orientation) are acting according to the values of their own culture when they do not follow through on a decision that is no longer to their liking. In their view, when it becomes difficult to live with a decision made previously, the intelligent man does not abide by it! This approach to decision-making does not lessen the responsibility of the Chinese to follow Christ. Missionary-evangelists who are called of God to work with the Chinese should be mindful of this approach to decision-making.

(2) There are varying possibilities with respect to any given decision. We usually think of a decision vis-à-vis any proposed change in attitude and/or action as involving

FIGURE 33

Alternatives in Religious Decisions

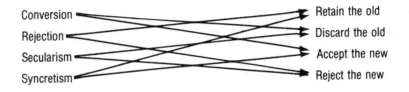

very limited possibilities: acceptance or rejection. This, of course, is an oversimplification. One can:

(a) Retain the old.
(b) Discard the old.
(c) Accept the new.
(d) Reject the new.

When we relate conversion to these four possibilities, it is evident that conversion really means "discard the old" (unbelief, sin, idolatry) *and* "accept the new" (faith in and obedience to Christ). Both elements are vital. There are other scenarios, however. It is possible to retain the old and reject the new. This is rejection. It is possible to discard the old faith without accepting the new. The result is secularism. It is also possible to accept the new without discarding the old. The result is syncretism. (See Figure 33.)

(3) Decision occurs at a point and as a process. Numerous scholars have pointed out that the process of decision-making needs careful study. We should be aware of the various steps in the process (though, of course, they can be elaborated differently).[11]

---

[11]David J. Hesselgrave, *Communicating Christ Cross-Culturally* (Grand Rapids: Zondervan, 1978), p. 447.

(a) Discovery. "Possibility X exists for me."
(b) Deliberation. "Should I choose possibility X?"
(c) Determination. "Yes, I will accept X."
(d) Dissonance. "If I had not chosen X, I would not be having this trouble."
(e) Discipline. "The implications of choosing X must be accepted."

These steps in the decision-making process are self-explanatory, with one exception—dissonance.[12]

Dissonance refers to the state of unsettledness that often occurs after one has determined that he will take a certain course of action—be it to purchase an automobile, to select a school, or to change one's religious faith. Dissonance arises when one experiences problems connected with the chosen course of action (e.g., low gas mileage in the case of the automobile; the "inordinate" educational requirements of the school; unexpected opposition to conversion).

What one does when he experiences dissonance depends on the kind of person he is. It also depends upon the kind of situation in which he finds himself. Once a down payment has been made on a new car, the buyer will probably not be able to return it no matter how low his gas mileage is! But one does not lose his freedom when making a decision for Christ. He can revert. (See Figure 34.)

A much more elaborate outline of the decision-making process as it relates to the Christian mission at home and abroad has been attempted by James Engel and H. Wilbert Norton in their book *What's Gone Wrong with the Harvest?*[13] The authors' basic contention is that Christian communicators have erred greatly in failing to ascertain where

---

[12]Cf. Leon Festinger, *A Theory of Cognitive Dissonance* (Evanston, IL: Row, Peterson Publishing Co., 1957), pp. 446–52.

[13]James F. Engel and H. Wilbert Norton, *What's Gone Wrong with the Harvest? A Communication Strategy for the Church and World Evangelism* (Grand Rapids: Zondervan, 1975).

FIGURE 34

Decision as Point and Process*

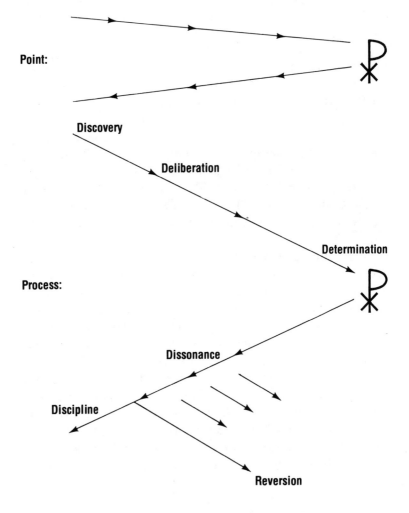

*Taken from David J. Hesselgrave, *Communicating Christ Cross-culturally* (Grand Rapids: Zondervan, 1978), p. 448.

their respective audiences are located in terms of their understanding of, and response to, the Christian message.

(4) Who can make what kind of decisions? Societies vary considerably as to who can legitimately make certain kinds of decisions and the circumstances under which they can be made. In many societies (e.g., Japan) decisions by children and even young adults will not be taken very seriously. Only at the time of economic independence and the establishment of a separate household are one's decisions accorded proper respect. As a result, Westerners should keep two matters in mind when they try to convert people in such societies: (a) Those who press for a decision by young people without conferring with their elders may be thought of as disrupters of family life and flouters of proper authority. (b) The real test of a younger person's resolve may not come at the time of decision, but rather when he enters an occupation or is ready for marriage.

(5) Group decision is sometimes possible. Generally speaking, cultures with lineage kinship patterns, rural (village and especially tribal) orientations, and "closed class" (caste) stratification will tend to stress group unity and the need for group decision. Cultures with the kindred kinship system and a significant degree of heterogeneity and openness will tend to stress individual decisions and the need for maintaining the integrity of individual convictions. Group decision, of course, obviates the problem of social dislocation. It has been demonstrated that even in the West, group decision is more lasting. Once a group arrives at a decision to act, the members are likely to carry it through.

In the context of Christian mission, group conversions may be called "*people movements*" or "*multi-individual conversion.*"[14] Group decisions do not necessarily mean that individuals have been overlooked. They usually mean that in-

---

[14]Donald McGavran, *Understanding Church Growth* (Grand Rapids: Eerdmans, 1970), pp. 296–305.

dividuals make choices in consultation and concert with others rather than independently of them.

Practical Reflection

A review of the above data on conversion and decision-making reveals a number of areas where some adjustment to biblical, social, and psychological realities could bring twentieth-century evangelical understanding and practice much closer to the New Testament ideal. There is perhaps no single area in which we are more circumscribed by traditional thinking and practice. Our practice has not always been faithful to New Testament teaching, nor has it kept pace with contemporary understanding. This is apparent enough within the North American context, but it becomes even more pronounced when we cross cultural boundaries. Missionary-evangelistic practice in cultures very different from our own reveals an insensitivity to basic cultural differences that is often appalling. As a consequence we often needlessly arouse antagonism by approaches which ignore decision-makers and confront their "charges." We sometimes make syncretists and secularists instead of Christians. We often resort to approaches which result in reversions and then think of those who revert as being fickle. We go to target areas with great potential for group conversion and still resort to methods conceived for individualistic cultures. It is to be hoped that we have now entered a time of transition during which missionaries and evangelists will become increasingly aware of the above factors.

It should be remembered that in conversion we are dealing with *men, not machines,* and with *souls, not statistics.* The major considerations in planning for actual decisions for Christ among any target people are related to what they experience as *individual persons* and as *persons in society.* Calls for decision should not only be Christ-centered, but also culturally-related and person-oriented.

Culturally-Related Decisions

Decision is to be called for in any society because the gospel demands response. But as we have seen, cultures differ so widely that cultural awareness is needful if missionary-evangelists are to evoke proper response.

(1) Plan for regular, frequent, and culturally appropriate opportunities for unbelievers to receive Christ. The time and place of such occasions will vary significantly. The important thing is that there be a general understanding that invitations to receive Christ may be given any time and will be given regularly.

ME-3 illustration: Pastor Rene Zapata of El Salvador has for years scheduled an evangelistic service in his church every Sunday night. All believers are informed that if they will invite their unsaved friends, they can be sure that the gospel will be preached and an invitation given. Souls regularly come to Christ. In areas of the world where Sunday evening meetings are impossible or attended only by believers, alternative times will have to be found.

(2) A great effort should be made to approach those leaders who are regarded by their respective cultures as being capable of making decisions as important as religious conversion. Even when they do not accept Christ, the understanding and goodwill that may be gained by recognizing their authority may make it easier for other members of the group who do become Christians. Christian workers whose evangelistic efforts are directed primarily to children, students, and women (those who, depending on the culture, may be regarded as lacking authority to make such a decision) would do well to give special attention to this advice.

ME-3 illustration: After years of evangelism in Kenya, a master plan for reaching new villages was prepared. The small planning group represented many years of missionary experience in Africa. They unanimously concluded that their previous strategy of going first and directly to those who were immediately accessible had been a mistake. They determined that in new areas, an initial presentation would be made to the village elders in order to secure their understanding and goodwill, or even their conversion and cooperation. Subsequent experience proved the validity of this approach.

(3) Group decisions should be encouraged. For altogether too long, Western individualism has determined our conversion patterns. Even in North America attention is now being given to approaching couples and whole (nuclear) families with the gospel. The possibility of encouraging group decisions should not be overlooked.

ME-3 illustrations: Some of the most outstanding examples of group conversion in recent times have occurred in West Irian, where whole tribes have burned their fetishes and come to Christ. An illustration with a wider applicability, however, may be the Sevav plan explained in some detail in the previous chapter. In Sevav there was a deliberate attempt to reach entire extended families as units, and to encourage group decisions for Christ. The relatively large number of those who decided for Christ and followed through, witnesses to the viability of the approach.

The Process-Sensitive Call for Decision

By using the phrase "process-sensitive call," we direct attention to the fact that in dealing with those for whom Christ died, we are dealing with people who have numerous questions, frustrations, and trials. Plan, therefore, to counsel some respondents concerning the issues of repentance and faith *over a period of time.* Do not minimize the importance of the decision point. But come to grips with the spiritual and psychological realities of the situation.

"Process decision," in the sense in which we use the phrase, has special reference to group decisions. However, it is also important to think in these terms when we are dealing with individuals who run the risk of ostracism as a result of conversion to Christ. To help these people counter dissonance is vital. Satan is not a good loser!

ME-3 illustration: Conservative Baptist missionaries in Kalimantan were interacting with a group of natives who were considering conversion to Christ. Many questions were asked and answered—seemingly to the satisfaction of all. Finally one elderly man found the courage and words to express a problem that was probably on the minds of all. He said, "We want to believe and follow your God, but tell us, can He make a rice field?"

How easy to give glib answers in such a situation. After all, our God made fields, rice, sun, and rain! And those offerings and prayers which attend farming in that part of the world add up to superstition and idolatry!

But these were responsible people with growing children to care for. They were sincere. And, given their view of the world up to that time, the question was entirely legitimate. Blessed are such a people when those who minister God's Word understand their view, and when they have ministers who refuse to leave them in idolatry or lead them into secularism, but rather lead them to Christ. Of course, God *can* make a rice field!

Baptism and Confession of Faith

Biblical Principles and Precedents

In New Testament times, when someone accepted Christ, he was expected to confess Christ. This was done in three ways: (1) in verbal confession of Christ as Lord; (2) in symbolic confession by water baptism; and (3) by good works and a changed life. None of these in and by itself was sufficient for salvation. All were the accompaniments of saving faith.

(1) *Verbal confession* can be seen in the letter to the Romans:

> That if you confess with your mouth Jesus as Lord, and believe in your heart that God raised Him from the dead, you shall be saved; for with the heart man believes, resulting in righteousness, and with the mouth he confesses, resulting in salvation. For the Scripture says, "Whoever believes in Him will not be disappointed." . . . for "Whoever will call upon the name of the Lord will be saved." (Rom. 10:9-11, 13)

The content of the confession is the lordship of Christ. But what is confession? Literally, it is a "saying of the same thing"—that is, saying the same thing about the Son as the Father says about Him. But in the context of Romans 10 "confession" is explained in a somewhat different way. There is a parallelism of sentence structure which can be seen by grouping similar statements:

(a) "believe in your heart that God raised Him"
(b) "with the heart man believes, resulting in righteousness"
(c) "whoever believes in Him will not be disappointed"

and

(a) "confess with your mouth Jesus as Lord"
(b) "with the mouth he confesses, resulting in salvation"
(c) "whoever will call upon the name of the Lord will be saved"

In this way it becomes clear that "confession" is equivalent to "calling upon the name of the Lord." Thus, confession of Jesus as Lord is an act of the believer which is based on faith in Christ as Lord and in which he calls upon His name.

(2) This verbal confession was followed by a *symbolic confession* before men. Baptism was enjoined upon the believer. It was emphasized in the Great Commission and practiced by the apostolic church. There is a danger in

regard to the doctrine of baptism, however. It is the danger of failing to distinguish between the baptism which saves (I Peter 3:21) and the water baptism which is only symbolic. We are not implying that there are two baptisms in Scripture, for that would be contrary to Ephesians 4:5. Rather, we are saying that water baptism is the visible representation of Spirit baptism. Just as Spirit baptism places all believers into the body of Christ at the moment that saving faith is placed in Him (I Cor. 12:13), so water baptism is performed upon confession of Christ as Lord, and the believer is then added to the church (Acts 2:41; 8:12–16).

(3) A third type of confession is apparent in the New Testament in that the believer was required to perform "deeds appropriate to repentance" (Acts 26:20). This type of confession is underscored in Titus 2, where the believer's conduct is that which adorns the doctrine of God (v. 10). Good works were to be done because "the grace of God has appeared" (v. 11). The works of the believer were a testimony to the grace of God. So essential were good works that James could affirm that their absence was a sign of dead faith (James 2:17) and their presence was an evidence of saving faith (James 2:18).

In summary, three types of confession were enjoined by the preachers in the apostolic church: The believer was to confess Jesus as Lord by word of mouth; he was to be baptized in water as evidence of Spirit baptism; and he was to produce works which demonstrated that his faith was a saving faith.

Relevant Research

(1) It would be well simply to note that researchers speak with a united voice on the intimate relationships that exist between knowledge and words on the one hand, and between communication and behavior on the other. It is difficult—perhaps impossible—to think without words. To

articulate one's beliefs is not only to convey them to others. It also has the effect of clarifying them and reinforcing them for oneself. As for nonverbal behavior, which is now widely referred to as "the silent language," people are constantly *communicating* their ideas, attitudes, feelings, and values without *saying* so much as a word.

(2) Research also indicates that it would be unusual if some kind of rite did not accompany so important an event as Christian conversion and the identification of the new believer with a new family and another way of life. Analogies to Christian baptism are to be found in most religions and pseudoreligious organizations—from Jewish circumcision, bar mitzvah, and priestly ordinances (cf. Num. 19:7), to Babylonian and Greek (especially Eleusinian) rituals, to the rites of modern Freemasonry. In fact, initiation rites which signify acceptance into the obligations and privileges of adulthood are common in many areas of the world. Christ did not overlook the significance of that kind of symbolic act in establishing His Church.

Practical Reflection

By and large, the Church has done well in emphasizing the importance of giving a verbal witness to one's faith and of living the kind of life which is consistent with that confession. (It should be noted, however, that in some societies and circumstances even verbal witness to unbelievers may not be advisable immediately upon conversion.[15]) Experience seems to indicate that the weaknesses of contemporary mission-evangelism are in the areas of "acts of repentance" and baptism.

(1) "Acts of repentance" are probably deemphasized today because we have misconstrued divine grace. Grace does not rule out the need for repentance, however. And

---

[15]Bruce Olson, *For This Cross I'll Kill You* (Carol Stream, IL: Creation House, 1973), p. 167.

restitution, reformation, and repentance go well together.

Another aspect of this problem comes to the fore in cross-cultural situations where acts of repentance may take unfamiliar forms. This is so because sin and unbelief have their own peculiar cultural expressions. For example, many pagan societies have household gods. In America, the house itself may become one's god. It is hardly appropriate to burn one's house. But what about household idols? What does repentance involve in these cases? Is it necessary that the household idols be publicly burned? Perhaps not. But neither should they be quietly stored in the closet!

ME-3 illustrations: At the time of their conversion, the Dani tribesmen of West Irian gathered their fetishes, amulets, and other accouterments of superstition and witchcraft, placed them in a large pile, and put the torch to them. Undoubtedly this clear break with the past was encouraged by the fact that the decision to convert was a group decision with tribal leaders showing the way. In the contexts of China, Korea, and Japan, where conversions tend to be individual and missions have a longer history, burnings of idols and talismans are not common. Perhaps they need not be. But neither can the issue raised by the prevalence of idols be overlooked.

(2) Verbal confessions should be encouraged. Since our Lord requires that we confess Him as Lord, we need to encourage spontaneous confessions of faith on the part of converts. We should also program some confessions lest this be overlooked in the busyness of our labors.

ME-1 illustration: Warren Bathke, until recently pastor of a church in Dix Hills, New York, made it a practice to give an invitation at the close of each Sunday morning service. His object was not only to invite unbelievers to the Savior, but also to give opportunity for those who had been converted in their homes as a result of the weekly visitation program to come forward and publicly witness to their new faith. Rarely did a Sunday go by without a response.

ME-1-3 illustration: In certain cultures church-planters have initiated a practice that seems very helpful. Before new converts are baptized, they are asked to carefully write out their testimony and confession of faith. This written testimony becomes a part of the church records, and a copy is given to the believer. Periodically through the years and whenever needful, these testimonies are reviewed by the believers. What a beautiful way to bring the grace of God in the life of individuals and of the church to remembrance!

(3) There are two basic reasons why baptism often becomes a problem instead of a blessing. First, much evangelism is carried on by parachurch groups and outside of the churches. As a result baptism becomes a moot subject or, at best, a subject which is conveniently filed for future consideration.

Second, many evangelical Christians have overreacted against the widespread notion that baptism is a means of grace. To this notion they rightly object. But as far as their practice is concerned, they seem to react by denying that baptism means anything. In this they are manifestly wrong. Baptism is biblical. It is meaningful. Its relationship to mission-evangelism needs another look; for, after many of the other perplexing problems of missionizing are solved, this one often remains. Why? Because in the New Testament the rite is initiatory, but, in practice, to baptize too soon seems to result only in an increase in the number of baptized pagans. Difficult though it may be, cooperating missionary-evangelists and pastors alike will need to decide on a procedure that seems to answer to biblical and local requirements.

ME-3 illustration: Shortly after World War II some Southern Baptist church-planting missionaries in Japan became distressed with the number of converts who reverted. In order to determine if there was any relationship between the time of baptism and the frequency of reversion, they carried out a limited test. In some evangelistic campaigns converts were baptized very soon after profession of faith. In other campaigns, converts were asked to take a prescribed course of Bible study before baptism. The missionaries concluded that the time of baptism was not a crucial factor in the incidence of reversion. Such factors as the quality of instruction received by the convert and his acceptance by older Christians seemed to be more important.

ME-3 illustration: Conservative Baptists in parts of Asia have taken a long look at the question of baptism. Several years ago they decided that baptism would not be administered to younger converts until they have reached legal age.

Master Plan Formation

Instruction Concerning Conversion

It is to be expected that non-Christians will not understand what is involved in true Christian conversion. The very concept of religious conversion is absolutely foreign to some cultural contexts. As a matter of fact, when we call for conversion, *any* given group of respondents will entertain some misconceptions which should be faithfully dealt with from the Word of God, whether in our preaching and teaching or in our witnessing and counseling.

A relatively easy way to deal with the situation is to note the likely misconceptions of the respondents (which can be surmised from study and interaction with locals) and then to counteract those misconceptions with preconversion biblical teaching. When we do this much, we can depend upon the Holy Spirit to do the rest (see Figure 35).

Analyzing Possible Motives for Conversion

The problem of motivation is best answered by putting things in proper perspective. The results of sin will be evident in every culture: poverty, slavery, hunger, strained

FIGURE 35

Audience Attitudes Concerning Conversion

Misconception (check or rank)	Required Biblical Emphasis
_____ **Opposition:** "Conversion is unnecessary."	"Repent and be converted."
_____ **Syncretism:** "We have been _____ (Hindus, Buddhists, etc.), but we want to be Christians too."	"You shall have no other gods before me."
_____ **Reversible Decision:** "We can always change our minds again if things don't work out."	"If any man, having put his hand to the plow, turns back. . . ."
_____ **Cheap Grace:** "Pray a prayer. That's all there is to it."	"Count the cost."
_____ **Private Matter:** "Religion is not something one talks about."	"With the heart man believes, . . . but with the mouth confession is made."
_____ **Other:** _____	

relationships, broken homes, greed, drunkenness, violence, ill health, ignorance, and many more. Depending upon a number of factors, conversion to Christ may or may not result in the resolution of these problems. *The first responsibility of the messenger of Christ is to speak to those spiritual needs which, on the authority of God's Word, he knows to be absolutely basic. His second responsibility is to take stock of the other needs of his respondents and to deal with them in biblical*

FIGURE 36

Analysis of Potential Motives for Conversion

Motives (check or rank)	Overall	Subgroup 1	Subgroup 2	Subgroup 3

1. Self-oriented Motivations
  a. To be able to cope with personal problems
  b. To obtain peace with others
  c. To gain prestige or power
  d. To escape obligations of another religion
  e. To procure employment or material gain
  f. To obtain health or medical benefits
  g. To gain happiness
  h. Other _____				

2. God-oriented Motivations
  a. The awareness of God's love
  b. A sense of sin and the need for forgiveness
  c. The desire to be at peace with God
  d. The desire for personal holiness
  e. A need for freedom from evil and satanic powers
  f. The desire to know God
  g. A conviction that the Christian message is true
  h. Other _____				

3. Society-oriented Motivations
  a. Natal influence (Christian parentage)
  b. The desire for acceptance by the Christian group or church
  c. Desire to marry a Christian
  d. Compliance with the decision of a converting group
  e. A reaction against the religion (or irreligion) of oppressing person or group
  f. Desire to gain entrance to a socially superior class or group
  g. Other _____				

ways, whether by word or deed. It would be unworthy of the servant of Christ to ignore the feelings and desires of his hearers. It would be illegitimate for him to appeal to those feelings and desires without regard to *God's response* to them! (See Figure 36.)

With the data from Figure 36 in mind, answer the following questions:

(1) Which of these needs constitute legitimate motives for conversion? Legitimate but insufficient? Clearly illegitimate? (Check off on the list.)

(2) Do the legitimate *felt* needs tend to obscure the *real* but unfelt needs? (For example, does the desire for acceptance in a Christian group cloud the need for forgiveness of sin?)

(3) Do illegitimate motives for conversion (e.g., expectation of instant happiness or wealth) indicate that the gospel has been miscommunicated?

(4) Will the convert tend to revert if the felt needs are not satisfied after conversion?

(5) What adjustments might be made in our evangelism and counseling?

Encouraging Meaningful Decisions

Once we understand what the Bible teaches concerning the decision to convert to Christ, it remains for us to determine *local* understandings and practices relative to decision-making. This can be done in several simple analytic steps.

Step One. Determine where the target group fits in on the continuum of the decision process (see Figure 37).

Step Two. Determine whether different target subgroups should be placed at different points on the continuum. In generations past, for example, adult Americans were at (a); they now are closer to (b). Not a few adolescents are at (c) or even (d).

Step Three. Determine which respondents will be consid-

FIGURE 37
The Continuum of the Decision Process

Once the group understands the gospel and individuals want to convert, respondents will . . .

Decide by themselves, without reference to peers or community.	Decide by themselves, but with careful consideration of the decisions of peers and community.	Deliberate and decide together, with reference to peers or community, but with no sanctions against those who do not concur.	Deliberate and decide together, and apply sanctions against those who do not join in the group's consensus.
a	b	c	d

ered capable of making decisions of the magnitude of religious conversion and which ones will participate only through their clan head, husband, parents, or some other authority figure. (In America, for example, a woman is considered competent to choose a religion independently of her husband, but a very young child may not have the same freedom.)

Step Four. Using the type of data which we have just discussed, answer the following questions:

(1) Shall we place a higher priority on individual or group decisions?

(2) Shall we give priority to certain segments (e.g., older people) in the society in calling for decisions for Christ?

(3) How much time will ordinarily be required in order to secure meaningful decisions?

(4) Is it advisable for the evangelist to *create* a peer group (e.g., a study class) whose members can deliberate a decision together?

If the evangelist follows the steps outlined above, decisions for Christ will tend to be more meaningful and genuine.

FIGURE 38

Cultural Factors Relating to the Timing of Baptism

Factors (check those which apply)	Implications		
	Early Baptism	Short Delay	Extended Probation
1. Delay would encourage group decision. _____			
2. Delay would discourage the convert. _____			
3. Converts are generally knowledgeable about the Christian faith and its requirements. _____			
4. There are previous practices in the locality important to timing. _____			
5. Other _____			

Determining Appropriate Forms of Confession and the Time of Baptism

(1) What does baptism signify to most members of the community? (A means of grace? Renunciation of one's heritage?)

(2) In what ways might the convert confess Christ and renounce his former religion without renouncing his culture and his people?

(3) Should the confession of faith be oral, written, or both?

(4) Should confession and baptism occur in a private or public place?

(5) What are the cultural parallels to baptism (e.g., graduations, initiations, rites of passage)?

(6) What do we learn from the cultural parallels? (For example, should baptism serve as a functional substitute for an initiation ceremony that is widely practiced but unchristian?)

(7) Closely related to these questions is the perennial problem of *when* to baptize converts. Unless the matter is dictated by the mission or denomination, or unless the church-planter feels strongly that biblical precedents dictate early baptism, cultural factors may be important in deciding the question. If so, the kind of reflection suggested in Figure 38 may be helpful.

While conversion is thought to be extremely important, the steps leading to and from conversion receive very little thoughtful planning by most missionary-evangelists. This is a most unhappy state of affairs. In faithfulness to God and in all fairness to potential and actual converts, they should be handled delicately and biblically. If the foregoing considerations aid us in doing this, they will have fulfilled their purpose.

twelve

The Believers Congregated

Once people have been converted, it is imperative that they feel themselves to be a part of the divine family, that they faithfully gather with other members of the family, and that they regularly participate in the activities of the family. Only in this way will they become strong, mature, fruitful members of the family of Christ. The present chapter is concerned with making this happen.

Objectives

(1) To establish times and places for the assembling of believers which will be in line with Christian practice and local customs and circumstances.

(2) To make meetings of believers (scheduled and unscheduled) as spiritually meaningful and helpful as possible.

(3) To introduce new believers into the fellowship and discipline of a local family of believers as soon as possible.

FIGURE 39
"THE PAULINE CYCLE"

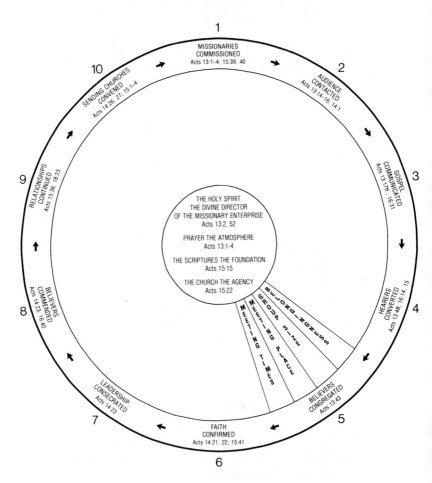

1
MISSIONARIES
COMMISSIONED
Acts 13:1-4; 15:39, 40

10
SENDING CHURCHES
CONVENED
Acts 14:26, 27; 15:1-4

2
AUDIENCE
CONTACTED
Acts 13:14-16; 14:1

9
RELATIONSHIPS
CONTINUED
Acts 15:36; 18:23

3
GOSPEL
COMMUNICATED
Acts 13:17ff.; 16:31

THE HOLY SPIRIT
THE DIVINE DIRECTOR
OF THE MISSIONARY ENTERPRISE
Acts 13:2, 52

PRAYER THE ATMOSPHERE
Acts 13:1-4

THE SCRIPTURES THE FOUNDATION
Acts 15:15

THE CHURCH THE AGENCY
Acts 15:22

8
BELIEVERS
COMMENDED
Acts 14:23; 16:40

4
HEARERS
CONVERTED
Acts 13:48; 16:14, 15

MEMBERS ORGANIZED
GROUP SIZE
MEETING PLACE
MEETING TIMES

7
LEADERSHIP
CONSECRATED
Acts 14:23

5
BELIEVERS
CONGREGATED
Acts 13:43

6
FAITH
CONFIRMED
Acts 14:21, 22; 15:41

". . . many of the Jews and of the God-fearing proselytes followed Paul and Barnabas . . ." (Acts 13:43).
"Not forsaking our own assembling together . . ." (Heb. 10:25).

(4) To provide as many ways into the fellowship of the family as possible.

(5) To adjust the program of evangelism so as to encourage both converts from the world and converts from nominal Christian backgrounds to enter the new fellowship.

Believing and Unbelieving Communities

Biblical Principles and Precedents

In the Old Testament era, God was concerned for His people, so He determined that they should be together and that He would dwell among them. We have a picture of the New Testament Church in the Old Testament gathering of the people of God around the tabernacle. Furthermore, God and His people lived and moved together (Num. 9:17-23).

In the New Testament, Jesus said, "Where two or three are gathered in my name, there am I in the midst of them" (Matt. 18:20, RSV). With the advent of the Holy Spirit, believers were baptized into the new body in which Jew and Gentile were one and Christ was the Head (I Cor. 12:13). Believers constituted the household of God (Eph. 2:19); all of them were accepted irrespective of ethnic background or social position. Believers were part of a supportive community called the Church and were to "bear one another's burdens, and thus fulfill *the law of Christ*" (Gal. 6:2, italics added).

The believing community in New Testament times bore certain similarities to ordinary unbelieving organizations, of course. They met together regularly; they accomplished certain objectives together; they encountered certain difficulties within the group; they sought out new members. But at the same time they were different. Luke writes that on the day of Pentecost Peter urged his hearers to "save themselves from their corrupt generation." Accordingly, those who accepted the message and were baptized gave themselves to:

(1) *Study*—"devoting themselves to the apostles' teaching."
(2) *Fellowship*—meeting together in the temple and homes.
(3) *Worship*—breaking of bread, praying, and praising God.
(4) *Stewardship*—giving themselves and their substance to one another as there was need.
(5) *Witness*—"having favor" with people so that the Lord added to their numbers (cf. Acts 2:41–47).

As time went on and as Christian communities multiplied, pagan culture and the unbelieving community became arrayed against the early believers. What made them suspect was not that they were "bad" but that they were "different"! Follow the apostles, for example. Wherever they went there was trouble! Jerusalem, Cyprus, Iconium, Lystra, Ephesus, Philippi, Thessalonica, Berea, Corinth—in all of these places the story was similar. Heathen temples lost their attraction, idol-makers lost customers, diviners lost their livelihood.

The Christian families of the first century were composed of people of different social class and, most likely, color. The believing community at Colossae included both Philemon and his slave, Onesimus, as brothers in Christ (Philem. 16). Certainly there were other masters and many slaves. Simeon Niger of Antioch was probably a Black (Acts 13:1). The apostle Paul made it clear that in Christ "there is neither Jew nor Greek, there is neither slave nor free man, there is neither male nor female" (Gal. 3:28a). That does not mean that such distinctions were totally disregarded among early Christians. It does mean that chromosomes, color, and class did not bring those communities together. Nor were they allowed to keep the believers of those communities apart.

In time, Caesar himself expressed opposition to the believing community. Even as the opponents of Jesus had accused Him of sedition and treason, the enemies of the early believing communities charged that believers acted contrary to the decrees of Caesar by undermining the Caesar cult.

A hostile culture, differences of class and color, the antagonism of Caesar—none of these could ultimately divide the believing communities or destroy their fellowship. Why? There are two basic reasons. First, they were united in Christ. "For you are all one in Christ," the apostle wrote (Gal. 3:28b). Theirs was a common creed. It was expressed in various ways and in greater or lesser detail. But its essence was, "Jesus Christ is Lord." So John could write very simply,

> Any one who goes too far and does not abide in the teaching of Christ, does not have God; the one who abides in the teaching, he has both the Father and the Son. If any one comes to you and does not bring this teaching, do not receive him into your house, and do not give him a greeting. (II John 9, 10)

Second, the early believers were attracted to one another by a common concern. They had real problems in their relationships. Nevertheless, they voluntarily gathered together in order to worship, pray, fellowship at the table of the Lord, be instructed in the faith, give of their substance, help one another, and carry out their mission. And these concerns so motivated them—and Christ so captivated them—that in spite of the antagonism of their culture, the differences of class and color, and the opposition of Caesar, they gathered together to worship and went forth to witness. And God caused the churches to grow (I Cor. 3:7).

Relevant Research

The Preservation of Culture and Cultural Change

Raymond Firth distinguishes between social structure and social organization. He points out that persons relate to each other in order to *preserve* traditional ways and values (social structure) and also to *effect change* and accomplish ends that would not otherwise be achieved (social organization).[1] The Church (and, therefore, the local churches, including embryonic local churches) is ordained by God to preserve and transmit His truth. In this sense it is a divinely-ordained structure. Unfortunately it sometimes becomes entrenched and intertwined with its respective "Caesars" and cultures in such a way that people born into the nation are automatically "born" into the church as well. When that happens, the church becomes a culturally-determined structure!

Basically, however, churches begin as organizations. This means that people voluntarily align themselves with one another in order to change people (themselves included) and circumstances, and to achieve certain other purposes and goals. That being the case, a certain amount of antagonism or, at the very least, disdain, can usually be expected from the larger society. Research shows that cultural disapproval does not mean that a religious organization cannot grow, however. In fact, Dean Kelley has shown that religious organizations which are more or less like the larger culture of which they are a part tend not to grow. Groups such as the Assemblies of God, Mormons, Jehovah's Witnesses, Seventh-day Adventists, and Black Muslims, on the other hand, grow rapidly while being "out of step" with the larger society.[2]

Differences in the Degree of Cooperation and Integration

Firth's distinction is not the only one that is important to an understanding of believing groups. There are at least two other well-known categorizations that emphasize the

---

[1]Raymond Firth, *Elements of Social Organization* (Boston: Beacon Press, 1963), pp. 29–40.

[2]Dean Kelley, *Why Conservative Churches Are Growing: A Study in Sociology of Religion* (New York: Harper and Row, 1972), pp. 20–25.

degree to which group members interact and cooperate with each other.

First, there is the *gemeinschaft/gesellschaft* distinction of the German sociologist Ferdinand Tonnies.[3] In *gesellschaft* (association) members are bound together by a system of exchanging goods and services, but they do not live and work in intimate relationship with each other. In *gemeinschaft* (community) the members of the group are intimately related to each other much as is the case, for example, in nuclear or extended families.

Second, there is the distinction between integrated and nonintegrated groups. Integration here does not have to do with ethnic background but with the degree of commonality of concerns and goals. Nonintegrated groups such as concert audiences and crowds at the ball park exhibit little by way of commonality. Integrated groups such as the faculty of a school or shareholders in a company exhibit a much higher degree of commonality.

If churches are to measure up to the New Testament standard, leaders and believers should pray and plan for warm personal relationships and a high degree of integration from the first. Believers are ordained to glorify God and promote the cause of Christ. Above all other groups they should evidence a united community and a common cause.

Homogeneous Units in Society

In the Church Growth movement especially there is special focus on the so-called homogeneous unit.[4] This is a rather nebulous term; based upon sound social-science data, it refers to a body of people who form a cohesive unit because of a common denominator such as ancestry, lan-

---

[3]Cf. Ferdinand Tonnies, *Community and Society,* trans. and ed. Charles P. Loomis (East Lansing: Michigan State University Press, 1957).

[4]Donald McGavran, *Understanding Church Growth* (Grand Rapids: Eerdmans, 1970), pp. 85–87.

guage, or life-style. Nuclear and extended families, clans and castes, ethnic and linguistic groups qualify as homogeneous units. Such units or groupings of people like to decide, work, play, and worship together. This being the case, Donald McGavran believes that churches should be planted by focusing on individual tribes, castes, and language groups, even though such a policy seems to be in conflict with the biblical principle that Christians of all languages, classes, and colors are one in Christ.[5] Roger Greenway, agreeing with McGavran, says that this is so even in the great cities of the world:

> Cities are "melting pots," but this aspect of urban life must not be overestimated. Beneath the surface there are still many differences. Much of the loneliness and frustration which rural-urban immigrants experience stems from their inability to communicate freely in the official language and from the foreignness of much of the urban culture. Religious services in their own language or dialect will attract them, and sermons and hymns they can understand will get through to their hearts. As tribe and caste distinctions break down in the course of time, the shift can be made away from ethnic congregations to "all peoples" churches. But until that time comes, it is best to recognize and accept the cultural heterogeneity of the city and proceed to multiply as many tribe, caste, and language churches as possible until all parts of the urban community have been leavened by the gospel.[6]

Practical Reflection

It is apparent from the above that cultural understandings, preferences, and ties, on the one hand, and Christian ideals and requirements, on the other hand, may be very much in conflict at the stage of the Pauline Cycle at which believers congregate (as well as at the conversion

---

[5]Ibid., pp. 289–91.
[6]Roger S. Greenway, *Guidelines for Urban Church Planting* (Grand Rapids: Baker, 1976), pp. 16–17.

stage). Just as the unbeliever is tempted to follow the crowd or stick with the clan and not convert to Christ, so the new believer, after an initial break, is tempted to return to the crowd or clan rather than following through and fully identifying with the believing group. If he does follow through, he is apt to seek out Christian fellowship among believers of the same cultural background. In either case, Christ and culture seem to be in conflict. What shall we do in congregating believers? Shall we capitalize on the ties of natural homogeneous units in order to overcome reversion and encourage growth? Or are such ties to be disregarded in view of the much more important bond that believers have in Christ?

Solutions to this problem are not easy to come by. But certain considerations can aid in its resolution:

(1) There should be no question of ultimate authority. We must conform to Christ, not to culture. However, the fact that in the divine Christ there are no distinctions of class, color, or sex does not mean that such distinctions are obliterated in human culture. It simply means that they are transcended. They remain significant but they do not reign supreme. Every local family of believers need not evidence the full, variegated social and cultural richness that characterizes the larger family or body of Christ. Furthermore, no social or cultural distinctive should be significant enough to exclude a believer from any family of believers, nor to alienate local church families from each other or the larger body of Christ.

(2) If our strategy has been sound at the contact, communication, and conversion stages of the Pauline Cycle, the problem may not be as acute in practice as it seems to be in theory. People with ethnic, class, linguistic, and other similarities tend to live in the same area, respond to the same kind of communication, and make decisions together. This being the case, as local families of believers grow, they will tend to be socially homogeneous. Charles Chaney distinguishes between "you all" and "howdy" Southern Baptist churches in the North Central states.

This distinction implies, not only that most Southern Baptist churches are composed of a large percentage of Southerners, but that some are largely made up of those originally from the Southeastern portion of the country while others are made up of Southerners originally from the Southwest. This does not mean that believers of different backgrounds should not be, or cannot be, assimilated into such churches.

(3) In situations that call for special "coping strategy," by patience and understanding we may be able to accommodate cultural preferences temporarily while moving toward the Christian ideal. Greenway's suggestion that in cities we begin with "homogeneous unit" congregations which eventually will become "all peoples" congregations would be an example. Again, we may have multiple meetings for believers, and thus appeal to different types of people. But we must keep the biblical ideal before us and find meaningful ways to express and experience our oneness in Christ, both in the local group and between believing groups.

(4) New local groups of believers will not become organized, integrated communities naturally and automatically. There must be a divine element—the operation of the Holy Spirit in the believing group. And a human element must be provided by the church-planter as the ultimate objective of glorifying Christ is made practical by means of clear and meaningful intermediate goals around which group members can rally their energies.

Belongingness:
The New Believer
and the Believing Community

Biblical Principles and Precedents

According to Scripture, the plight of unsaved men is complete separation from God and His family. They are "excluded from the commonwealth of Israel, and strangers to the covenants of promise, having no hope and without God in the world" (Eph. 2:12). Even in eternity they are consigned to "the eternal fire which has been prepared for the devil and his angels" (Matt. 25:41). Lack of belongingness is so evident everywhere that Karl Marx used the term *alienation* to describe the desperate situation of the proletariat. Unsaved men are alienated.

Believers, on the other hand, "are no longer strangers and aliens, but . . . fellow-citizens with the saints, and are of God's household" (Eph. 2:19). In other words, *they belong!* Relevant to this truth are two important facts presented in Scripture.

The first fact is that man is a social being. When Adam was created, God declared that it was not good that man should be alone (Gen. 2:18). Eve was created and the first society was formed. But man fell and God created a new man (II Cor. 5:17; Gal. 6:15; Eph. 4:24; Col. 3:10). This new man is also a social being. He, too, is made for fellowship with God and with other men. To recognize the social responsibilities of the new man, one has only to observe the way the apostle Paul immediately plunges into a discussion of social relations when he speaks of the new man (Eph. 4:24-32; Col. 3:10-14). Redeemed or fallen, man by nature is a social being. This truth cannot be ignored.

The second fact is that God has created a new society for the redeemed man. This new society is the Church. Belonging to the Church is not optional for the believer. By divine action he is united to the body of Christ (I Cor. 12:13). No believer is excluded nor exempted on grounds of race or social class (I Cor. 12:14). All believers are part of the new society.

The early church understood these truths. To the embryonic new society of 120 believers, 3,000 were added in one day (Acts 2:41). There was no waiting period while the new converts learned basic doctrine or attained to a certain state of holiness. This pattern was repeated again and again (Acts 4:4; 6:7; 11:21; 16:5). The new convert was not left alone. The Spirit joined him to the body of Christ and the early church identified him as one of their own.

As one who belonged to the Church, the new believer had identity. He was a Christ-follower. In the new society he received spiritual nourishment through the action of the believing group (Eph. 4:11–16). He was loved and was taught to love in return (Heb. 10:24, 25). All the security and stability which come from belonging to a group were his. This sense of belongingness was so intimate that the group was called a body and each person was a "body part." When one part suffered, all parts suffered. When one member was honored, all members were honored (I Cor. 12:26).

Identification with the group, however, did not destroy individuality. As an individual the new believer had been given special capacities which enabled him to make unique contributions to the body (Rom. 12:3–8; I Cor. 12:7–11; Eph. 4:7–16). These spiritual gifts gave him status. He was needed by the group and the group could not function properly without his abilities. At the same time, he needed the group since he could not function apart from it. His individuality contributed to his "social beingness" and his social nature contributed to his individuality. In the new man and the new society, alienation is completely overcome. The believer belongs!

Relevant Research

From a scientific point of view also, man is a communal creature. He lives in the context of community. Not only is this in accord with man's nature, it also is in accord with his predicament, because cooperation is essential to coexistence. Therefore, human beings relate to each other— especially to those of the same race, language, class, upbringing—in order to serve psychological and sociological needs. Throughout the literature there is emphasis on

the need of the individual for belongingness and acceptance in the community. We will briefly look at three concepts which relate to this need.

1. Incorporation

Incorporation refers to the acceptance of the new
member into the group of which he becomes a part. Incorporation is of two kinds. Informal incorporation is accomplished by simply making the new member feel that he
is indeed a member of the group. Formal incorporation
involves some kind of ritualistic reception of the new
member into the group, usually in the presence of all or
most of the members.

The activities and rites of incorporation are so important that almost every organization, including churches,
has them in some shape or form. Nevertheless, we Christians are liable to err in this regard. In the first place, we
might put so much emphasis on the decision *point* that we
forget that the decision *process* involves incorporation into
the new group and the acceptance of its discipline. In the
second place, we place such an emphasis on accepting
Christ and being accepted by Him that we may take it for
granted that the new believer feels accepted by the believing group. If the new believer has a responsibility to join
the believing group, the believing group has a responsibility to do everything possible to incorporate and integrate
the new believer into the family of faith!

2. Anomie

Perhaps more than any other sociologist, Emile Durkheim stressed the role of society in human life. In fact, he
went so far as to suggest that religion is important primarily as a supporter and interpreter of the social order. It
goes without saying that we cannot wholly agree with Durkheim at that point. Nevertheless, we can learn much from
him.

Durkheim elaborated three very different types of relationships that exist between an individual and the moral order represented by society.[7]

In the first type, the individual is related to a society in which he is made to see himself as separate and responsible for his own affairs. He does not have recourse to the community when things go wrong. The result may be "egoistic suicide."

In the second type of relationship, the individual is bound to society in an intense way. In fact, he is willing to give his life for the community in an act of altruism.

In the third type, the individual is transferred from one social pattern or order into another. He suddenly acquires a new "social character." For example, he may become rich overnight with the result that he is alienated from his impoverished friends without being accepted by the established wealthy. Durkheim called this condition *anomie*— the state which results from being put into a place where norms are ill-defined, contradictory, or absent.

If Durkheim's position seems extreme, it should be remembered that he was reacting against Charles Darwin, who saw everything from a biological perspective. In spite of our quarrel with Durkheim's position, it is important to view his concept of *anomie* from a Christian perspective. How often do new believers come into the company of believers without receiving clear signals as to what is expected of them and what it means to be a member of a Christian group or church? What may seem clear to us may well be altogether unclear to the new believer! Spiritual "anomic suicide" may be just another name for reversion or, to use the older term, backsliding. But when it occurs, at least part of the onus falls upon more mature believers.

---

[7]Cf. Emile Durkheim, *Suicide: A Study in Sociology* (New York: Free Press of Glencoe, 1951).

3. Conformity

Analyzing the adaptation that individuals must make in relating to one another in order to achieve group goals, Robert K. Merton stresses that members must accept both the goals of the group and the means of attaining them.[8] If the individual member accepts the goals but not the means of attaining them, the result will probably be *innovation*. If he accepts the means but not the goals, *ritualism* will result. If he accepts both the goals and the means, the result will be *conformity*.

Building upon Merton's ideas, Lawrence Richards believes that churches tend to give priority to means rather than to goals. As a result, Christians tend to become ritualists, going through the motions of worship, service, and so forth, but not really maturing as fellow believers in Christ.[9] The concept of conformity is usually frowned upon (in American society at least); but when conformity means adherence to true faith and practice, when it means becoming more Christlike, when it means that the believing group can go forward in the plan and program of God—then it is a positive concept!

It seems that Richards himself is advocating innovation, because he accepts the goals of the churches but not the means that are being used to attain them. In any case, his observation merits consideration when we are planning for the first meetings of new believers as well as for the ongoing ministry of the churches. Worship, service, witness, and fellowship are long-term goals. But from the very first, new believers must be introduced to them and to the biblical means for attaining them. Otherwise either ritualism or innovation may result, and innovation for the new believer may also spell reversion.

---

[8]Robert K. Merton, *Social Theory and Social Structure*, rev. ed. (New York: Free Press of Glencoe, 1957), pp. 139–40.

[9]Lawrence O. Richards, *A New Face for the Church* (Grand Rapids: Zondervan, 1970), pp. 50–51.

Practical Reflections

This little parody of hymnody may seem humorous but it has a sting:

> To live above with saints we love,
> That will be the glory,
> To live below with saints we know,
> Well, that's a different story.

Put yourself in the place of a new convert in your target area. A radical reordering of beliefs, values, lifestyle, and relationships is in order. Take time to reflect: What would your questions be? The words of Pastor Baldemore of Manila are worthy of mention: "When a Filipino considers the possibility of conversion, one of his first questions is, 'With what group would I be associated?'" Perhaps this question is of greater importance than we imagine in *most* cultures and instances of conversion (except in some cases of group conversion). Note again the large percentage of Japanese whose motivation for converting to Lutheranism was a desire for the love and fellowship of the Church (p. 242).

In light of these considerations, there are several questions we should ask about our policies in the past:

(1) Have we put too much responsibility for "follow-through" upon the convert and not enough on those who are already believers?

(2) Have we given insufficient and one-sided directions to converts?

(3) Have we put too much confidence in traditional ways of treating (or neglecting) new converts?

Group Functions and Optimum Size

The notion of "optimum size" will be new to most readers. We are referring to the proper size of a group with a view to the goals and functions of that group. It is somewhat analogous to so-called normal body weight. Obviously, every human body should not be the same weight. Normal weight depends upon the height, body frame, and, to a certain extent, the kind of activities in which one engages. With a view to the activities and aims of a group we will call the "right" number of members the "optimum size."

Biblical Principles and Precedents

The Bible does not give all the information that we might like when it comes to the number of believers present in any given situation. But it does give some significant information in this regard. We are sure of the following:

(1) Christ had three disciples who had a special relationship to Him—Peter, James, and John.

(2) Our Lord chose twelve disciples to be with Him as He went about His ministry. When one betrayed Him, another—Matthias—was chosen to take his place (Acts 1:26).

(3) After sending out the Twelve on a mission, the Lord sent out seventy (or seventy-two) to go ahead of Him to towns and places He was about to visit (Luke 10:1).

(4) Our Lord appeared to a group numbering in excess of 500 after His resurrection (I Cor. 15:6).

(5) There were some 120 believers in the Jerusalem church at the time of Pentecost. After Pentecost the number of believers swelled to 3,000 and then 5,000 (men) and probably more (Acts 1:15; 2:41; 4:4).

It would be interesting to know exactly how many believers there were in those churches mentioned in the New Testament. The number must have varied greatly. We know that "all" in Lydda and Sharon turned to the Lord (Acts 9:35). The number of believers in some other places, such as Athens, must have been very small indeed. The early churches were modeled somewhat after the synagogue, and the fact that there had to be ten adult men in order to organize a synagogue may have had some significance for church practice. Some scholars have conjectured that the congregation at Antioch numbered between 300 and 500 souls. The fact that believers often met in private homes (as well as in public places) meant that many of the gatherings were necessarily small.

Relevant Research

Once again, we cannot present firm figures for the optimum size of various types of groups, but there are some general indications in the literature:

(1) *Core leadership* groups such as those which run corporations and lead military campaigns seem to number in the range of three to twelve members. Edward T. Hall writes, "Eight to twelve persons can know each other well enough to maximize their talents."[10]

(2) The *small group*, which is so prominent in sociological literature, is usually defined as a group of such a size that (a) its members can establish a face-to-face relationship and (b) the absence of any member from a meeting would be noticed. The small group seldom numbers more than twenty-five or thirty members, and usually less. It is well-suited to effect group learning, fellowship, and corporate action. Howard Snyder notes the importance of small groups:

> Early Pietism was nurtured by the *collegio pietatis,* or house meetings for prayer, Bible study and discussion. The small group was a basic aspect of the Wesleyan Revival in England, with the proliferation of John Wesley's "class meetings." Small groups undergirded the Holiness Revival that swept America in the late 1800s and led, in part, to the modern Pentecostal movement. More significantly, the

---

[10]Edward T. Hall, *Beyond Culture* (Garden City, NY: Anchor Press, 1977), p. 203.

road to the Reformation was paved by small-group Bible studies. If nothing more, these facts surely suggest that small groups are conducive to the reviving ministry of the Holy Spirit.[11]

We have emphasized elsewhere that the extremely rapid growth of Soka Gakkai Buddhism in Japan is related to the prominence given to small discussion groups.[12] In a lecture at Trinity Evangelical Divinity School, George Cowan of Wycliffe Bible Translators emphasized that according to law the Mexican government recognizes only groups of forty members or more.[13]

(3) One definition of *community* is the "maximum number of people who can reside together in face-to-face relationship." This is usually taken to be about 1,000 people. In his study of nativistic movements in Africa, David Barrett suggests that the number 1,000 may be very significant. Using statistics for 1966, he notes that the average size of some 600 Protestant mission churches or dioceses in Africa was 36,000 members. Three hundred Catholic dioceses averaged 97,000. But the independent churches which have been mushrooming in Africa tended to be considerably smaller—the overall average was 1,400, and only about 1,000 in Ghana, South Africa, Nigeria, and other "long-involved" nations. Barrett suggests that the size of a true Christian community may be smaller than the Western world has realized, and that the size of some of our church groupings may have to be scaled down in order to reintroduce *philadelphia*.[14]

---

[11]Howard A. Snyder, *The Problem of Wineskins: Church Structure in a Technological Age* (Downers Grove, IL: Inter-Varsity Press, 1975), p. 140.

[12]David J. Hesselgrave, "A Propagation Profile of the Soka Gakkai" (Ph.D. dissertation, University of Minnesota, 1965), pp. 249–64.

[13]The lecture was delivered in April, 1970.

[14]David Barrett, *Schism and Renewal in Africa* (Nairobi: Oxford University Press, 1968), p. 171.

Practical Reflection

The implications of "optimum size" may be much greater than is realized in most churches and missions.

(1) Leadership should be in the hands of a few recognized, gifted leaders. If leadership is not shared, it runs the risk of being dictatorial and occasioning division. If it is shared too widely, it runs the risk of being unwieldy and ineffective.

(2) In some cultures it may be extremely difficult for local churches to grow much larger than the upper limits of the size of the small group. Cultures that emphasize the group rather than the individual make it difficult for individuals to follow Christ. When some do believe, the believing family becomes very important to them. But unless an unusual vision and superior strategy for outreach are evident, the need for acceptance and fellowship is met in the small group, and growth may level off at that point.

(3) As embryonic churches grow into established churches with ever-increasing numbers of believers, it is crucial to remember that the small-group life of the believers must be maintained. Howard Snyder emphasizes:

> Theologically, large- and small-group gatherings are the structural implications of the church's being the people of God and the fellowship of the Holy Spirit. . . . Peoplehood implies the necessity of large-group gatherings while community requires small-group structures.[15]

The Place of Meeting

No doubt about it, the bottleneck in many an effort in church-planting is the meeting-place. In country after country, missionary-evangelists and other church leaders

---

[15]Snyder, *Problem of Wineskins*, p. 163. Note that Snyder's use of the word *community* does not refer to group size per se.

say, "Solve the church building problem for us, and our
program of planting new congregations will go into orbit."
It is hard to believe that the Church of Christ cannot advance without a generous supply of brick and mortar. At
the same time, most of us who have been involved in
pioneer efforts over a number of years will confess that an
adequate building is usually a big boost to growth.

Biblical Principles and Precedents

It is worthwhile to reflect on the fact that Jehovah's first
provision for a special place in which to meet with His
people was a tent or tabernacle. At Jehovah's command the
people moved. At His command, the people camped.
Jehovah was present with His people within the tabernacle
(Num. 9:17–23). Then came the day when David proposed
that a temple be built. He said to Nathan, "See now, I dwell
in a house of cedar, but the ark of God dwells within tent
curtains" (II Sam. 7:2). In response, Jehovah said:

> Go and tell my servant David, Thus saith the Lord, Shalt
> thou build me an house for me to dwell in? Whereas I have
> not dwelt in any house since the time that I brought up the
> children of Israel out of Egypt, even to this day, but have
> walked in a tent and in a tabernacle. In all the places
> wherein I have walked with all the children of Israel spake
> I a word with any of the tribes of Israel, whom I com-
> manded to feed my people Israel, saying, Why build ye not
> me an house of cedar? (II Sam. 7:5–7, KJV)

After discussing the relevant passages, Howard Snyder
concludes, "The truer sign of the presence of God in his
earthly church is the tabernacle, and only secondarily the
temple. The tabernacle is the truer symbol, for it more
accurately shows how God acts in history."[16]
In a sense the New Testament seems to bear out this

---

[16]Ibid., p. 63.

contention, though it would not be true to say that our Lord neglected the temple. He was taken there as a child. He visited the temple during His ministry, and He cleansed it of merchants and proclaimed that as His Father's house it should be a house of prayer (Matt. 21:13; Luke 19:46). But to the Samaritan woman He said that the time would come when men would not worship Him either on Mount Gerizim or in Jerusalem, but in "spirit and in truth" (John 4:23). And He promised that wherever two or three believers would gather in His name, He would meet with them (Matt. 18:20).

After the ascension of their Lord, the early believers met in the temple and in homes (Acts 5:42). As Christianity spread throughout the Empire, believers met in the synagogues (Acts 9:20; 13:5; 18:26), publicly (Acts 18:28; 20:20), and in the open air (Acts 16:13). From the very beginning and throughout the New Testament era, house gatherings were a common feature of Christian corporate life (Acts 2:46; Rom. 16:5; I Cor. 16:19; Col. 4:15). In fact, there were no church buildings as we know them for the first 150 years of the Church's existence.

We conclude, then, that Christianity has no one sacred spot or shrine on earth and that God will meet with His people wherever they gather to worship and call upon His name. In this, true Christianity is uniquely *the* universal religion.

Relevant Research

Research in this area is certainly not as voluminous and significant as is the case in many areas, but the following observations based upon case studies of rapidly growing religious movements in other cultures may be worthy of consideration.[17]

---

[17]David J. Hesselgrave, "What Causes Religious Movements to Grow?" in *Dynamic Religious Movements: Case Studies in Rapidly Growing Religious Movements Around the World*, ed. David J. Hesselgrave (Grand Rapids: Baker, 1978), pp. 313–14.

(1) One obvious advantage of the house meeting is that it serves to keep the group small. The small-group meetings lend themselves to mutual recognition of participants, dialogue, interaction, and the building of friendships. When a member is absent, the others are aware of it and establish contact. Neighbors, friends, and acquaintances find it relatively easy to accept invitations to the house meeting and are rather easily assimilated into the small group. When the group outgrows the limitations of the house (and small-group size), it is quite simple for part of the group to start a new group in the home of another member. In this way the number of meetings, meeting-places, groups, and individual members multiply rapidly.

(2) Most religious groups do have central locations where the faithful gather. Every group of believers may not have such a meeting-place in their own community. Nevertheless, they most likely have some accessible building which serves as a center for certain religious activities.

The Grand Main Temple of the Orthodox Sect of Nichiren Buddhism is a modern wonder reputed to be the largest temple on earth. Built to endure, the *Sho-Hondo,* as it is called, seats 6,000 in such a way that all may view the *Honzon* without interference. The *Honzon,* a tablet allegedly inscribed by Nichiren some seven hundred years ago, is the central object of worship for the Soka Gakkai. Standing near the *Sho-Hondo* are other buildings both contemporary and quaint which depict Japan's history during the eras of growth of Soka Gakkai.[18] The Soka Gakkai claim this temple area is the earth's center and the location of the coming kingdom.

Some other groups also display architectural grandeur. Consider the Mormons' Temple Square in Salt Lake City. Still others have meeting-places characterized by extreme simplicity. Most do have some site or cultural possessions which are meaningful to them.[19]

---

[18]Hesselgrave, "Nichiren Shoshu Soka Gakkai—The Lotus Blossoms in Japan," in *Dynamic Religious Movements,* pp. 129–30.
[19]Hesselgrave, "What Causes Religious Movements to Grow?" p. 313.

FIGURE 40
The Zone of Participation*

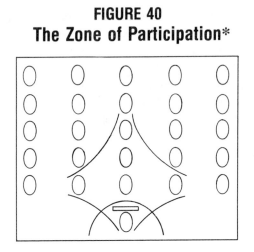

*See Mark L. Knapp, *Nonverbal Communication* (New York: Holt, Rinehart and Winston, 1972), pp. 26–27. Copyright © 1972 by Holt, Rinehart and Winston. Reprinted by permission.

(3) Research shows that the shape of the meeting-place and the arrangement of its furniture affect the process of communication. Mark Knapp emphasizes that there is a "zone of participation" which is roughly in the form of a triangle with the base immediately in front of the speaker.[20] People sitting in this area are most likely to respond to what is being said and done in the pulpit area. (See Figure 40.) The long, rectangular sanctuaries characteristic of many churches and other places of meeting are not well designed for effective communication. If sanctuaries were better designed for effective communication, much less energy would need to be spent trying to urge people to move to the front pews!

Practical Reflection

There can be no doubt that in many parts of the world the lack of an adequate meeting-place is one of the fun-

---

[20]Mark L. Knapp, *Nonverbal Communication* (New York: Holt, Rinehart and Winston, 1972), pp. 26–27.

damental obstacles to planting new churches. Whatever else we might conclude, the following must be said:

(1) More God-given ingenuity, creativeness, and patience will probably be required of missionary leadership during this stage (unless or until a permanent meeting-place is secured) than at any other stage in the Pauline Cycle.

(2) The development of new churches ultimately cannot be dependent upon the provision of a church building, as desirous as that might be.

(3) To broach the problem of a permanent building too soon after beginning a new work may discourage new converts.

(4) This is a point where the promise of some kind of assistance from the supporting constituency may be a source of great encouragement.

The Times of Meetings

Biblical Principles and Precedents

The writer to the Hebrews clearly stated that Christians should not neglect to assemble themselves together (Heb. 10:25). The primitive church followed the practice of meeting often. In fact, in the period after Pentecost, they met daily (Acts 2:46).

It cannot be established, however, that there was one certain time when a congregation was required to meet. The Colossians were told not to allow anyone to judge them in regard to feast days or Sabbath days (Col. 2:16). The Romans were told that there was no agreement among Christians in regard to days: "One man regards one day above another, another regards every day alike. Let each man be fully convinced in his own mind" (Rom. 14:5). When entering a city, Paul customarily joined with those meeting in the synagogue on the Sabbath (Acts 17:2). For Christian believers, however, the first day of the week became the customary day to meet. On the first day a collection was to be made for the poor (I Cor. 16:2). It was on the first day of the week that the Lord had been resurrected (John 20:1). Therefore, as a testimony to Christ's death and resurrection, it was natural to celebrate the Lord's Supper on the first day of the week (Acts 20:7). It came to be known as the Lord's day (Rev. 1:10). So, although there was no command to meet on a certain day (unless I Cor. 16:2 be construed to be such a command), the first day came to be the normal meeting day.

Similarly, it cannot be established from Scripture that the primitive church was required to meet at any specific hour of the day. Some meetings were held at night (Acts 12:6, 12; 20:7). Others were held during the day (Acts 3:1; 19:9). It seems that the churches picked times that were convenient for the worshipers.

Relevant Research

Recent anthropological research has revealed that, with respect to the concept of time, there is a marked difference among cultures. In part these differences reflect different philosophies of history. For example, cultures that have a cyclical philosophy of history, according to which history is constantly repeating itself and goes forward at an almost imperceptible rate, can be expected to have a very different approach to time than will a culture with a philosophy where time is always "running out." Local conditions and lifestyles will also have a profound effect. Accordingly, two considerations become especially important to churchmen.

"Time-orientation" Versus "Event-orientation"

For better or worse, some audiences will have a good feeling about a meeting only if it begins and ends on time. Other audiences will be relatively unconcerned about punctuality (in this sense), and will entertain a good feeling only if the meeting meets their expectations in terms of what should occur. In the former case the "good" meeting starts—or, at least, is dismissed—on schedule. In the latter case, the "good" meeting begins when the people are ready and closes when the objectives for the gathering have been achieved. The differences between these two cultural (and subcultural!) orientations are crucial.

Variation in Schedules

Not nearly so subtle as the previous distinction, but of vital importance to the church-planter, are the differences that result from varying local lifestyles. In Nigeria, for example, the week is determined by the market day that occurs every four or eight days (depending on the tribe). For the Igbo, the day is marked off by three separate gatherings of liquid from the raffia palm. All appointments are made in accordance with these events.[21]

In our culture, the differences between urban and rural schedules frequently are of significance in the determination of meeting times.

Practical Reflection

Christian leaders need sensitivity to the kind of data we have been considering. They have a tendency to say, "Sunday (A.M.) only," or "no special day," or "meetings begin promptly at 7:00 P.M.," and so forth, in accordance with their own upbringing and personal preferences. The Bible seems to require that believers meet frequently and place special emphasis on the first day of the week. Research indicates that some sort of flexibility will be very important when it comes to setting the schedule for meetings in any given locality. Especially at the beginning of a

---

[21]Margaret Green, *Igbo Village Affairs*, 2nd ed. (London: Cass and Co., 1964), pp. 22, 34.

work, local ideas about time and local lifestyles will be crucial if believers are to be congregated and discipled effectively. Only by consulting Scripture and assessing the local situation can it be determined how many meetings are needed and when the meetings should be held. Only by a study of Scripture and applying its teachings to the local situation can we be sure that meetings will be pleasing to God and rewarding to His people.

ME-3 illustration: The leaders of one church in Hong Kong took stock of their situation and decided upon two worship meetings on Sunday—one in the morning and one at night. They correctly reasoned that many business people who were required to work until 5:00 or 6:00 P.M. on Sundays would seldom have the opportunity to meet for regular worship unless a Sunday evening worship service became a part of the church schedule. Meetings of several thriving youth groups were scheduled at the same time. In addition, frequent evangelistic services were held at times other than Sunday evening and were well attended, due to the location of the church at a busy commercial intersection.

Master Plan Formation

Belongingness

Perhaps the two things most needed by new believers immediately following their conversion (whether as individuals or in groups) are clear instruction as to what God expects of His family members and caring Christian friendship. It is the responsibility of the missionary-evangelist to see to it that these two essentials are supplied right away. New believers should receive instruction orally. They should also be given culturally appropriate written materials such as a Bible (or portions thereof), a brief

FIGURE 41

Christian Family Initial Care Card

Name of new believer(s) _____

Address _____

Phone (if any) _____ Date of profession of faith _____

Name of Christian counselor/friend assigned _____

_____

(Counselor, please note: Those areas where the new believer has already been helped are filled in below. In Christian love, please carry out the other assignments, remember the new convert daily in prayer, and fill in the form and return it to the undersigned by ___[date]___.)

1. Early contacts:
   First contact (date) _____   Second contact _____
   Third contact _____   Fourth contact _____
   Fifth contact _____   Sixth contact _____

2. Early instruction. Information and counseling provided concerning:
   Private (home) prayer and Bible reading _____
   Group (church) meetings and activities _____
   Confession of faith _____
   Preparation for baptism _____

3. Materials provided:
   Bible or Bible portion _____
   Manual or other printed material _____
   Schedules of meetings, etc. _____
   Other _____

4. Introduction to believing community (as appropriate):
   New believer introduced to church or full group   (date)_____
   New believer introduced to the following church groups (classes, etc.):
   _____ (_____date)
   _____ (_____date)
   _____ (_____date)

                   Assignment made by _____
                   Counselor completing this form _____
                   Date form returned _____

manual for new believers, and information on meeting-places and times. In most cases identity with the believing group will be aided significantly if some tangible insignia is provided for new converts—a Bible portion with a special imprint, a pin, a small card.

One of the most important things the Christian worker can do for new converts is to introduce them (as believing individuals, families, or groups) to mature believers who will act as counselors and friends while they are being established in the faith. *It is imperative that this be done immediately, since the first forty-eight to seventy-two hours after profession of faith are often absolutely crucial.* However this introduction is made, the Christian counselor/friend should receive and later provide specific information regarding the new convert(s) for whom he is responsible. Three simple steps should be followed:

Step One: A list of Christian believers who are mature and willing to take this kind of responsibility should be compiled.

Step Two: The believer best suited to help the new convert(s) should be prayerfully chosen, and counselor and convert(s) made known to each other.

Step Three: A form such as the one in Figure 41 should be filled out (as far as possible) and then given to the counselor, with the request that he fill in the remaining sections and return it. This should be done within a specified time, in most cases within six weeks.

Groups Projected for the Church

It is just as important to meet the needs of believers and the objectives of the church as it is to add to the total number of believers. This being the case, it is well to plan and (eventually) provide for various groups of believers in the emerging church. Such factors as age, sex, ethnic origins, educational background, and so forth, must be taken

FIGURE 42

Potential Places of Meeting

	Ease of transportation (distance, parking, etc.)	Availability and economic feasibility	Psychological factors (neighborhood, building, etc.)	Appropriateness for Christian activity (noise, size, atmosphere).
Believers' Homes				
Church Building				
Public Hall				
Theater				
School Building				
Factory				
Office				
Dormitory Lounge				
Other: _____				
Other: _____				
Other: _____				

FIGURE 43

Potential Meeting Times

Time	Compatibility with working hours, school schedules, traditional meeting times in the community, etc.	Transportation factors (availability of private and public transportation, proximity to believers' residences, etc.)
Sunday: Morning		
Afternoon		
Evening		
Weekdays:		
Monday: Morning		
Afternoon		
Evening		
Tuesday: Morning		
Afternoon		
Evening		
Etc.		

into account in planning for these subgroups. Give consideration to the following:

(1) Emerging-leadership groups.
(2) Small groups for Bible study, discipling, Christian service, etc.
(3) Eventual optimum size for the congregation. (At what point should consideration be given to starting satellite congregations?)

Place(s) of Meeting

In concert with knowledgeable locals, rate possible places of meeting as good, fair, or poor for each of the factors which will affect the believers' willingness to participate. Remember to rank potential meeting-places for the congregation as a whole and for subgroups separately (see Figure 42). Since circumstances change, be prepared to reevaluate these places periodically.

Times of Meeting

In a manner similar to evaluating meeting-places, rate possible meeting times as good, fair, or poor in relation to those factors which will affect believers' participation. Remember to rank possible meeting times for the congregation and each subgroup separately (see Figure 43).

In this chapter we have been concerned with bringing new believers together in a Christian fellowship. This stage in the Pauline Cycle is exceedingly important, initially in gathering believers together as an embryonic congregation and subsequently in bringing converts into the fellowship. For every new congregation and for every new believer, this stage is a very temporary one. But it is also very crucial. Many a congregation has experienced a significant setback because the factors involved were not thoroughly thought and prayed through. And myriads of "lost sheep" have been found and lost again because undershepherds procrastinated in folding and feeding them.

thirteen

The Faith Confirmed

Confirmation should not be thought of as simply a mental exercise for church youth. Confirmation is for *all* believers and it is for believers *only*. Conversion without confirmation and confirmation without conversion are theological contradictions. Conversion is *to* a new faith and a new life. It anticipates confirmation. Confirmation is *in* the new faith and life. It presupposes conversion. Let every missionary-evangelist—indeed, every church leader—give serious thought to this indispensable phase of Christian life and ministry.

Objectives

With the foregoing in mind, the following objectives are important in church-planting:

(1) To establish believers in the faith so they know what they are to believe and how they are to live.

(2) To provide opportunities for worship that will be uplifting and God-honoring.

FIGURE 44
"THE PAULINE CYCLE"

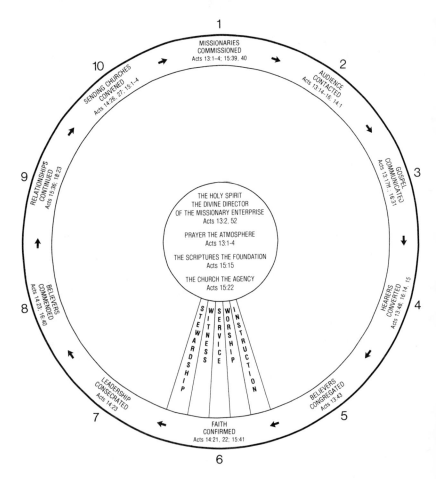

"And he was traveling through Syria and Cilicia, strengthening the churches" (Acts 15:41).

(3) To exhort believers to serve under the authority of Christ by the power of the Holy Spirit so that as citizens of heaven and earth they will make both spheres richer by their contributions to God and man.

(4) To help believers in their witness—"giving away their faith," to use Paul Little's expression.

(5) To encourage believers to practice faithful stewardship in accordance with the time, talents, treasure, gifts, and energies God has given them.

Faith and Instruction

Biblical Principles and Precedents

The Old Testament is clear that believers were to be confirmed in the faith. God said through Moses:

> Hear, O Israel! The Lord is our God, the Lord is one! And you shall love the Lord your God with all your heart and with all your soul and with all your might. And these words, which I am commanding you today, shall be on your heart; and you shall teach them diligently to your sons and shall talk of them when you sit in your house and when you walk by the way and when you lie down and when you rise up. And you shall bind them as a sign on your hand and they shall be as frontals on your forehead. And you shall write them on the doorposts of your house and on your gates. (Deut. 6:4–9)

In the New Testament, the command of God is equally clear. Jesus told His disciples to teach "all things whatsoever I have commanded you" (Matt. 28:20, KJV). Paul closely followed this instruction. He wrote, "For I received from the Lord that which I also delivered to you" (I Cor. 11:23). Timothy was exhorted to teach faithful men so that they in turn could teach others (II Tim. 2:2). Teaching the Word of God to believers is just as imperative for us as it was for Paul and Timothy!

It is obvious, however, that the "all things" must be taught in a space-time context. Not everything can be taught or learned at once. This fact makes the question of priorities important. What truths or practices are so important that they must be taught early in the Christian life?

Truths to Be Taught to New Believers

The author of the Epistle to the Hebrews makes a striking statement about the truths to be taught early in the development of the believer. In chapter 6, after expressing his regret that his readers had not become teachers as he had expected and after affirming that some truths are "milk" and other truths constitute "solid food," he says:

> Therefore leaving the elementary teaching about the Christ, let us press on to maturity, not laying again a foundation of repentance from dead works and of faith toward God, of instruction about washings, and laying on of hands, and the resurrection of the dead, and eternal judgment. (Heb. 6:1, 2)

The "elementary teaching about Christ" is those truths presented in the first five chapters of the letter. Christ is seen as superior to the prophets in that He gave a final revelation of the very nature of God when He made a purification for sins. He is superior to the angels in that He is the Sovereign God to whom the angels direct their praise. He is superior in that He partook of flesh and blood and tasted death for every man, providing salvation. He is superior to Moses in that Moses is a servant in the house while Christ is the Son. Christ has provided a rest for the believer and has become our faithful high priest. These are elementary truths.

Other elementary truths are repentance and faith, baptism, resurrection, and eternal judgment. A comparison of this list with the Pauline Epistles which were directed to infant churches reveals that Paul followed a similar pattern in his teaching. In I Thessalonians the sufferings, death, and resurrection of Christ are seen as having already been taught (2:14, 15; 4:14; 5:9). Faith has clearly been taught (1:3; 2:10; 3:7; 5:8). The teaching of repentance is implied (1:10), while eternal judgment is specifically mentioned (1:10; 3:13; 5:9). In I Corinthians Paul writes that he is determined to emphasize the cross (2:2). Resurrection is taught in a detailed manner (15:12-58) and judgment is also presented (3:10-15; 4:5). Paul clearly followed the pattern of presenting truths which the author of Hebrews labeled "elementary."

However, the passage in Hebrews contains the complaint that the readers had not progressed from the elementary stage because they had not become doers of the Word (Heb. 5:12-14). The implication is that Christian practice was taught along with elementary Christian doctrine. This also is seen in the epistles Paul wrote to very young churches. For example, purity in sexual relations is presented as an integral part of holy living (I Cor. 5:1-10; 6:9-20; I Thess. 4:1-7). Believers are exhorted to show brotherly love (I Cor. 13; I Thess. 4:9, 10). Explicit instructions are given about marriage and divorce (I Cor. 7). Industriousness is urged upon those awaiting the coming of the Lord (I Thess. 4:11, 12). The problem of eating meat offered to idols is discussed (I Cor. 8; 10:14-22). We conclude, therefore, that the teaching given to new believers in the early churches was a mixture of instruction in elementary doctrine and practical Christian living.

The Teaching Given to the Mature Churches

The author of the letter to the Hebrews states that his readers are now ready for deeper teaching (6:1). So he proceeds to discuss the priesthood of Melchizedek and of Christ, and the doctrine of the new covenant. In similar fashion Paul demonstrates that there are deeper teachings which should be given to the more mature believer (I Cor. 3:1, 2). These teachings are best seen in his letters to the older, established churches. The letters to the Philippians,

Ephesians, and Colossians should be studied in this regard. What could be more profound than the *kenosis* passage of Philippians 2, the great Christological passage in Colossians 1, and the tremendous soteriological passage of Ephesians 1? It is plain that Paul reserved deeper teachings for more mature Christians.

Furthermore, Paul expected more mature practice from these churches. Believers were to seek those things which are above, while mortifying their members upon the earth (Col. 3:1–14). They were to be filled with the Spirit and give evidence of it (Eph. 5:18—6:9). They were to exhibit the unity of the Spirit (Eph. 4:13) and be joyous in all circumstances (Phil. 3:1).

Relevant Research

Growth and Instruction

Studies show that rapidly growing religious (and other) movements tend to stress that those who wish instruction should master a basic doctrinal core and, once that has been mastered, go on to the deeper teachings of the movement. One could call this process "indoctrination." It is too bad that this term has been linked with brainwashing and therefore has a bad connotation. When coercive methods are employed, indoctrination is to be deplored. Otherwise, it is a good word. But by whatever name, the process is a common one. The fact that we disagree with both the methods and the teachings of Communism, Scientology, the Unification Church, Jehovah's Witnesses, the Mormons, and Soka Gakkai Buddhists should not blind us to their strengths. Immediately upon believing, Gakkai converts (for example) are introduced to a carefully-thought-out program of instruction in the basic teachings of the sect. Instruction in small groups, special lectures, a believers' manual, a series of voluntary examinations, advancement according to the degree of doctrinal knowledge attained—all of these are parts of the program.[1]

Formal, Informal, and Technical Learning

A most helpful distinction has been made by the anthropologist Edward T. Hall. He believes that learning takes place at three levels: the formal level (mistake-correction); the informal level (imitation of models); and the technical level (from a teacher). One of Hall's major contentions is that a far greater proportion of learning than we may suppose takes place at the informal level.[2] One of the implications of this is that much more attention needs to be given to the modeling of biblical truth. Unless truth is exemplified and modeled in terms of changed behavior, its mere recitation probably is not nearly as effective as we ordinarily suppose. This is especially the case in the pioneer situation.

Learning by Listening and Seeing

Studies indicate that, all things being equal, 10 percent of the subject matter of a given lesson is remembered when the lesson has been taught by speech alone, while twice that amount (20 percent) will be recalled if the lesson is communicated by sight alone. But if listening and seeing are combined, 65 percent of the material will be recalled![3]

Learning by Doing

It is a fundamental law of pedagogy that one learns by doing. Learning is not simply a matter of cognition. It is

---

[1]David J. Hesselgrave, "Nichiren Shoshu Soka Gakkai—The Lotus Blossoms in Japan," in *Dynamic Religious Movements: Case Studies in Rapidly Growing Religious Movements Around the World*, ed. David J. Hesselgrave (Grand Rapids: Baker, 1978), pp. 129–48.

[2]Edward T. Hall, *The Silent Language* (Greenwich, CT: Fawcett Publications, 1959), pp. 63–91.

[3]Statistics quoted in David R. Mains, *Full Circle: The Creative Church for Today's Society* (Waco, TX: Word Books, 1971), p. 87.

FIGURE 45

Learning by Doing*

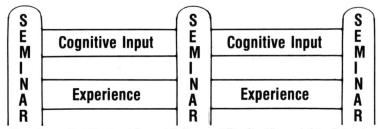

*Based upon Ted Ward and Samuel F. Rowen, "The Significance of the Extension Seminary," *Evangelical Missions Quarterly*, vol. 9, no. 1 (Fall 1972), pp. 17–27. Reprinted with permission of the *Evangelical Missions Quarterly*, published by the Evangelical Missions Information Service, Box 794, Wheaton, IL 60187.

also a matter of action. Learning that is divorced from life, that is only a matter of the accumulation of data, is hardly worthy of the name. The best education, therefore, is that which combines the classroom and the laboratory, that which involves the learner in the employment of information. Ted Ward sometimes uses the analogy of a split rail fence to communicate this approach to learning. The idea is that theory and practice go together and that periodically there should be an opportunity to discuss and analyze what one has learned and experienced (see Figure 45). Though the "split rail diagram" with its reference to seminars and cognitive input seems especially applicable to colleges and universities, it would be a mistake to think that it does not apply to the local church and, indeed, to any learning situation.

Practical Reflection

(1) While Roland Allen is concerned that basic Christian doctrine be taught to new believers in pioneer areas, his observations and experience lead him to believe that in many cases our practice is to maintain standards and sys-

tems of doctrine that are extrabiblical. And how are these standards and doctrinal systems maintained? First, by making it mandatory that candidates for baptism learn that which is, for many of them, very difficult verbal lessons. Second, by training teachers in the system and seeing to it that they, in turn, maintain the standard. The results have been sterility, dependency, and immaturity.

Allen acknowledges that there is a fine line between teaching the doctrine so that it *reveals* the person of Christ and teaching it so that it *usurps* the place of Christ. But he insists that we so preach Christ that men are truly converted to Him, and that we so instruct the convert that he will endeavor to answer the questions of life by seeking out true doctrine. Only in that way will the churches grow spontaneously:

> It is vain to say that the doctrine was false or falsely stated, and therefore it failed. It failed not because it was false or falsely stated, but because it was mere doctrine divorced from experience. And the preaching of that power of Christ is Gospel; but the other by itself is mere doctrine, and like all doctrine, in itself lifeless.[4]

(2) Perhaps influenced by Allen, and certainly informed by his own experience, Donald McGavran criticizes missionary-evangelists for the "tremendous pressure to perfect" which he believes to be characteristic of the Protestant missionary enterprise. He points out that we have a seemingly irresistible urge to leave off discipling (i.e., making new converts) in order to make "good Christians" out of those who have already come to Christ.[5]

These criticisms by Allen and McGavran are well taken. But they betray a natural tendency to overreact and go too

---

[4]Cf. Roland Allen, *The Spontaneous Expansion of the Church*, 2nd ed. (London: World Dominion Press, 1949), pp. 57–79. The quotation is from p. 68.

[5]Donald McGavran, *How Churches Grow* (New York: Friendship Press, 1966), pp. 93–101.

far in the opposite direction. The antidote to a lifeless, though true, doctrine is not to be found in a lessened zeal for true doctrine, but in a greater dependence on the Holy Spirit and an increased confidence in true converts. And the root of the "perfection problem(!)" is not so much our urge to perfect believers, but our failure to continue with evangelism. The diagnoses, therefore, are partly correct, and remedies are required. But we must exercise care lest the cure be worse than the disease.

(3) If our analysis of the usual approach in pioneer situations is correct, it may account in part for the state of affairs in existing churches as well. To what do we attribute the seeming general dearth of Bible knowledge? Have we a lack of Bible instruction in our churches? Perhaps. But it may be that the problem goes even deeper. If a person attends three religious gatherings a week totaling four hours, he will have attended a cumulative total of 8,320 hours of religious services by the time he is forty years of age. By contrast, the average university student receives his bachelor's degree after spending but 2,176 hours in the classroom![6] The amount of instructional time may be a factor, but we are persuaded that the quality of the instruction is the basic problem and that for two reasons.

First, a significant program of instruction is not available or is not apparent to the believer (particularly the new believer) in most churches. The Bible and various other books are utilized. But much instruction is hit-and-miss (more miss than hit) and is neither carefully laid out so the believer can see the sweep of it, nor carefully programed to proceed in stages from the elemental to the complex. As a consequence, the believer seldom knows where he is in the program, and hardly ever has a sense of progressing from one plateau to another.

---

[6]Statistics quoted in Paul Benjamin, *The Growing Congregation*, rev. ed. (Cincinnati: Standard Publishing, 1972), pp. 33–34.

Second, all too often doctrine is divorced from life. "Unfortunately," writes Lawrence Richards, "we evangelicals have been trained to think of and to read Scripture in terms of 'truth to be understood' rather than 'reality to live.'"[7] Instead of fencing off doctrine from life, or the sacred from the secular, it would appear that we need to mend our instructional fences in the way suggested by Ted Ward!

ME-3 illustration: The work of the Wycliffe Bible Translators among the Tzeltals of Mexico is a scintillating example of the kind of instruction which, according to the data just examined, is most effective. In this particular case the problem of giving Christian instruction to the converts was compounded by the illiteracy of the Tzeltals. Once the church came into existence, believers were gathered for Sunday services that were approximately six hours long! The services were led by Tzeltal leaders on a rotating basis. Comparatively new believers who nevertheless had qualifications for preaching and teaching assumed those responsibilities after being checked out by missionary teachers on the Scripture passages being used. During the Sunday school time the entire congregation was divided up and assigned to classes where the Bible was taught. Each class and its teacher(s) had one primary lesson that was given week after week. During the week they were to share with a neighbor what they had learned. The basic ideas and Scripture passages were memorized. Questions were answered by pointing to the relevant Scripture passage, even if the student was illiterate. Believers were allowed to progress to the next class (with its more advanced teaching) only upon passing an "examination" and on the testimony of a neighbor to the effect that they were living according to the truth of the lesson! Within a few years the Tzeltal Church had grown to 8,000 believers, including 120 be-

---

[7]Lawrence O. Richards, *A New Face for the Church* (Grand Rapids: Zondervan, 1970), p. 178.

lievers who could read and possessed the spiritual qualifications of a pastor!

Faith and Worship

Biblical Principles and Precedents

Recently in a church in Venezuela, a missionary was conducting a Sunday morning worship service. After the singing of some hymns and choruses, the giving of the announcements and the collecting of the tithes and offerings, the question was asked of the congregation, "How many of you believe that you have worshiped God this morning?" Not a single person responded affirmatively. The missionary then asked, "What is worship?" No one seemed to know. Let us see what the Bible says about worship.

The Biblical Definition of Worship

There are at least six Greek words in the New Testament which can be translated worship. Each one reveals some aspect of what worship is.

(1) *Proskuneō* is the most common word for worship. It is a composite word which literally means "to kiss towards." It could easily be translated "adore."

(2) *Sebazomai* depicts an act of reverential awe and fear. Its noun form was used as a title of the Roman emperors from Caesar Augustus onward. In Acts 25:21 this title is used of the tyrant Nero.

(3) The word *eusebeō* is related to *sebazomai* and indicates piety or reverence. The noun form is often translated "godliness."

(4) *Therapeuō* literally means "to heal" and this by manipulation of the hands as in a massage. In Acts 17:25 worship in the form of such service with the hands is expressly

denied to be a legitimate form of worship as far as the true
God is concerned.

(5) and (6) *Latreuō* and *leitourgeō* both mean a service
rendered to God. "*Leitourgeō* is the fulfillment of an office
in a representative sense while *latreuō* is service to the deity
on the part of both priest and laity."[8]

In summary, the New Testament meaning of worship is
adoration accompanied by some sort of service rendered
to the one who inspires reverence.

A good illustration of true worship is seen in the leper
who came to Jesus (Matt. 8:1–4). A literal translation of
verse 2 would be: "And behold, when a leper had come to
him, he worshiped him by saying, Lord, if you will it, you
are able to make me clean." Here the word for worship is
proskuneō. It involves three elements: (1) realization of the
lordship of Jesus Christ; (2) recognition of His sovereign
will; and (3) recognition of His power. This is true worship. The leper did not worship because he was going to be
healed nor was he healed because he worshiped. He worshiped by recognizing the sovereign power resident in the
Lord. If he had not been healed, he still would have worshiped.

The Biblical Pattern of a Worship Service

Strangely, the Pauline Epistles do not use the word *proskuneō* except in I Corinthians 14. But this passage is very
instructive. It teaches us how true worship is to be encouraged and carried out.

If therefore the whole church should assemble together
and all speak in tongues, and ungifted men or unbelievers
enter, will they not say that you are mad? But if all proph-
esy, and an unbeliever or an ungifted man enters, he is
convicted by all, he is called to account by all; the secrets of

---

[8]C. Abbott-Smith, *A Manual Greek Lexicon of the New Testament* (Edinburgh: T. and T. Clark, 1964), p. 266.

his heart are disclosed; and so he will fall on his face and worship God, declaring that God is certainly among you. What is the outcome then, brethren? When you assemble, each one has a psalm, has a teaching, has a revelation, has a tongue, has an interpretation. Let all things be done for edification. (I Cor. 14:23-26)

It is disclosure of the secrets of the heart and the detection of the presence of the Lord, accompanied by the realization of accountability to God, that provoke worship. The activity described by Paul is characterized, first of all, by a heavy reliance upon revealed truth. The psalm, the teaching, the prophecy, the revelation, and the tongue all have their origin in God and are revealed to man. Second, there is a total participation by believers. "Each one" is said to have a part. Third, there is clarity of expression. This is the theme of the passage. Prophecy is more useful than tongues because it can be understood. Fourth, there is orderliness. Although each one participates, the participation is by turn (v. 27). Fifth, there is critical reception of the message. While the prophets are speaking, the listeners pass judgment on what is being said (v. 29). It is this kind of simple service designed to edify the believer that provokes worship.

Worship and the Lord's Supper

The Lord's Supper was instituted just before Jesus' betrayal (Matt. 26; Mark 14; Luke 22). It became a regular observance of the early church (Acts 2:42-47; 20:6, 7; I Cor. 11:20-34). The most complete passages on the Lord's Supper are the Synoptic accounts of its institution and the Pauline direction as to its practice in the Corinthian church. Though the other apostles had been present when Jesus instituted the Lord's Supper, the apostle Paul claimed to have received his instructions concerning its observance directly from the risen Lord (I Cor. 11:23), just as he had received his gospel (Gal. 1:11, 12). Paul found it necessary to correct certain abuses that had characterized Corinthian practice of the Supper and he did so in I Corinthians 11:20–34. Due to its relevance to local church practice, we concentrate here on some important lessons to be gained from this passage.

First, the mode of observance of the Lord's Supper had the appearance of a common meal, even though it had a very special significance (v. 21).

Second, the observance involved the giving of thanks and praise (v. 24). The word *eucharisteō,* which means to give thanks, is used here and in Luke 22:19. In Matthew and Mark *eucharisteō* is used with reference to the cup, while *eulogeō,* which means to speak well or ascribe praise, is used with reference to the bread.

Third, the Supper was in remembrance of the Lord (vv. 24, 25). *Anamnēsis* does not mean simply "memory of," however; it connotes a realization of the abiding presence of the Lord.

Fourth, the frequency with which the Lord's Supper is to be observed is not specified, but the implication of the phrase "as often as" (v. 26) is that it is to be observed regularly and frequently. This interpretation of the phrase is in accordance with what we know of early church practice.

Fifth, observance of the Lord's Supper is a means of proclaiming (*katangellō*) the Lord's death until He who is spiritually present comes corporeally (v. 26).

Sixth, the Lord's Supper is for those who are worthy; that is, those who are believers and have examined themselves to make sure that they are in right relationship with the Lord (vv. 27, 28).

Seventh, chastening results from participating in the Lord's Supper unworthily (vv. 29–32).

In planting a new church in the Third World, three erroneous assumptions are commonly made. The first assumption is that if people come to faith in God through

Christ they will naturally know how God desires to be worshiped. This is true only in part, if at all. Instruction is needed.

The second assumption is that the worship which is part of the missionary-evangelist's tradition is biblical worship. The likelihood is that genuine biblical worship would entail much more participation, spontaneity, and feeling.

The third assumption is that all aspects of indigenous worship are inherently wrong. Not necessarily so. Silent prayer, drums and other native instruments, and certain forms of drama and dance may be used to make worship more biblical and meaningful. In short, neither Western nor indigenous forms of worship should be introduced or discarded uncritically.

The Relation of the Holy Spirit to Worship

No discussion of worship would be complete without some mention of the role of the Holy Spirit in worship. When Jesus spoke to the woman by the well, He said that the hour had come in which true worshipers should worship in Spirit and in truth (John 4:23). In I Corinthians 14, which deals with the gifts of the Spirit, the simple worship service is described. From this we may infer that the true worshiper is equipped by the Spirit. When taken together the two passages teach that the Spirit both motivates the believer to worship and equips him for that worship. Thus it would seem that no true worship is offered until the worshiper is controlled by the Holy Spirit and is using the gifts of the Spirit. When this happens, the very life of the believer is to be described in terms of a service of worship (Eph. 5:18-20).

Relevant Research

The Nature of Worship

Anthropologists are in general agreement that worship has been a part of the experience of mankind from the

earliest times.[9] As might be expected, anthropologists
characterize early worship in accordance with their own
biases. To the naturalist, worship is usually seen as an effort to placate, cajole, or appease supernatural powers of
one sort or another.[10] In his popular book *The Silent Language,* Edward T. Hall classifies religious ceremonies
under the category of "defense"—along with military defense and health practices![11] As a matter of fact, those who
have had any appreciable exposure to non-Christian
religions—those who have seen non-Christians at their various shrines, temples, and home altars—will attest to the
fact that much, if not most, of such worship tends to cor-
roborate the conclusions of social scientists. In fact, the
worship of many people degenerates to appeasing the
supernatural. But true Christian worship is first and
foremost the honoring of God as God, and the ascription
of praise and thanksgiving to Him for what He is and has
done. It does not exclude petition for provision and protection because God invites His children to approach Him
for help in time of need. But worship is not wholly, or even
primarily, petition. It is a recognition that God is and that
He has already provided life and sustenance and salvation.
Thus Christian worship is—or should be—something
much different from anything practiced by the unregenerate man and something which will be all but impossible
for the unregenerate man to understand or interpret.

Worship and Environment

Worship is often associated with certain sacred places,
and, if not *confined* to those places, is nevertheless rendered more significant and efficacious when practiced in
those places. The Samaritan woman entertained just such

---

[9]Cf. John B. Noss, *Man's Religions,* 3rd ed. (New York: Macmillan,
1963), pp. 4–31.
[10]Cf. Peter B. Hammond, *An Introduction to Cultural and Social Anthropology* (New York: Macmillan, 1971), pp. 258–93.
[11]Hall, *Silent Language,* pp. 57–59, 92.

an idea (John 4:20). Indeed, Judaism with its temple worship reinforced such a notion. Biblical Christianity is a universal faith in that it knows of no spot on earth that is more sacred than any other, or where one ought to worship in preference to any other. At the same time, corporate worship does require a place of meeting, and a group of Christians—just as any other religious group—will be affected by environmental factors.

Most such factors will be obvious to all. In many pioneer situations, however, the matter of providing a place for worship will loom so large as to obscure other environmental factors that are important. How else can one explain the lack of provision of simple embellishments (a flower arrangement, for example) which, in even the most simple surroundings, help create an atmosphere for the worship of the God of creation and order? Or, how else can one explain the mistakes that are built into numerous houses of worship from the very first? James White, for example, decries both the long, narrow hall and the separated-transept types of church buildings and predicts that, in the future, church architecture will be much more conducive to true Christian worship.

> Probably the present-day experiments which have placed the congregation in transepts or other separate areas will be little imitated. Such arrangements make preaching very difficult. They also foster the illusion of two or more separate congregations instead of one body gathered about the Lord's table.
>
> Most likely the audience hall type of long naves, sloping floors, and comfortable pews will be rare in the future. It is quite possible that galleries will be little used. With the liturgical centers as close as possible to the congregation, the people will have easier access to them and the notion of certain places in the church as holy spots, monopolized by the clergy and choir, will be lessened considerably. The impression that God is beyond the east window—will be avoided by centrally planned buildings.[12]

---

[12]James White, *Protestant Worship and Church Architecture* (New York: Oxford University Press, 1964), p. 177.

Practical Reflection

Perhaps no aspect of corporate Christian experience has been the object of more criticism recently than has the hour or so of formal worship on Sunday morning. The criticism is much more evident in the Western world (especially North America) than it is in the non-Western world. Perhaps that is because Westerners tend to be more self-critical. Perhaps non-Westerners simply "grin and bear it," or, quite possibly, they register their disappointment by staying away. In any case, reflection is called for.

Third World peoples probably find the usual Christian worship service too Western. Western hymns, Western instruments, Western sermons, and Western abruptness—all of these and more give Christian worship a stamp of foreignness which does not necessarily reflect true spirituality.

In the West one difficulty is that of meeting the expectations and needs of various segments of the average congregation: resident older believers, younger believers, and new believers; and visiting believers, and unbelievers. This difficulty can be partially resolved by instructing the congregation in the true nature of worship and by striking a balance as far as the expectations of the various segments are concerned (see Figure 46).

FIGURE 46

The Balanced Worship Service

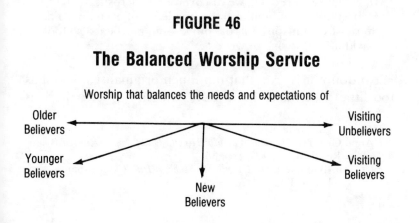

Worship that balances the needs and expectations of

Older Believers

Younger Believers

New Believers

Visiting Unbelievers

Visiting Believers

Another problem in the West is that many congregations feel that the worship service is uninteresting. Representing more progressive evangelical pastors, David Mains uses the phrase, "worship that is pompous and dull," to describe the ordinary Protestant worship service.[13] His basic contentions are that leaders err in a number of ways: (1) they mistake the real meaning of worship; (2) they call our hodgepodge of independent and unrelated activities at the 11:00 o'clock hour on Sunday morning a "worship service"; (3) they see a necessary connection between pews, maroon carpets, elegant chandeliers, and vaulted ceilings, on one hand, and "worship," on the other; (4) they fail to plan for meaningful worship.

Anne Ortlund, wife of the pastor of a thriving congregation in Los Angeles, agrees—for the most part at least. She insists that we must be scriptural, that we must give creative thought to our worship services, and that neither the repetition of traditional forms nor the supposedly spiritual unstructured service is the answer.

> Where does the idea come from that if you're "in the Spirit" you can eliminate preparation?
> I'm not sympathetic to the philosophy behind it. . . .
> But all of our ideas of worship must be rooted firmly in the Scriptures, and I find in them no high praise that was just off-the-cuff. . . .
> Psalm 34 is a great hymn of praise. Did it just flow out of David like water? Well, we discover it's an acrostic, with the Hebrew alphabet built into the first letter of each line. The Spirit of God inspired it, of course—but maybe it also took David a lot of work to write it.[14]

No doubt it is true that too much originality (as well as too little) can make for a dull church.[15] But if there is

---

[13]Mains, *Full Circle,* pp. 52–55.

[14]Anne Ortlund, *Up with Worship: How to Quit Playing Church* (Glendale, CA: Regal Books, 1975), p. 36.

[15]Cf. Dan Baumann, *All Originality Makes a Dull Church* (Santa Ana, CA: Vision House Press, 1976).

anything that we don't need in a new work for Christ, it is simply more of the same thing that we have known previously and elsewhere—especially when it comes to the worship service.

ME-1 illustration: Numerous churches have revived interest in their worship services by initiating meaningful change. Some new churches have attracted large numbers of people from the very first by means of innovative worship. One such church is Chicago's Circle Church.[16] The new congregation has not had the advantage of stained-glass windows and maroon carpets! In fact, they meet in a Teamsters' Union Hall! Chairs are arranged in such a way that the congregation is seated in a semicircle around a raised platform in one corner where the ministers are located. The choir and other musical groups may be placed along the side or in the rear of the hall.

Founding pastor David Mains defines worship in terms of praise and adoration to God. Since emphasis is placed upon the preaching of the Word during the Sunday morning service, he calls it the "Service of Worship and Instruction."

The "Service of Worship and Instruction" is usually divided into three sections (though flexibility is the rule):

The Approach to God in Worship
God Speaking Through His Written Word
The Response of Obedience

The first section is given exclusively to worship (in the sense of praise and adoration). In special and congregational music, emphasis must be placed on the words more than on the style of music. In prayer and Scripture reading, the words must be addressed to God and speak of His greatness and worth. Mains writes that it is not unusual for

---

[16]Cf. Mains, *Full Circle*, pp. 71–81, for a complete description of the services at Circle Church.

a staff member to spend one or two hours writing the invocation!

The second section of the service highlights Scripture reading and the sermon. Mains's practice is to emphasize a single basic theme in the sermon—a theme echoed throughout the entire service. This theme is expressed in a single "purpose sentence" which is formulated weeks in advance by whoever is scheduled to preach. The sermon is reinforced by teaching aids such as overhead transparencies, slides, recordings, and so forth.

The third section of the service encourages appropriate response to God on the part of the congregation. This response is not a perfunctory rendering of a responsive reading, but asks for genuine commitment to truth expressed in behavioral terms.

Biblically-oriented and culturally-relevant worship services such as those at Circle Church are bound to attract believers and unbelievers alike.

Faith and Service

Biblical Principles and Precedents

The Basis of Service

One of the more extensive themes running throughout Scripture is that of service. It is said that when the Son of God became a man, He became similar to a slave; the implication is that the very nature of man is that of a servant (Phil. 2:7). Man is commanded to serve (Matt. 4:10). The early church believed that men are "remade" in order to serve (I Thess. 1:9). A solid basis for service is seen, therefore, in man's nature, God's command, and the beliefs and practice of the early church.

The Semantics of Service

The New Testament uses several words in connection with the service of the believer: *doulos, diakonos, leitourgos, latreuō* (from *latris*), *oiketēs* and *hupēretēs*.

The *doulos* was a slave. This word in its various forms is the one most commonly used in the New Testament in connection with service. The Lord had much to say about this type of servant. No one can be a *slave* of two masters (Matt. 6:24). When told to do something, the good *slave* does it (Matt. 8:9). Those who wish to be great in the kingdom of heaven should first be *servants (slaves)* (Matt. 20:27). The *slave* is never greater than his master (Matt. 10:24). An alert *slave* of God will be rewarded when Christ comes again (Matt. 25:21; Luke 12:37). This and much more was spoken by Christ about the *doulos*.

Paul also spoke about the *doulos*. He confessed that he was a *slave* of Jesus Christ (Rom. 1:1; Gal. 1:10; Titus 1:1). Men are *slaves* to whom they render obedience (Rom. 6:16). All were *slaves* to sin (Rom. 6:17, 20). But the believer should be a *slave* of righteousness (Rom. 6:18). Obedience to his master is the chief characteristic of a *slave* (Col. 3:22). Thus if one tries to please men, he may place his *servant (slave)* relation to Christ in jeopardy (Gal. 1:10).

Another common word for servant is *diakonos*. While the derivation of this compound word is doubtful, the meaning is clear from its usage. It (including cognates) is often used in connection with the serving of food (Matt. 8:15; 25:44; Mark 1:13; Luke 17:8; Acts 6:2). It is used of bringing relief money to the poor saints of Jerusalem (Rom. 15:25; II Cor. 8:4). The idea always seems to be: "Give to another or do for another that which is necessary to his life." In the spiritual realm it is used of bringing to men things necessary for their spiritual life. Thus there are the ministry of the Word of Christ (I Cor. 3:5), the ministry of reconciliation (II Cor. 5:18), and the ministry of the Spirit in bringing life (II Cor. 3:6).

While *doulos* relates the believer to the *person* of his Lord, *diakonos* relates the believer to the *work* of his Lord—work to be carried out in the world. Jesus came into the world to be a *diakonos* (Mark 10:45). Greatness requires faithfulness at the level of servant (Matt. 23:11). Very soon after the birth of the Church, the apostles established the office of deacon (Acts 6:2-6). These men ministered to the physical body (Acts 6:1-3) and to the spiritual man (Acts 8:5). Those who wished to be deacons had to be highly qualified (Acts 6:3; I Tim. 3:8-10).

A third kind of servant was the *leitourgos*. He was one "who discharged a public office at his own expense."[17] The word (and its cognates) is used in connection with the public ministry of the priest in the temple (Luke 1:23; Heb. 10:11), monetary giving (II Cor. 9:12), the physical affliction of the apostle Paul on behalf of the Philippians (Phil. 2:17), the aid which the Philippian church gave to Paul (Phil. 2:30), government officials ruling for God (Rom. 13:6), the angelic ministry (Heb. 1:7), Christ's high-priestly ministry in the heavenly sanctuary (Heb. 8:2), and the duties of the apostles and teachers in the Antioch church (Acts 13:2). By virtue of the fact that believers constitute a royal priesthood, the *leitourgos* ministry belongs to all of them (I Peter 2:5).

The word *latris* also describes a servant. While the noun form is not found in the New Testament, the verb form, *latreuō*, is used in reference to the service of both priest and people. This type of service was to be rendered exclusively to God (Matt. 4:10). The heathen perverted this service and worshiped the creature rather than the Creator (Rom. 1:25). Now, it is this service which Paul has in mind when he speaks of the offering of the believer's body to God as one's "reasonable service" (Rom. 12:1, 2).

The *oiketēs* was the domestic servant who lived in the house of his master (Acts 10:7; Rom. 14:4; I Peter 2:18). Being a *house*-servant, the *oiketēs* had a closer relationship to the family than did most other servants. It is significant that Jesus uses this word when He affirms that no servant can serve two masters (Luke 16:13).

Finally, *hupēretēs* is also used for "servant." This com-

---

[17]Abbott-Smith, *Greek Lexicon*, p. 267.

pound word literally means "under-rower." It was used to describe the rowers on the ships of the Mediterranean Sea. In the New Testament it is used to describe officers of the Sanhedrin or synagogue (Matt. 26:58; Luke 4:20). It aptly describes the work of John Mark as he accompanied Paul and Barnabas (Acts 13:5). Note that the word conveys the idea of being a servant to a government minister in an official capacity. John Mark was serving the apostles on an official mission. Therefore, he is described as a *hupēretēs*. Paul, in fact, uses the word to characterize himself as an "officer of Christ" (I Cor. 4:1).

All of these words are used to describe the servant of God. Underlying each word is the idea of "doing the will of another." This is the gist of being a servant. The servant of God is one who does the will of God.

Relevant Research

In his book *East to Eden?*[18] Charles Corwin points out something that has been almost universally observed by those who have lived and worked in the Orient for a period of time. Despite the popularity of some of the non-Christian Eastern religions in the West, down through history those religions have not produced anything like the outpouring of compassionate service to mankind that has characterized biblical Christianity. Hospitals, leprosaria, literacy campaigns, and many other humanitarian services have accompanied the progress of Christianity across the face of the earth. Christianity's rivals cannot begin to match that record. In fact, research will reveal that works of compassion undertaken by Buddhists or adherents of some other Eastern religion usually originated after Christian enterprises of the same stripe were initiated in the same general area.

---

[18]Charles Corwin, *East to Eden?* (Grand Rapids: Eerdmans, 1972).

Practical Reflection

It is unfortunate that Christian service and witness often seem to be competing concerns in Christian outreach when, in fact, both are biblical and complementary. Paul said that he was called to be a minister *and* a witness (Acts 26:16). One reason for this tension is that service enterprises such as hospitals and educational institutions have a way of preempting finances and energies so that evangelism and witness tend to get crowded out. Another reason is that some of those in the service enterprises have downgraded verbal witness and insisted that acts of compassion are the only witness that is needed. Still another reason is that some specialist organizations have majored in certain types of Christian service, and others in evangelism—a fact that tends to foster competitiveness within the Church.

In any case, when we come to a localized ministry such as planting a new church, the matter of service ministries both within and without the church is often disregarded or unduly delayed. *As soon as men and women are converted,* the matter of their service within and without the church should be considered. As George Peters writes, "Service is not only for the perfect, it is a means of perfecting the saints."[19] The fact that service has often been neglected should not be allowed to set the precedent. Scripture is our guide. Even the emerging church should constitute itself as a caring community. Every believer should have something to do for Christ.

First, special attention should be given to needs within the group of believers. Some way of ascertaining these needs should be determined. Then these needs should become concerns for prayer *and* service. Of course, the needs which arise as a product of church life (such as cleaning, ushering, child care, etc.) become opportunities for service as well.

---

[19]George Peters, "Pauline Patterns of Church-Mission Relationships," *Evangelical Missions Quarterly,* vol. 9, no. 6 (1973), p. 116.

Second, the believing community should make it a matter of high priority to find out the felt and real needs of
the target community. Most communities will be so sur-
prised by the presence of a group of believers who really
want to serve that they will sit up and take notice of the
church—some for the first time.

ME-1 illustration: Several years ago the young people of
the Evangelical Free Church in Lincoln, Nebraska, considered what they could do in order to better serve Christ.
They realized that there was not a great deal of poverty in
their area, but they knew that there were needs, many of
them both *felt* and *real.* Which ones could they meet? They
decided that they could serve best by offering themselves
as tutors of retarded children and slow learners in the
community. This they did on a regular basis. For the first
time many local citizens looked upon the church as a servant of the community. Unlike the vast majority of their
peers whose lifestyle made demands upon the community,
these young people were giving themselves in meaningful
service to others. As a result, the church experienced a
renewed growth.

Faith and Witness

Biblical Principles and Precedents

To whom was the Great Commission directed? That
question has plagued the Church down through the centuries. Generally speaking, the sixteenth-century Reformers believed that it was given to—and fulfilled by—the
original apostles, and that it does not directly apply to
anyone who came after them. However, such men as Adri-
an Saravia (1531–1613), Justinian von Weltz (1621–1668),
and William Carey (1761–1834) argued that the Great
Commission applies to the Church wherever and whenever it exists.

There is a sense, of course, in which the various commissionings of those early followers of Christ had special application to them. In the first place, only certain individuals could qualify to be witnesses (*martures*, Acts 1:8) in the sense of having been personally present during our Lord's ministry, death, and resurrection. This was a special qualification of apostleship (Acts 1:21, 22). In the second place, the risen Lord did give certain persons as special gifts to His Church—apostles and evangelists among them. However, it is apparent that witnessing and evangelizing in the early church were not confined to those designated as special apostles. Yielded to and directed by the Holy Spirit, ordinary believers witnessed and evangelized. They went everywhere preaching the Word (i.e., *euaggelizō*, evangelizing—Acts 8:4). In fact, as John Nevius asserts, "A great advance had been made before the Apostle Paul was called from his home by Barnabas to assist the disciples already gathered at Antioch."[20] Unquestionably, Nevius is correct when he concludes that it was largely through the efforts of ordinary Christians that Christianity found its way to "Cyprus, Syria, Cilicia, Egypt and as far west as Rome."[21] And it should be remembered that those believers were still young in the faith. *Believers were testifying while learning.* And, after being formed, *churches witnessed while growing* (I Thess. 1:8).

While there were distinctions in the early church which were analogous to the distinction we make between the clergy and the laity today, the difference was not that the "clergy" did the witnessing and evangelizing while the "laity" simply supported them in such endeavors. Rather, there was a spontaneous witness on the part of the believers that was little short of earthshaking in the Mediterranean world. In the manner of Christ, who instituted the "master plan of evangelism,"[22] the leaders of the early

---

[20]John L. Nevius, *Planting and Development of Missionary Churches* (Nutley, NJ: Presbyterian and Reformed, 1958), p. 59.

[21]Ibid.

[22]Robert E. Coleman, *The Master Plan of Evangelism* (Westwood, NJ: Fleming H. Revell, 1963).

church both served as models and prepared the believers for these tasks (I Cor. 4:16; Eph. 4:11, 12). Had the witness of the early church been confined to that of the apostles and evangelists, the picture of the growth of that church would have been very different from that which we see in the New Testament.

Relevant Research

The "Strachan Theorem"

After doing research on Communism, Islam, Jehovah's Witnesses, the Latter-day Saints, and other movements, and after a careful study of relevant literature, the late director of the Latin America Mission, K. Kenneth Strachan, settled on a principle which became the cornerstone of *Evangelism-in-Depth* strategy. It is now known as the "Strachan theorem": "The successful expansion of any movement is in direct proportion to its success in mobilizing and occupying its total membership in constant propagation of its beliefs."[23] As George Peters points out, it is regrettable that Strachan did not go on to discover other dynamic principles of evangelism and church multiplication, but this theorem is indeed an important principle.[24] Its importance has been demonstrated in "saturation evangelism" movements around the world as well as in the study of still other growing religious movements.[25]

Life-related Witness

It should be noted that witness seems to be especially effective when it is related to contemporary issues with which people are concerned. One need not completely agree with Gabriel Fackre's indictment of contemporary

---

[23] *Evangelism in Depth* (Chicago: Moody Press, 1961), p. 25.
[24] George W. Peters, *Saturation Evangelism* (Grand Rapids: Zondervan, 1970), p. 53.
[25] David J. Hesselgrave, "What Causes Religious Movements to Grow?" in *Dynamic Religious Movements*, pp. 319-20.

evangelism in order to appreciate his emphasis on relating Christian faith and witness to contemporary issues such as nuclear war, ecological disaster, abortion, marriage, and biomedical engineering.[26] This is a most natural way of witness, and research into the rapid growth of other religious movements supports Fackre's contention.[27]

The Weakness of Campaign Evangelism

In spite of the potential in lay witness to effect world evangelization and growth in the local church, research indicates that not all efforts to harness this potential are successful. In fact, such highly organized efforts as *Evangelism-in-Depth* and *Here's Life, America* have often failed to produce the anticipated church growth.[28] The limited success of these and similar campaigns, however, is not attributed by researchers to the employment of lay witness but rather to the *programing* of lay witness. If lay witness is to result in church growth, it is doubtful that it can be imposed upon the churches from outside the churches or be geared only or primarily to one specific period of time. Witness must come from within the churches as a part of their ongoing outreach. In other words, research seems to indicate that if believers in the churches are not revived and spiritually alive to their ongoing responsibility in the world, churches will not grow and multiply as they did in the New Testament era.

Practical Reflection

There can be little doubt that when it comes to church growth, both the professionals and the nonprofessionals

---

[26]Gabriel Fackre, *Do and Tell: Engagement Evangelism in the '70s* (Grand Rapids: Eerdmans, 1973), pp. 56–57.

[27]Hesselgrave, "What Causes Religious Movements to Grow?" p. 306.

[28]Cf. Peters, *Saturation Evangelism*, pp. 72–77, for an analysis of *Evangelism-in-Depth's* contribution to church growth; and C. Peter Wagner, "Who Found It?" and James F. Engel, "Great Commission or Great Commotion?" *Eternity*, September 1977, pp. 13–19, for an analysis of the results of the *Here's Life, America* campaign.

must be involved in witness—the former equipping, modeling, and participating, and the latter learning and doing. When this is the program, God will cause churches to grow.

Where and why have breakdowns in this normal pattern of Christian witness occurred?

(1) Breakdown number one occurs within the hearts, not the heads, of leaders and laity alike. The apostles had three years of instruction at the feet of the master Teacher and Example, but they were faltering witnesses at best until they were infused and empowered by the Holy Spirit at Pentecost. Post-Pentecost believers were powerful witnesses *before* there was opportunity for them to receive prolonged instruction. The essential ingredient for witness, then, is the inner working of the Holy Spirit. We must wait upon the Spirit before we proceed to witness (Acts 1:8).

(2) Breakdown number two occurs when church leaders fail to encourage the spontaneous witness of new believers. There are risks in such witness, of course. But God takes a risk with every one of us. What is needed is encouragement that engenders confidence. The new believer has a fresh experience to report. He has numerous contacts with the world. Little is to be gained by putting him on the shelf until he matures, except staleness of experience, separation from unbelievers, and sterility of witness.

(3) Breakdown number three occurs when leaders prescribe witness without preparing witnesses, and when they challenge believers to witness without channeling that witness. This may seem to contradict what we have said above, but in reality it is no contradiction at all. All of us have known certain Christians who maintain the spontaneity and simplicity of their initial witness over long periods of time—even throughout a lifetime. But most Christians soon encounter problems and questions from unbelievers, problems and questions that deserve intelligent, biblical answers. Discouragement and withdrawal from the arena of encounter may result. When this occurs, simply to pre-

scribe witness and challenge the believer to spread the gospel may accomplish little more than to arouse feelings of guilt. Experience teaches us that the wise leader *trains* his people in soul-winning and *channels* that effort in a program of outreach. All may not witness in the same way, or with the same effect, because Christians are people and people differ from one another. But all Christians can be fruitfully engaged in some aspect of a well-rounded program of outreach and witness. Such involvement accomplishes more than a witness to nonbelievers. It also confirms the faith of the Christian!

(4) Breakdown number four (closely related to number three) occurs when the outreach programs of churches in missionary circumstances (emerging churches) are patterned after those of the older churches. New churches require a larger proportion of their membership to be actively engaged in outreach than is usually the case in established churches. Donald McGavran emphasizes that if new churches are to grow, a larger number of church leaders must be "heading out" into the community, rather than simply serving the church *within* the church.[29]

(5) Breakdown number five occurs when church leaders place a higher value on special imported programs and personnel than they do on the potential inherent within the local church. This is not to denigrate the importance of such programs. Robert Schuller emphasizes the value of imported personnel who can attract the attention of the public to the new work.[30] Eugene Nida points out that something akin to entropy in the physical realm also occurs in religious movements such as churches—that is, they tend to "cool off."[31] Personnel and programs periodi-

---

[29]McGavran, *How Churches Grow*, pp. 139–40.

[30]Robert H. Schuller, *Your Church Has Great Possibilities* (Glendale, CA: Regal Publications, 1974), pp. 114–16.

[31]Eugene A. Nida, "Dynamics of Church Growth," in *Church Growth and Christian Mission*, ed. Donald A. McGavran (New York: Harper and Row, 1965), pp. 170–75.

cally imported from without the local church may serve to revive God's people in addition to winning some who are lost. But when such special programs supplant the ongoing outreach of the local believers, or upset that outreach in such a way that it becomes difficult to keep it going, then something is seriously amiss and reevaluation is in order. It seems to us that precisely this is happening over and over again today.

ME-1 illustration: One of the best-known programs of lay witness leading to growth in the local church is that of the Coral Ridge Presbyterian Church in Fort Lauderdale, Florida. In 1961 Pastor D. James Kennedy accepted the invitation of some 45 people who wanted to organize a church. The number dwindled to 17 before the church began to grow. As a result of a program of visitation-evangelism, the membership increased to 2,000 by 1970. As of 1978, Sunday morning worship attendance exceeded 5,000.

The basic program of the Coral Ridge church is set forth in the book *Evangelism Explosion.*[32] Warren Bathke summarizes the essence of the plan:

> Kennedy's plan is a simple one. Train briefly—then go out immediately. He instructs a small class of ten or twenty people for thirty minutes. Then he sends them out in groups of three into homes in the area. After sixteen weeks, each home visitor becomes a trainer for another person in the program. After nine years of training sessions he had three hundred home visitors going out on visitation.
>
> The emphasis of the training is on learning to tell the Gospel in a positive and gracious manner. Detailed instructions are given from initial contact to total involvement of an individual in a church.
>
> As one might imagine, to put together the elements of many specialists into one harmonious program is a difficult

---

[32]D. James Kennedy, *Evangelism Explosion*, rev. ed. (Wheaton, IL: Tyndale House, 1977).

task, yet that seems to be part of the purpose of the church. To have the visitation program stand the test of time is quite another matter.

A church's doctrine does indeed design its mission. For evangelical churches its Gospel mandates outreach and growth. There are many specialists' programs in America that are waiting to be incorporated into one harmonious operation. This is the task of the local church.[33]

The value of Kennedy's approach is attested to, not alone by the growth of his own congregation, but also by the fact that literally hundreds of other congregations have adopted the plan and profited thereby. Nevertheless, it is only one plan among many. It will not work in every community.

Faith and Stewardship

Biblical Principles and Precedents

Stewardship has to do with all that a Christian "possesses"—time and talent as well as treasure. Here, however, we are concerned with stewardship of money and material wealth. The essence of biblical teaching on the subject can be reduced to three very simple but important statements: (1) All that we have is given by God (I Cor. 4:7); (2) That which God gives us is really ours to do with "as we please" (Acts 5:4); (3) Since God has given freely to us, we should also freely give to God and those in need (Matt. 10:8; I John 3:17).

Upon investigation of the biblical record, it will come as a surprise to many that God has much to say about money and material possessions. It is obvious that God had communicated to Cain and Abel the desirability of sacrifice

---

[33]Warren E. Bathke, "Visitation Evangelism: Do We Need It?" *Evangelical Beacon*, 11 July 1978, p. 19.

(Gen. 4). Abraham paid tithes of all that he possessed (Heb. 7:2). The children of Israel were commanded to bring sacrifices and offerings to God (Exod. 30). Jesus reminded us that we should lay up treasure in heaven and that our heart will be where our treasure is (Matt. 6:19–21). We are told that the "love of money" (not money itself) is the "root of all evil" (I Tim. 6:10).

Ralph Martin notes that Paul's teaching on these matters is summed up in seven basic principles emphasized in II Corinthians 8 and 9:[34]

(1) The basis of stewardship is that God has given bountifully to His people.

(2) The most important offering is the commitment of one's own life to God.

(3) All Christian giving is prompted by divine grace, yet is voluntary, eager, and cheerful.

(4) Stewardship is to be offered in accordance with one's ability and the needs of others.

(5) God is no man's debtor.

(6) Churches and their people should be fair and open in their financial dealings.

(7) Concern for the welfare of others creates a bond of love between giver and recipient and calls forth the praise of God.

Relevant Research

The "Protestant Ethic"

It was the sociologist Max Weber who developed the concept of the "Protestant ethic," but the ethic itself has long been a part of Protestantism. Weber simply provided a construct and an analysis of a phenomenon that came to characterize Protestant believers soon after the Reformation. Namely, that as a by-product of attention to the bibli-

---

[34]Ralph P. Martin, *Worship in the Early Church* (Grand Rapids: Eerdmans, 1975), pp. 84–85.

cal teaching on stewardship, Protestants tended to be characterized by industriousness and thrift.[35]

Donald McGavran's studies of world missions and churches have led him to a very similar (if not identical) conclusion. Namely, that once people are redeemed and enter God's family, they tend to raise their standards of living and productivity. He calls this "redemption and lift."[36]

Astute churchmen recognize that while this kind of industry is commendable, it is not an unmixed blessing. John Wesley, for example, realized that this ethic is likely to result in prosperity and wealth, and is apt to lure the affections of believers away from single-hearted devotion to Christ. He concluded that the only solution to the problem is that as believers *earn* more, they should *give* more!

The Sacred and the Secular

Western man especially has a deep-seated inclination to make a radical distinction between the sacred and the secular, neatly dividing his concerns and activities into these two airtight compartments. The distinction has now become a commonplace both in scientific analysis and in the popular mind.

Many non-Western and non-Christian societies, on the other hand, do not make this distinction. All of life is intimately related to deities and spirits, worship and ritual. An informative research project was carried out some twenty years ago at a mission station in the Sepik district of New Guinea.[37] (Perhaps only in a virgin mission field could this kind of study be successfully carried out.) The mission station was a large one with seventy permanent buildings.

------

[35]Max Weber, *The Protestant Ethic and the Spirit of Capitalism*, trans. Talcott Parsons (New York: Scribner, 1958).

[36]Donald McGavran, *Understanding Church Growth* (Grand Rapids: Eerdmans, 1970), pp. 270-88.

[37]O. E. Fountain, "Religion and Economy in Mission Station Relationships," *Practical Anthropology*, vol. 13, no. 2 (1966), pp. 49-58.

The closer each village was to the mission station, the more it was involved in the ordinary business concerns of the station. To study the effect of the business relationships upon the spirituality of the churches, certain measurable qualities of spirituality (attendance, stewardship, etc.) were investigated. It was found that the closer the churches were (geographically) to the mission station, the greater their economic involvement was; *the farther they were from the station, the greater their spirituality proved to be!* Among other conclusions it seems clear that the Western tendency to think of the "business" of living as distinct from stewardship, worship, and "spirituality," had a negative effect in a society that, in spite of its lack of the knowledge of God, nevertheless did not put worship, sacrifice, and ritual in a separate compartment from the production and marketing of goods!

The Psychology of Value

There seems to be a principle (true in many cases if not all cases) according to which the perceived value of something is correlated with one's investment in it. Put in another way, intrinsic value is not the only yardstick by which we evaluate things. If, for example, a person invests energy, money, and time in something, its perceived value goes up accordingly even though the intrinsic value does not change.

This principle is easily testable. Some years ago in our family–owned store we placed identical items in separate displays, one of which was marked at a lower price and the other at a higher price. Though not adjacent, the displays were in the same general location. Our hypothesis was substantiated. Many customers examined the merchandise in both displays and still purchased the higher-priced items, assuming that whatever cost more *had* to be superior.

We feel a certain ambivalence about this kind of phenomenon. On the one hand, it is irrational to place a greater value on an item simply because one pays more for it. But there is a principle here that is powerful and pervasive enough to have influenced the policy of many dynamic religious movements—many of them sell their publications (for example) rather than give them away, or give them only with the understanding that the one who gives them has actually paid for them on the recipient's behalf. This is true of some of the fastest growing religious movements in the world, such as the Jehovah's Witnesses and Soka Gakkai.

Practical Reflection

There are some pronounced tendencies in many church-planting situations which betray the fact that missionary-evangelists do not give enough attention to basic biblical and psychological principles as they relate to stewardship.

(1) There is a tendency to postpone instruction concerning the stewardship of money and material goods. This is perhaps more pronounced in the Third World, but it is not confined to the Third World. There are various reasons for this tendency. One reason is that salvation is a free gift of God (though it cost heaven's best) and we want people to understand that they cannot buy it or merit it. Another reason is that religion in the East, and increasingly in the West, is associated with begging and money-making; and we want people to understand that we are not charity-seekers or charlatans.

Of course, we do not err when we do not seek money for God's work from people who do not know God. But we do err when instruction in Christian stewardship is not given to those who do know God and when we do not encourage them to give proportionately, generously, and gladly.

ME-3 illustration: Two churches are located within a few miles of each other in a certain Asian country. One was founded some twenty-five years ago by a dear missionary lady who appealed for support from the homeland but did no more than pass the collection plate in her congregation of nationals. The other was started somewhat later by a missionary and national pastor working as a team. In this church, as soon as people became believers, they were instructed concerning stewardship and challenged to give so God's work might prosper. Several years ago leaders of both churches were interviewed. Both congregations include some prominent and well-to-do people within their membership. But the first congregation had about thirty members and an average Sunday offering of about ten to twenty dollars. It was still without a pastor because the members "could not afford" to hire one. The second congregation numbered almost two hundred members and had an average Sunday offering of fifteen hundred to two thousand dollars. And in addition, it was starting two daughter churches!

(2) There is a tendency in some situations to allow the church-planting effort to become primarily a financial operation. This is one of the concerns of Roland Allen. He feels that we greatly retard the multiplication of new churches if missionary work becomes a secular operation and finances the chief concern.[38] His reasoning is not difficult to follow. Taking a long look at the apostolic churches he concludes that we are far removed from apostolic practice. In the New Testament period every province and every church was financially independent and assumed obligation for its own teachers and poor. Modern practice in founding churches is to begin by securing a dwelling for the church-planter, some land for a building, necessary equipment for the church, and so forth. Consequently, the planting of churches early becomes a basically "secular business" (Allen's phrase) involving negotiations for real estate, agreements with contractors, and

---

[38]Roland Allen, *Missionary Methods: St. Paul's or Ours?* (Grand Rapids: Eerdmans, 1962), pp. 49-61.

supervision of construction as well as the raising of funds for the entire operation. In this we are as far removed from apostolic practice in action as we are in time.

One must remember that, in part, Allen's conclusion represents a *reaction* against his missionary experience which was not balanced by a corresponding *action* in successfully applying his own principles. With the coming of age of the churches, there is no reason to disdain interdependency, particularly in the founding of new churches. Nevertheless, Allen's criticism should not be brushed aside without serious reflection. When church-planting and renewal cannot occur without the endless importation of foreign funds, and when church-planters become first "ministers of finance" and only secondarily "ministers of the Word," we have strayed from New Testament principles and have jeopardized the future of our mission in the world.

Master Plan Formation

In the preceding chapter we were concerned with the initial care of new converts. Here our concern is for their continued welfare and strengthening. We suggest that two types of records be kept for each believer. First, a record to be filled out by the new believer (perhaps over a period of time) which will reveal his assessment of his talents, interests, and commitments as a Christian (see Figure 47). Second, a record of the progress of each new believer to be kept by his counselor/friend until he has received basic instruction and has been fully integrated into the life of the emerging church (see Figure 48). The time required to accomplish this objective will vary with the individual and cultural environment, but from six to twelve months might be considered average. (Church leaders will be greatly aided in planning the program of the local church if they will use questionnaires to get a reading on older believers as well as new ones.)

FIGURE 47

Questionnaire for New Believers

Name: _____ Sex: _____

Address: _____

Telephone: _____ Date of profession of faith: _____

Age: Under 20· _____; 20 to 30 _____; 30 to 40 _____;
     40 to 50 _____; over 50 _____

Marital status: Married _____; Single _____; Widowed _____;
     Divorced _____

Family members and relationship to the above: _____

_____

- -

1. Do you have a Bible? Yes_____ No_____

2. Will you join a Bible Instruction Class? Yes_____ No_____

3. Which of the following worship opportunities will you observe?
   a. Public: Sunday A.M._____ Sunday P.M._____ Other_____
   b. Family_____
   c. Personal_____

4. What abilities and interests do you have which might be used in the
   service of Christ? _____

   _____

5. In accordance with Romans 12 and I Corinthians 12, will you look
   to the Lord for the provision of such spiritual gifts as He may give
   you? _____
   And are you desirous to receive counseling as to the presence and use
   of those gifts in Christ's service?

   _____

6. Have you shared your testimony of faith in Christ with your family?_____ friends?_____ fellow believers?_____

7. Are you willing to share your testimony with others as the Lord and
   church leaders provide opportunity?_____

8. In accordance with Acts 20:35 and I Corinthians 16:1, do you recognize
   the importance of stewardship of material goods?

   _____

FIGURE 48

Report on New Believer

A new report form should be completed by the counselor or other leader at regular intervals until the new believer has been fully integrated into the life of the believing community.

Believer's name _____

Counselor's name _____

Date _____

Date of profession of faith_____ Date of baptism_____

Date of acceptance into informal membership in group or church_____

Date of acceptance into full membership in the church_____

— —

Bible Instruction record:

    Date of completion of lesson series #1 _____

    Date of completion of lesson series #2 _____

    Date of completion of lesson series #3 _____

Etc.

Participation in worship:

    Public worship: Regular_____ Irregular_____

    Family worship: Regular_____ Irregular_____

    Personal worship: Regular_____ Irregular_____

Service involvement:

    Form of service   Supervisor

    _____   _____

    _____   _____

Witness:

    Form of witness   Supervisor

    _____   _____

    _____   _____

Stewardship:

    Involved_____   Not involved_____

Some will object that the keeping of such records is too laborious and time-consuming. We would argue that secular institutions such as schools keep records and that, above all other institutions, the Church of Christ should be interested in individual people. Furthermore, if the original counselor *and* the new believer are given the responsibility of keeping the records up-to-date, the burden on the missionary-evangelist and local leaders is actually reduced. By keeping the records accessible to the leaders (no highly personal information is included) the spiritual welfare and progress of the group can be more readily monitored. When the new believer encounters spiritual difficulties or fails to progress, the counselor can bring this to the attention of the leaders, who will be able to minister accordingly. When individuals come to Christ in groups, it will be helpful to find some way of grouping the individual records so that the progress of the group as well as of its individual members can be monitored. In cases where, by virtue of the vast numbers of new converts or other factors, the church-planter decides not to use individual records, he must continue to evaluate carefully the progress of the church as a whole.

There should be a record of the progress and commitment of new believers in the areas of instruction, worship, service, witness, and stewardship. Let us briefly consider each of these areas separately.

Faith and Instruction

The basic principle with which we are concerned here is that all believers should master a common set of fundamentals of the Christian faith. If available, a catechism or instructional manual provided by the sponsoring church or mission should be used. Otherwise, depending upon the culture and background of the people, some general work like John Stott's *Basic Christianity*[39] may be used. The

---

[39]John R. W. Stott, *Basic Christianity* (Grand Rapids: Eerdmans, 1958).

material may be taught in a Bible instruction class in the Sunday school or at a special hour. Instruction in worship, service, witness, and stewardship will, of course, be included in the study program.

Faith and Worship

Assuming, then, that the meaning and practice of Christian worship constitute part of the instruction provided for all new believers, our concern shifts to the believers' actual experience in public worship, group (e.g., family) worship, and personal worship. Are the believers actually participating regularly? Are they being strengthened spiritually as a result of worship? Do they feel that God is pleased with their worship? Is the observance of the Lord's Supper an integral part of their worship? The answers to these questions will be important in planning public worship and counseling concerning private worship.

Faith and Service

The key here is to find out precisely what talents and spiritual gifts for Christian service are possessed by believers, and then to provide opportunities for them to develop their talents and spiritual gifts and to use them in Christ's service. Believers have a responsibility to aid one another both in the recognition and in the utilization of these talents and gifts. If this dual responsibility is reflected in progress records, and the information is acted upon, the chances of the new believer's actually serving Christ will be greatly enhanced.

Faith and Witness

We can anticipate that, as a result of the inner working of the Holy Spirit and proper instruction at the time of turning to Christ, converts will bear a spontaneous witness to family, friends, and the believing group. Nothing is quite so refreshing and convincing as the witness of the newly reborn member of God's family. In most cases, however, it will be important that Christian leaders provide inspiration, models, and occasions for a continuing witness. It is precisely at this point that many cults outdo the Church. Then let the church-planter settle on a program of evangelistic outreach for the local group (simplified, perhaps, at first). And let all believers have the privilege of participating in it, in ways great or small.

Faith and Stewardship

Churches have a wide variety of approaches to the stewardship of money and material goods. Single or multiple freewill offerings, the pledge system, faith-promise plans, offerings in kind, monies given directly to a church treasurer—these and various other approaches are used in churches around the world. It is not our intention to evaluate these various approaches here, but rather to suggest that all believers should be provided with information and materials designed to encourage them to exercise generous stewardship on a regular basis.

The twentieth-century Church and its missions have been criticized on two seemingly contradictory counts. On the one hand, we are told that churches in new areas have not grown because of the tendency to concentrate on the first believers until they become "good Christians." This to the neglect of a continued outreach to the unconverted. On the other hand, we are told that many of our churches are weak because believers are not instructed and built up in the faith.

Who is right? It would seem that if either criticism is valid, the other must be invalid. But it may be that both are true! Urging believers to be "good"—and even praying that they will be "good"—is not the same as confirming them in the faith! Instruction in the Word, worship of God, service for Christ, witness to the world, stewardship of means—these are the elements of confirmation. It is hard to imagine that churches composed of confirmed believers will not grow. And it is hard to imagine that churches without confirmed believers can be pleasing to the Lord of the Church.

fourteen

The Leaders Consecrated

It is common for church-planters to desire that groups of new believers organize as soon as practicable. The emphasis can be somewhat misguided, however. No organization can be stronger than its leadership. Therefore, to think, pray, work, and plan with a view to raising up spiritual leadership for the organizing church should be of first priority. When spiritual leadership emerges, organization will become practicable and essential.

Objectives

With the above in mind, we will establish three objectives for this stage of the Pauline Cycle:

(1) Efforts should be continued to promote the spiritual maturity of all believers in the congregation.

(2) The believers should be taught how to recognize and select men and women who are gifted and spiritually qualified for leadership in the local church.

FIGURE 49
"THE PAULINE CYCLE"

"And when they had appointed elders for them in every church. . ." (Acts 14:23a).

(3) A permanent organization of the church should be established that is scriptural, functional, effective, and expandable.

Developing Qualified Leadership for the Local Church

Biblical Principles and Precedents

The Synagogue Background

The churches which Paul founded were not organized in a religious vacuum. Most of the early converts had been members of synagogues. It was natural for these believers to follow the synagogue traditions of worship and patterns of organization.

Briefly look at the synagogue pattern. In order to organize a synagogue or hold meetings it was necessary to have at least ten men. The elders of the congregation selected a ruler (or possibly several of them). The ruler was responsible for synagogue services and properties. He often designated others to conduct the expressions of praise, prayers, readings of the Law and the Prophets, and the giving of exhortations. Several assistants carried out menial duties, inflicted corporal punishment or otherwise disciplined members, and dispensed alms received from the members.

New Testament believers, therefore, had a model for church leadership and organization. It is not to be inferred that they followed this synagogue pattern rigidly, however. The point is that the early believers were aware of basic ways and means for conducting corporate spiritual life and business.

The Officers of the Church According to the New Testament

At least five offices of the early churches can be readily distinguished in the New Testament: the apostle, the prophet, the evangelist, the pastor (elder, overseer), and the deacon. The two latter offices require special consideration here. Local churches need pastors (or elders) and deacons.

(1) It seems that, in the New Testament, the terms *pastor, elder,* and *overseer* (or *bishop*) are used more or less synonymously. However, the three terms designate functions which may have been performed by more than one man. Since the oft-used word *elder* normally occurs in the plural, it seems likely that most early congregations had more than one such person (Acts 14:23; 15:2, 4, 6; 20:17). Passages such as Ephesians 4:11 and I Timothy 5:17 seem to differentiate between those elders who primarily governed and those who ministered the Word and shepherded the flock. The common distinction between "pastor" and "elder," therefore, may have more validity in terms of *function* than in terms of *office* as such.

Specific functions of such leaders were: (a) to govern the congregation (I Tim. 5:17), not by "lording" (*katakurieuontes*) over it but by example (*tupoi*) (I Peter 5:3); (b) to minister the Word of God (Acts 20:28; Eph. 4:11; I Peter 5:2); (c) to equip believers in the church so they could minister and build up the body (Eph. 4:11); (d) to protect the congregation from false teachers (Acts 20:28–30); and (e) to visit the sick and pray for them (James 5:14).

Polycarp, who was both a disciple of John and an early church leader, summed up the duties of the elder in the following words:

> And let the presbyters be compassionate and merciful to all, bringing back those that wander, visiting all the sick, and not neglecting the widow, the orphan, or the poor, but always "providing for that which is becoming in the sight of God and man"; abstaining from all wrath, respect of persons, and unjust judgment; keeping far off from all covetousness, not quickly crediting [an evil report] against anyone, not severe in judgment, as knowing we are all under a debt of sin. If then we entreat the Lord to forgive us, we ought also ourselves to forgive; for we are before

the eyes of our Lord and God, and "we must all appear at the judgment-seat of Christ, and must every one give an account of himself." Let us then serve Him in fear and with all reverence, even as He Himself has commanded us, and as the apostles who preached the gospel unto us, and the prophets who proclaimed beforehand the coming of the Lord [have alike taught us]. Let us be zealous in the pursuit of that which is good, keeping ourselves from causes of offense, from false brethren, and from those who in hypocrisy bear the name of the Lord, and draw away vain men unto error.[1]

(2) Concerning the office of deacon there is little room for question. The deacons in the New Testament churches carried out such duties as "waiting on tables" and dispensing church funds. By inference we may conclude that they did whatever menial tasks were necessary in order to make it possible for those who ministered the Word to give full attention to that ministry (Acts 6:1-6). It should be emphasized that the deacons had a spiritual and essential ministry. Without them corporate activities would have suffered, individual needs might not have been met, and the ministry of the Word would have been hampered. Note also that worthy women participated in this diaconal ministry (Rom. 16:1, 2).

The Qualifications of Local Church Leaders

(1) The pastors (elders, overseers).
  (a) Pastors must be above reproach (I Tim. 3:2; Titus 1:6, 7).
  (b) They must be the husband of one wife (I Tim. 3:2; Titus 1:6).
  (c) They must be temperate and self-controlled (I Tim. 3:2; Titus 1:8).
  (d) Pastors are to be prudent, sensible, and just (I Tim. 3:2; Titus 1:8).
  (e) They must be respectable (I Tim. 3:2).

---

[1]Polycarp, "The Epistles of Polycarp to the Philippians," *Ante-Nicene Christian Library*, vol. I in *The Writings of the Apostolic Fathers* (Edinburgh: T. and T. Clark, 1867), pp. 72-73.

(f) And hospitable (I Tim. 3:2).

(g) And able to teach (I Tim. 3:2).

(h) No pastor should be addicted to wine (I Tim. 3:3; Titus 1:7).

(i) Nor pugnacious (I Tim. 3:3; Titus 1:7).

(j) Nor contentious (I Tim. 3:3).

(k) Pastors must be gentle (I Tim. 3:3).

(l) They must be free from the love of money (I Tim. 3:3; Titus 1:7).

(m) They must manage their household well (I Tim. 3:4).

(n) Pastors should not be new converts (I Tim. 3:6).

(o) They must have a good reputation with unbelievers (I Tim. 3:7).

(p) They must not be self-willed (Titus 1:7).

(q) Nor quick-tempered (Titus 1:7).

(r) Pastors must love what is good (Titus 1:8).

(s) They must be devout and just (Titus 1:8).

(t) They should hold fast to sound thinking (Titus 1:9).

(u) They should exhort others to sound teaching (Titus 1:9).

(v) And refute those not holding sound doctrine (Titus 1:9).

(2) The deacons (and deaconesses as appropriate).

(a) Deacons must have a good reputation (Acts 6:3).

(b) They must be full of the Holy Spirit and wisdom (Acts 6:3).

(c) They must be competent in administration (Acts 6:3).

(d) Deacons should possess dignity, seriousness (I Tim. 3:8).

(e) They must not be double-tongued (I Tim. 3:8).

(f) Nor addicted to much wine (I Tim. 3:8).

(g) Nor fond of sordid gain (I Tim. 3:8).

(h) Deacons should hold the mystery of the faith with a clear conscience (I Tim. 3:9).

(i) They must be tested, not new converts (I Tim. 3:10).

(j) Deacons must be the husband of one wife (I Tim. 3:12).

(k) They must be good managers of their children and households (I Tim. 3:12).
(l) Deacons must possess strong personal faith (I Tim. 3:13).
(m) They should not be given to slanderous gossip (I Tim. 3:11).
(n) They must be sober (I Tim. 3:11).
(o) And reliable in all things (I Tim. 3:11).

Relevant Research

Defining "Leader" and "Leadership"

Leadership has been defined in various ways. Some definitions are most instructive:

(1) Field Marshal Montgomery said, "Leadership is the capacity and will to rally men and women to a common purpose, and the character which inspires confidence."[2]

(2) To a question asked by General Charles Gordon concerning leadership, an old Chinese leader, Li Hung Chang, answered, "There are only three kinds of people in the world—those that are movable, those that are immovable, and those that move them."[3]

(3) Philip K. Bock, an anthropologist, writes, "Leaders are specialists in decision-making."[4]

(4) Bock gives another definition, which may be the most useful one for our purposes. He says that leaders are those who have a "role involving legitimate exercise of authority over other persons."[5]

The more one thinks about the matter of leadership, the more one is impressed that authority is the key to understanding it. Of course, the kind of authority involved is extremely important.

---

[2] J. Oswald Sanders, *Spiritual Leadership* (London: Lakeland, 1967), p. 19.
[3] Ibid., pp. 19–20.
[4] Philip K. Bock, *Modern Cultural Anthropology—An Introduction*, 2nd ed. (New York: Alfred A. Knopf, 1974), p. 118.
[5] Ibid., p. 117.

Four Kinds of Leaders

Four types of leaders may be distinguished on the basis of the source of their authority.[6]

(1) *Hereditary leaders.* The authority of hereditary leaders is based on their position in a kinship group (e.g., the oldest living male in a royal lineage). They are leaders because of *who* they are rather than *what* they can do.

(2) *Bureaucratic leaders.* The authority of bureaucratic leaders comes by systematically progressing through positions of lesser authority. They have advanced because of both competence (in the narrow sense) and seniority.

(3) *Charismatic leaders.* Unique persons may rise to authority in times of great social crisis. By the force of personality they command enthusiastic followers.

(4) *Representative leaders.* Representative leaders are chosen by their followers through general consensus or election. They are then responsible to their followers. Many of these leaders possess the distinctive qualities of the other types of leaders, but these qualities are not the basis of their authority.[7]

The "Peter Principle"

Lawrence J. Peter emphasizes that there is a common tendency to promote faithful members of any organization with little regard to their ability to produce at a higher level of responsibility. When an individual is elevated to a level above his capability he becomes frustrated and unproductive.[8] Therefore, success in one position of responsibility in and of itself does not assure success at another position where the demands may be significantly different and greater.

Churches *do* need to recognize faithfulness, compe-

---

[6]Ibid., pp. 118–20.
[7]Ibid.
[8]Cf. Lawrence J. Peter, *The Peter Principle* (New York: Bantam Books, 1970), pp. 19–27.

tence, and a job well done. Rapidly growing sects are often much more objective and generous in this regard than are the churches. Nevertheless, spiritual gifts and natural abilities must be taken into account in the encouragement and selection of church leaders. Only those who *can* preach should be *required* to preach. Only those with the *gift* of teaching should be *asked* to teach. And only those with the *ability* to administer should be *called* to administer.

Practical Reflection

Differentiating Natural and Spiritual Leaders

Though the characteristics selected are especially true of Western-type leadership, the comparison that J. Oswald Sanders makes between natural and spiritual leaders is worthy of careful consideration.[9]

The Natural Leader	The Spiritual Leader
(1) Self-confident	(1) Confident in God
(2) Knows men	(2) Also knows God
(3) Makes his own decisions	(3) Seeks to find God's will
(4) Ambitious	(4) Self-effacing
(5) Originates his own methods	(5) Finds and follows God's methods
(6) Enjoys commanding others	(6) Delights to obey God
(7) Motivated by personal considerations	(7) Motivated by love for God and man
(8) Independent	(8) God-dependent

Selecting Natural Leaders as Church Leaders

Leadership in the larger society must be distinguished from leadership in the churches. Much has been written on making contact with the leaders of a community and

---

[9]Sanders, *Spiritual Leadership*, p. 21.

winning them to Christ with a view to a resultant positive effect on Christian witness and church life. This is well and good provided unconverted and unspiritual leaders of society do not enter the church and become leaders there primarily by virtue of their social status and natural leadership ability.

ME-3 illustration: What amounts to an unusual experiment in "transplanting" natural, societal leaders to positions of leadership in the churches was carried out by the Rhenish Mission in conjunction with their work among the Bataks on Sumatra.[10] Those who were the natural leaders in the society were baptized and appointed as leaders in the churches. The result was that the churches had leaders, but in many cases the leaders were the occasion of numerous and aggravated problems. Those with natural leadership ability and leadership status in society are not thereby qualified to take positions of leadership in the churches. One of the easiest courses to follow in the organization of churches is to select those of demonstrated leadership in society for a similar role in the church. In the case of the Rhenish Mission this was by design. In most cases it happens by default. In both instances, adverse results can be expected. *A spiritual church must have spiritual leaders.*

The Church Leader as a "Representative Leader"

The spiritual leader is a person *under* authority and *with* authority. He is most like the "representative leader" in larger society in that the basis of his authority does not lie in natural qualities of leadership (even though he may well possess them), but in the fact that he is equipped by God and chosen by Holy Spirit-directed churches. As Vergil Gerber writes, "A man cannot normally exercise authority in the church *until that authority has been recognized by the church.*"[11]

---

[10]Peter Beyerhaus and Henry Lefever, *The Responsible Church and the Foreign Mission* (Grand Rapids: Eerdmans, 1964), pp. 50–53.

[11]Vergil Gerber, *Missions in Creative Tension* (South Pasadena, CA: William Carey Library, 1971), p. 284.

If this is to occur, it is imperative that believers be instructed concerning the biblical standards for leadership in the local church. These must be held up before believers so that they have a yardstick against which to measure spiritual growth. Not all believers will become leaders, for not all will have the right combination of gifts and abilities. But all should aspire to the highest standards of godliness, and those who attain them should be recognized and invested with special responsibility and authority.

ME-1 illustration: The Fellowship Bible Church of Dallas, Texas, constantly and explicitly keeps the qualifications for church leaders before new converts and church members. Pastor Gene Getz and his colleagues have organized the church into small groups, each of which is led by an elder or undershepherd. When a believer thinks that he measures up to the standard, and the leaders agree, he is given responsibility for one of these groups. Since this has been the plan from the beginning of the church, organization and leadership have developed simultaneously. Twofold growth—numerical and spiritual—has been the result.[12]

Training Leaders in the Churches

It is not enough that certain believers have the potential for leadership. As they give evidence of spiritual growth, they must be given opportunities to utilize their potential and develop as church leaders. This process will make special demands on both missionary-evangelists and the emerging leaders. But the results will justify any sacrifice.

ME-3 illustration: A missionary in Japan, Jim Blocksom, developed a simple and effective program for training potential elders for a newly emerging church in the Kansai area. Each week he met with five mature and able laymen whom the Lord had added to the believing group. They reflected on and evaluated Blocksom's expository message

---

[12]Gene Getz, *Sharpening the Focus of the Church* (Chicago: Moody Press, 1974), pp. 105–08.

of the previous Sunday. Then they studied the Scripture text which had been announced for the following Sunday's message. After determining the meaning of the text they suggested specific applications for the Japanese context.

When some months had passed, Blocksom arranged to be away for a Sunday and told the laymen that one of them would have to preach. With one accord they all excused themselves on grounds of inability and inexperience. But Blocksom was ready for them with an unanswerable argument: "Since you have helped me so considerably with criticisms and suggestions for all this time, certainly any one of you can be expected to do quite well."

One layman was chosen to preach, and preach he did. Strangely enough, the missionary found it necessary to minister elsewhere with increasing frequency! By the time the church was organized and a paid pastor was installed, the church had five laymen who could preach, teach, and lead with remarkable ability.

Leaders "Heading Out" and Leaders "Heading In"

In his own unique and captivating style, Donald McGavran makes a distinction between church leaders who are "heading out" and those who are "heading in."[13] His point is that, once churches become established, the majority of their leaders are given responsibilities that have to do with training the children of Christian families, ministering to the needs of the congregation, keeping the church organization running smoothly, and maintaining church facilities. Now all of this is good and necessary. But it also hinders growth and results in an ecclesiastical form of "Parkinson's Law" (which we will consider shortly). The church is constituted to find *lost* sheep, not just to fold and feed the *saved* sheep. If, therefore, a new church models itself after the average established church, it will soon find

---

[13]Donald McGavran, "Principles of Training Leaders for Growing Churches," a lecture given at Trinity Evangelical Divinity School on October 16, 1969.

that the attention and efforts of most leaders will be focused inward and few will be reaching out to the lost. Stagnation will result. Only by continual and careful study and action will the proper proportion of attention, time, and effort be given to outreach, even in the pioneer situation.

Effecting Permanent Organization in the Local Church

Biblical Principles and Precedents

The Emergence of Church Organization in the New Testament Period

Contrary to the thinking of some, much New Testament church organization was formal. Otherwise the churches would not have been able to take required actions in a decent and orderly manner. Many early churches undoubtedly were patterned after the synagogue, but the New Testament reveals a distinct development in church organization and administration.

The germ of New Testament church organization existed previous to Pentecost. In the Epistles, believers are "saints" and "brethren" and they are found in "churches." As such they shared a mutual priesthood (I Peter 2:9) and a common ministry (Eph. 4:11–15). Only regenerate persons were members of local churches. And all regenerate persons were members of the churches, as far as we know. It does not seem to be the case that any definite number of believers was required in order to organize a local church (as was true of the synagogue). After all, Christ had promised His presence where even two or three gathered in His name (Matt. 18:20).

The early emphasis in the ministry of Paul and others was upon preaching. With the passing of time more attention was given to matters of church organization. Before any of the Pauline Epistles were written, in the Book of James (written about A.D. 48) we have reference to the "elders of the church" (James 5:14). And in Paul's first epistle, reference is made to those who are "over you in the Lord" (I Thess. 5:12).

Organization and leadership go hand in hand. In the case of the Jerusalem church, the leaders were the special apostles themselves. In the case of the Antioch church, some of the first leaders came from Jerusalem (Acts 15:22, 27). In the cases of the missionary churches, leaders were chosen by the missionary-evangelists and/or the local believers.

Congregationalism and the New Testament Churches

The fact that, as congregations developed, they had some leaders who did not come from the local congregation and some who were appointed by missionary-evangelists does not rule out congregationalism. A. H. Strong offers convincing arguments that in the New Testament era church government was democratic or congregational:[14]

(1) It was the duty of the whole church to preserve unity in its action (Rom. 12:16; I Cor. 1:10; Eph. 4:3).

(2) The whole church had responsibility for maintaining pure doctrine and practice (II Cor. 11:1–3; I Tim. 3:5; Jude 3; Rev. 2 and 3).

(3) The ordinances were committed to the whole church to observe and guard (I Cor. 11:23, 24).

(4) The whole church elected its officers and delegates (Acts 6:3, 5; 13:2, 3; 15:2, 4, 22, 30; II Cor. 8:19). (This is a critical point, of course. Strong cites works by Meyer, Hackett, Baumgarten, and others in making his case. He understands Acts 13:2, 3 as referring to the whole church at Antioch. And regarding passages such as Acts 14:23 and

---

[14]A. H. Strong, *Systematic Theology* (Philadelphia: Judson Press, 1907), pp. 887–929.

Titus 1:5 it is maintained that the "appointing" by the apostles or Titus does not refer to the *mode* of appointment and therefore does not rule out the authority of the church community, which is upheld in other passages.) (5) The whole church had the responsibility and authority to exercise discipline (I Cor. 5:4, 5, 13; II Thess. 3:6, 14, 15).

We must not press these arguments too far. There seems to have been a flexibility in New Testament organization that served the purposes of the churches. The pattern probably differed somewhat from church to church. At the same time, as Donald Lake says:

> Churches can have deacons, elders and pastors or only pastors . . . but the issue of congregationalism is: Where does the authority to elect reside, upon whom does the responsibility fall, and to whom does the power of discipline belong?[15]

Episcopalians will answer, "With the bishops." Presbyterians will answer, "With the elders." Those of us who espouse congregational polity will, of course, answer, "With the congregation."

Relevant Research

Human Government

Leadership and organization are human necessities. Anarchy is "practically impossible." But forms of government do vary radically, and with them the types and authority of leaders, and the methods of their selection. The basic types of human government parallel the alternative forms of church polity:

---

[15]Donald Lake, "Congregationalism: Does it Matter?" in *The Evangelical Beacon*, 16 March 1976, pp. 10-12.

(1) Autocracy—absolute authority exercised by one man.

(2) Oligarchy—authority exercised by a select and privileged group within the larger society.

(3) Democracy—authority vested in the members of the society.

It should not be overlooked that most human governments can (and perhaps to some degree usually do) exhibit some characteristics of more than one of these basic types. A pure form of government is a rarity. Sometimes the form of an autocracy (monarchy) is retained while functionally the government is a democracy. Sometimes the form of a democracy is retained while functionally government is either an autocracy (dictatorship) or an oligarchy. Form and function need not necessarily coincide.

Social Structures and Social Organizations

What has been said previously about the distinction between social structure and social organization (i.e., a voluntary or free association) is pertinent here. Depending upon one's personal experience and perspective the local church could be thought of as displaying the characteristics of either or both of these. To new members who come into the church by profession of faith or transfer (and to many believers who do not actually join a local church) the churches sometimes appear to be structures in which people are required to assume added responsibilities with but little hope of having a significant voice in changing programs and policies enacted by an entrenched hierarchy. Actually the local church *is* somewhat different from a free association where individuals are organized in a way that suits the pursuance of certain goals. Such organizations may be initiated, defined, directed, and discontinued at the discretion of the membership. Certain liberals have described the churches in such terms and with great violence to both Scripture and Christian practice. Nevertheless, the local church does exhibit some of the characteristics of a voluntary association. A. H. Strong recognizes the implications of this dual role (structure and organization) of local churches.[16]

"Parkinson's Law"

There is a pronounced tendency on the part of human governments and most social organizations to grow ever larger and consume an unnecessary and disproportionate part of the total resources upon themselves. This they often do without a commensurate increase in effectiveness in terms of the original and basic goals. Although C. Northcote Parkinson developed this law from his research into business organizations, it has a much wider application.[17]

Decision by Consensus

It may be well to take another look at the method of decision-making called "decision by consensus." A consensus is a shared conviction that a particular decision is the right one. It is arrived at by a full discussion of the problem in which all members are encouraged to share their true feelings as the discussion progresses. Members make known which of the alternatives they can support in view of the goals of the group. If and when the decision to act is reached, it represents the best wisdom of the entire deliberative body (though not necessarily the first choice of each individual member). Decisions reached in this way promote the achievement of the goals of the organization and help assure group harmony in pursuing them. Decision by consensus is as adaptable to democratic institutions at the grassroots level as is the method of decision by "discussion and vote."

---

[16]Strong, *Systematic Theology*, pp. 892–93.
[17]C. Northcote Parkinson, *In-Laws and Outlaws* (Boston: Houghton Mifflin Co., 1962), p. 233.

Practical Reflections

Generally speaking, missionary-evangelists who have seen their task as including the planting and developing of local churches have had the best of intentions. Not only so, they have also been relatively successful in establishing churches all around the world. No one who is familiar with pioneer work at home or abroad, however, would be willing to say that what has been accomplished has been done in the most biblical and effective way. At perhaps no other stage in the Pauline Cycle will it be easier to make mistakes that have more far-reaching effects. Happily, by taking another look at the biblical record, the secular scene, and the experience of churches around the world, it is possible to pinpoint potential problems and, perhaps, avoid them.

Autonomous or Christonomous Churches?

From the days of Henry Venn and Rufus Anderson, strategists have stressed the "indigenous church." It has usually been defined as self-supporting, self-governing, and self-propagating. Overall, when properly conceived and wisely applied, this has been a good emphasis. Recently, however, it has received some healthy reevaluation. The question has been raised, "Is it proper to define churches in terms of *autonomy* (i.e., *self*-governance), etc.? Would it not be more biblical and fruitful to describe them in terms of *Christonomy*, i.e., under the rule of Christ?"[18] Moreover, and in line with this, is it not true that, properly conceived, churches modeled on the New Testament *will be* indigenous ("related to the soil")? *Is it not our cultural expectations that make churches something other than indigenous?* And for that matter, is it not possible for a church to be indigenous according to the classical definition (self-supporting, self-governing, self-propagating) and still be more or less unrelated to the soil in which it must grow?

---

[18]Beyerhaus and Lefever, *Responsible Church*, pp. 112–13.

These questions deserve careful consideration. They point at the heart of church organization.

Church Polity as a Reflection of Local Practice

A careful study of representative church polities will reveal that historically they have tended to reflect the social structures of the times and places of their inception. In spite of what we have concluded about congregationalism, the early churches did exhibit some episcopal characteristics due to the presence of the apostles. Given the social setting of the early centuries, it is easily understood how episcopal characteristics were continued and even amplified after the death of the apostles themselves, and how a doctrine of apostolic succession was later devised in order to reinforce them. The Reformation churches—developed where feudal concepts and clan structures were strong—tended to be presbyterian. Congregational forms as we know them are a more modern development which unfolded along with revolts by minorities against authoritarianism. It should be borne in mind that the congregational form of church government does not necessarily preserve the independence of the local congregation, nor do episcopal or presbyterian forms necessarily abrogate it.

While the form of church polity is important, the function is just as important or more so. A form of church government that is foreign to the target culture will tend in one of two directions. Either it will adapt functionally to local ways of governance, or it will greatly impede the growth of the church.

ME-3 illustration: In Zaire some years ago, there was a district business meeting of congregationally-organized churches. Three times the meeting had to be recessed when the democratic method of nominating a chairman occasioned pandemonium and worse. The fact is that the participants were working with an unfamiliar form that could not be expected to function well if closely adhered to! Little wonder that a veteran missionary in attendance remarked, "I wish that we could go back fifty years and undo the mischief we have caused by the organization we imposed."

We err when we push any church polity too far from the form and functioning of local socio-political expressions of government. The church can learn from the local *structures* (society organized to preserve the traditions) because it too must preserve certain teachings, values, and ways of life. The church can learn from local *organizations* (groups organized to effect change) because it too is an agent of change both within the Christian community and in the larger society.

Putting Local Organization "Up for Grabs"

One of the most common errors of church-planters who espouse congregational polity is the rather common practice of involving the new church in the construction of its own constitution. The reasons for the practice are obvious. They stem from democratic ideals and notions of congregational responsibility. But the practice is misguided.

In the first place, a new congregation of believers is usually composed of a number of people who are in the process of adjusting to one another and, in many cases, to biblical teaching. Misunderstandings can easily occur.

In the second place, the construction of a biblical and practical instrument of organization is a time-consuming task which diverts attention away from outreach to unbelievers and confirmation of new believers at a time when the fledgling church can least afford it.

In the third place, a locally devised constitution (like all other constitutions) will be an imperfect instrument which will soon need revision on the basis of experience. Moreover, it will often prove to be most difficult to revise a constitution in which there are vested local interests.

It is, therefore, far better to propose a model constitution which has been prepared by the sponsors of the emerging church than it is to put a constitution "up for grabs." When the (charter) members realize that they will be able to revise it according to their needs at a later date, they will usually welcome emancipation from this arduous task.

ME-3 illustration: The personal experience of one of the authors in organizing a local congregation is relevant here. The hours spent in constructing a constitution came within a hair's breadth of being rewarded with a church split—a division at the hour of birth! In similar subsequent situations he proposed acceptance of a model constitution under which the congregation could operate for the first several years of its existence. In each case, the results were much happier!

The Tendency to Overorganize

The trouble with many constitutions and the efforts of missionary-evangelists along these lines is that both tend to impose organizational yokes upon fledgling churches that even mature churches have found it difficult to bear. "Parkinson's Law" is operative in many churches, including new ones!

Churches and their derivative missions and organizations must come to grips with this natural tendency. One church spawned twenty-nine committees! Ultimately a thirtieth committee was appointed to check up on the other twenty-nine! Now, of course, the mere fact that there are numerous committees in a church is no more than prima facie evidence that "Parkinson's Law" applies. We must ask what they are doing and how well they are doing it. But the fact remains that Western churches, at least, are often afflicted with too many committees, committees that are too large, and committees that are working too hard and too long on the wrong objectives. To keep the church wheels turning does not mean that the church is going anywhere.

Decision by Consensus or by Discussion and Vote?

No church polity (including congregational polity) need be locked in to decision by discussion and vote. That procedure is certainly allowable but there are at least two aspects of it that may be inimical to Christian purposes. First, the more carefully and passionately the alternatives are presented, the more likely that sides will be taken and feelings hurt. Not all heat produces light! Second, decisions affecting the total life of a congregation that are made by a bare simple majority seem out of keeping with the unity of the body and divine guidance. To introduce decision by consensus in a society that is not acquainted with the process may not be easy, but the change may be like dew from heaven. To introduce any other process in a target area where decision by consensus is traditional may be tragic.

Maintaining Scriptural Discipline

Biblical Principles and Precedents

No good purpose is served by idealizing the early Christian congregations. On the contrary, it is very important that we recognize that they had problems. Only then can we fully understand the importance of discipline in the first century and in the twentieth.

There were cases of immediate, severe, corporal punishment in the early congregations. The cases of Ananias and Sapphira (Acts 5:1–11) and those Corinthians who participated in the Lord's Supper unworthily (I Cor. 11:28–32) readily come to mind. In those cases, God dealt directly with offenders on the basis of His knowledge of their inner motives. God may deal directly with erring believers today as well. But that is up to Him. When the churches began to exercise discipline, the conditions (but not necessarily the principles) changed radically.

The New Testament teaching on church discipline can be summarized by considering three basic questions: *Who? Why?* and *How?* [19]

Who Was Disciplined in the Early Church?

(1) *Those guilty of serious doctrinal deviation.* When the purity of the gospel (soteriology) and the truth about the person of Christ (Christology) are at stake, the Bible leaves no room for carelessness or indecisiveness. Such cases are to be dealt with forthrightly and without delay (Gal. 1:6-9; I Tim. 1:19, 20; II John 7-11).

(2) *Those guilty of continued ecclesiastical insubordination.* Diotrephes is a classic example of insubordination (III John 9, 10). Not only did he put himself and his own interests first, he also turned a deaf ear to the apostle and the local believers. He even excluded true Christian brothers from the church. He exhibited those precise characteristics of evil that John had talked about in his first letter—lawlessness and lack of love for the brethren (I John 2:9-11). There is no room for such behavior in the churches.

(3) *Those guilty of flagrant moral indiscretion.* In the First Epistle to the Corinthians we are told of an instance of intrafamily fornication within the church (I Cor. 5:1-5). The offender of common morality is by no means excused. Paul indicated in no uncertain terms that the one who was guilty in Corinth must be disciplined.

(4) *Those guilty of voluntarily being indigent.* Evidently there were some people in the early churches who stopped working but did not stop eating! Paul knew of such per-

---

[19]J. Robertson McQuilkin, "Whatever Happened to Church Discipline?" *Christianity Today*, vol. 18, no. 13, 29 March 1974, pp. 8-12.

sons in Thessalonica. They lived "in idleness, mere busybodies, not doing any work." He commanded that they "do their work in quietness and . . . earn their own living." Otherwise they were to be disciplined (II Thess. 3:11–14, RSV).

We should not suppose that this is a complete register of those who merit discipline, or that Scripture supplies a complete register. Paul took the occasion of immorality in Corinth to mention idolaters, revilers, drunkards, robbers, and greedy persons, and he prescribed discipline for them also (I Cor. 5:9–13). It is clear that churches had a divine directive to discipline their members, and they were to do so evenhandedly according to God's standards and not their own.

Why Were People Disciplined in the Early Church?

(1) Discipline was exercised in order that offenders might be punished and justice done (I Thess. 4:6, 7). We hasten to add that this was not the chief grounds for cases of New Testament church discipline. Nevertheless, church discipline was to be considered as part of the judgment of God upon wrongdoers.

(2) Discipline was to be exercised in order that offenders might be instructed and reclaimed (I Cor. 5:5; 11:32; II Thess. 3:15). This is one of the dominant notes of the biblical teaching on discipline. How could erring believers be brought to their senses, to repentance, to new usefulness, and to all that accrues to salvation? How else, if not by being forced to experience something of the consequences of their evil ways? This biblical teaching needs new emphasis in today's churches. Church discipline is remedial. It is to be undertaken with great sorrow and compassion, and in the hope that the erring brother or sister will be restored to obedience and fruitfulness.

(3) Discipline was to be exercised in order that others might be warned and fear God (Acts 5:11). If sin had been overlooked or winked at in the church, sinners might have

been encouraged to think that they could continue to sin with impunity. This was not to be.

(4) Discipline was to be exercised in order that the church might be purified and protected. This important reason for discipline is underscored by Paul's apt metaphor: "A little leaven leavens the whole lump" (I Cor. 5:6). That is why those who were in the church and who persisted in sinning could not be allowed to go on without correction. Both unscriptural teaching and ungodly living are infectious in Adam's sons.

How Was Church Discipline Carried Out?

This is certainly an important consideration. Church discipline itself becomes an evil when exercised in an unscriptural manner because it becomes hurtful to the body and to the testimony of Christ.

(1) Private grievances and public sin were to be differentiated and dealt with accordingly (Matt. 18:15-17; I Cor. 5; Gal. 2:11-14; I Tim. 5:20). In the passage from Matthew it would seem that the problem was between private individuals. It was to be dealt with by enlisting the aid of other believers and, if the offender would not listen, by having nothing more to do with him. In the other passages the problems were matters of public record. To deal with them only in private would have been to disregard both the nature of the offenses and the reasons for discipline.

(2) Discipline was to be exercised only on the basis of factual knowledge (Matt. 18:15-18; I Cor. 5:1; I Tim. 5:19). Discipline was serious. Hearsay evidence was insufficient. Our Lord's requirement that there be two or three witnesses fell within the Mosaic pattern, but it had a wider application, as evidenced by Paul's requirement that elders were not to be charged with wrongdoing unless there were two or three witnesses.

(3) Discipline was to be carried out with a proper spirit on the part of those who enforced it (Matt. 7:1-5; Rom. 15:1, 2; II Cor. 2:6-8; Gal. 6:1-4). A spirit of vindictive-

ness or self-righteousness had no place in church discipline. Rather, responsible believers were to judge themselves, and then to deal with offenders in a spirit of meekness and helpfulness.

(4) Discipline was to be carried out by exclusion from *koinōnia* (Matt. 18:15–17; I Cor. 5; II Thess. 3:14; II John 7–11; III John 9–11). These passages deal with somewhat different circumstances, but the basic method of discipline was the same in each case. One of the greatest gifts God has bestowed on believers is fellowship with the saints. One of the most severe punishments the churches can inflict is the withholding of it.

Relevant Research

Guilt Cultures and Shame Cultures

In spite of the fact that a great deal of relevant research and writing on the subject has occurred since Ruth Benedict made her well-known differentiation between guilt cultures and shame cultures,[20] the basic distinction is worth noting. Among other differences, the people in guilt cultures are more concerned with separate, discrete acts and deplore the transgression of a specific code. Those in shame cultures are more concerned with the overall self and deplore falling short of an ideal. In relation to church discipline, erring believers in guilt cultures tend to suffer inwardly irrespective of whether or not others in the church fellowship know about those sins. In fact, sin is likely to be thought of as a matter between the individual and God, with little thought given to the consequences of sin to the body of Christ. Erring believers in shame cultures will tend to suffer when they fail to live up to the expectations of others and therefore "lose face."

Of course, the Bible reflects some aspects of both types

---

[20]Ruth Benedict, *The Chrysanthemum and the Sword* (Boston: Houghton Mifflin Co., 1946).

of cultures. In guilt cultures, like the traditional United States, believers need instruction as to the effect of sin upon the church. And *koinōnia* needs to be developed to the point where the withholding of it would cause real remorse. In shame cultures, such as traditional Japan (or the United States of tomorrow?), believers must be taught that God sees our sin even when our neighbors don't, and that unconfessed sin breaks our relationship with Him even though fellow believers are unaware of the problem.

Belongingness as a Primary Motivation

Numerous studies point to the importance of belongingness in, and acceptance by, a group as a primary motivating force. Abraham Maslow's "motivational pyramid," for example, indicates that when elementary physiological and safety needs are cared for, higher motivations take over.[21] One such higher motivation is the need for "belongingness." No man is an island. When it comes to church discipline, the implications of this need for "belongingness" are obvious.

Discipline and Group Progress

It is self-evident that groups which have a large proportion of disciplined members who are committed to group goals and programs will grow faster than those that do not. The importance of this principle stands out in bold relief when we consider the rapid growth of conservative churches in America[22] and the even more rapid growth of such groups as the Church of Jesus Christ of Latter-day Saints and Jehovah's Witnesses.[23] Of course, various factors must be taken into consideration in studying the

[21]Abraham Maslow, *Motivation and Personality,* 2nd ed. (New York: Harper and Row, 1970).

[22]Dean Kelly, *Why Conservative Churches Are Growing* (New York: Harper and Row, 1972), pp. 20–31.

[23]Ibid., pp. 20–31; and David J. Hesselgrave, *Dynamic Religious Movements* (Grand Rapids: Baker, 1978), pp. 308–09.

growth of these movements. But the inescapable fact is that church organizations with great numbers of nominal believers generally are not growing, while those with a high proportion of committed, disciplined members are growing.

Practical Reflection

Whatever Happened to Church Discipline?

This question, as posed by J. Robertson McQuilkin, is both pertinent and practical. Discipline, in the churches of the Western world especially, has fallen prey to an easygoing religiosity that bears little resemblance to New Testament Christianity. The reasons are not hard to find.

First, the attitudes and values of Western culture have adversely affected the churches. Therefore, Christians tend to lose sight of the holiness of God and the sinfulness of sin. In addition, the general lack of discipline in Western culture has invaded the churches.

Second, the availability of many churches in the same area makes it more difficult to maintain discipline in the churches. When a church member is in danger of discipline in one church, he is apt to look for another church in the same area. Only rarely will the shift of allegiance be questioned when he applies for transfer of membership.

Third, church membership is downgraded in many Christian circles. It is often deemed sufficient to be a member of the Universal Church. All too often, membership in a local church is considered to be a matter of personal preference.

Little wonder, then, that existing churches do not serve as good models for new churches. Unless missionary-evangelists hold scriptural principles and models before the new congregations, they cannot be expected to become New Testament churches.

Discipline Based on the Unity of the Church

It is obvious that discipline has to do with the purity of the church and its testimony. Often overlooked is the fact that discipline is also related to the unity of the church. In fact, as Roland Allen notes, there was a real sense in which Paul put the whole church under discipline when calling for the discipline of one member.[24] Western individualism tends to diminish the pain that the entire body should feel when one member falls, and the shame that the errant believer should feel when disciplined. By contrast, Paul emphasized the unity of the body—not only in theory but also in practice. Therefore, when discipline was exercised in those times, the whole church was intimately involved.

Discipline from the Conscience of the Church

It is important that church discipline be just that— *church* discipline. Pioneers and, later, other church leaders play important roles in investigating accusations of wrongdoing and in dealing with offending members. But discipline is something less than biblical when the conscience of a few leaders is imposed upon the church. Only when the larger body of believers agree that God's standards have been violated, that the purity of the body is jeopardized, and that a certain course of action is in accordance with the revealed will of God—only then can something so distasteful and disagreeable accomplish its divinely intended ends.

Self-exposure, the Key to Church Discipline

In a singularly helpful article on church discipline, Jacob Loewen illustrates how important it is for church leaders, including the missionary-evangelist, to expose themselves as being subject to the same temptations and weakness as

---

[24]Roland Allen, *Missionary Methods—St. Paul's or Ours?* (Grand Rapids: Eerdmans, 1962), pp. 123–25.

other believers.[25] By discreetly but candidly revealing that they too are tempted, sometimes fail, and are always in need of the prayers of God's people, they encourage others to deal honestly and biblically with the problem of sin in themselves and in the church.

Master Plan Formation

Developing Qualified Leadership for the Local Church

Leaders must be both discovered and developed. Essential to both processes is a recognition of the qualities or characteristics of leadership whether natural or spiritual. When both the church-planters and the local believers are aware of these characteristics, they will also become aware of the leadership that the Lord of the Church is providing for the emerging congregation. Then, giving priority to the development of spiritual qualities, these leaders can become a blessing to the entire congregation.

The master plan will involve three steps.

Step One: Plan for some teaching and preaching that clarify the distinction between the characteristics of natural and spiritual leadership, and that hold up the latter as the "measure of a spiritual man or woman."

Step Two: Single out those whose ability and testimony occasion the confidence of other believers. In part this will be an automatic process. There is a natural tendency, however, for those who are leaders in secular society to become leaders in the church. Unless spiritual qualities are assigned high priority in this selection process, the emerging congregation may be headed for trouble.

Step Three: Special responsibilities and training should be given to those who are recognized as leaders and poten-

---

[25]Jacob Loewen, "Self Exposure: Bridge to Fellowship," *Practical Anthropology* 12 (1965), pp. 49–62.

tial leaders. If the attention that is involved in praying for and working with this small group is balanced by delegated responsibilities, the specter of favoritism will be avoided. Previously we discussed the notion of "optimum size" (pp. 284–88) and the relationship between the size of the group and group objectives. In the nature of the case the core leadership group in any church will be relatively small. But in many ways its formation and training are most important aspects of church-planting because these leaders will not only manage church affairs, they will model the faith for good or ill. Whether leaders number one, three, or twelve, therefore, they are worthy of the concern, time, and effort of missionary-evangelists.

Effecting Permanent Organization in the Local Church

When leaders have developed to the point where believers will follow them, the time for permanent organization has arrived. Two aspects of this organization are all-important and require careful planning: *preparation* for the organizational meeting and the *proposal* of an organizing document.

First, then, the organizational meeting should be preceded by a period of preparation and prayer. The following checklist will aid in this preparation:

(1) Do leaders agree that the time is ripe for organizing the church?

(2) Is it clear who will be invited to the organizational meeting?

(3) Are the agenda and procedure to be followed understood by all?

(4) Has the suggested document of organization been made available to everyone?

(5) Have the leaders of the organizational meeting been selected and prepared?

(6) Has there been an ample period for discussion and prayer on the part of God's people?

If a temporary organization has been functioning effectively, it should not be difficult to plan for the organizational meeting and provide adequate answers to these questions. Second, special attention should be given to the organizing document or constitution of the church. It should be simple enough to allow for flexibility and initiative in church life, comprehensive enough to provide a common ground for action, and indigenous enough to insure effective decision-making and smooth functioning in the congregation. If, as we suggest, the church-planters put forth a model organizing-document for the congregation, it should include information concerning the following:

(1) Purpose and goals
(2) Duties of leaders
(3) The qualities of leaders and methods of electing them
(4) The process of decision-making
(5) Standards for membership
(6) Standards of belief
(7) Standards of behavior
(8) Matters of discipline
(9) Matters of finance
(10) Ownership of property
(11) Items required by the local government

Maintaining Scriptural Discipline

The church which is lax in discipline after its formation will have great difficulty in recovering a biblical level of discipline later. It is imperative that leaders and members of the new congregation apply constitutional and biblical principles of discipline from the very beginning. This is true in relationship to two groups of people: those who are already members and those who will apply for membership. Church-planters, therefore, should plan to encourage the new congregation to deal decisively and Christianly with defections from biblical faith and practice. And they should assist where possible in the preparation and examination of new members.

One of the results of the emphasis in Western cultures on the rule of law has been the tendency to see church organization as something separate from the spiritual life of the church. Business meetings of the church are seldom characterized by fervent prayer and warm fellowship. Discipline is often lacking because it is regarded as punitive and not as a means of restoring the erring brothers and of preserving the purity of faith and testimony of the church. Of course, non-Western cultures also have their inbuilt biases and prejudices. Missionary-evangelists can escape these cultural traps by consciously planning for church organization with sensitivity to Scripture *and* culture.

fifteen

The Believers Commended

If there is any one subject in church-planting evangelism that does not receive adequate attention either in the literature or in the actual planning for a new work, it is that of the withdrawal of the pioneer worker(s). This is not to imply that this topic necessarily needs a voluminous literature or an exhaustive study. But sound strategy for planting churches cross-culturally *must* include plans for the withdrawal and redeployment of the pioneer worker(s). In most cases it is almost as important that pioneers know when and how to leave a new work, as that they know when and where to undertake it in the first place.

Objectives

With the foregoing in mind, our objectives for this stage should be:

(1) An amicable withdrawal of the pioneer(s) from the established congregation at the best possible time (as soon as practicable).

FIGURE 50
"THE PAULINE CYCLE"

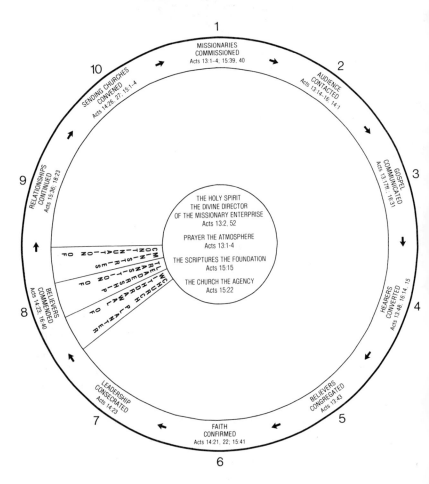

".. . having prayed with fasting, they commended them to the Lord in whom they had believed" (Acts 14:23b).

(2) An orderly transition of pastoral leadership in the congregation.

(3) A continuation (where possible) of effective ministries that have been undertaken by the pioneer worker(s).

Preliminary Considerations

The stage of development with which we are presently concerned has posed major problems for both home and overseas missions. Though many of the problems are similar in both cases, some are unique to overseas missions.

Similarities in Home and Foreign Missions

(1) In both home and foreign missions we have often lacked the wisdom to carefully prepare and deploy (and redeploy) missionary-evangelists.

(2) In both cases the temptation to build our own "little kingdoms" instead of Christ's "great kingdom" must be resisted.

(3) In both cases a special bond often develops between "pioneer leaders" and "pioneer followers." Usually this bond is hard to break. Planning for separation with its tearful farewells is similar psychologically to planning for one's own funeral!

(4) In both situations any given church polity has unintended adverse effects unless compensations are made. Congregationalism especially can result in a long period of agonizing search for a new pastor unless proper procedures are made clear ahead of time.

The Unique Problems of Foreign Missions

(1) Some of the most difficult decisions for ME-2 and ME-3 cross-cultural missions are those which have to do with the transference of authority from mission to national

church and from the church-planting missionary to the planted church and its leaders. Theorists have talked about stages of growth leading to independence. Henry Venn coined the phrase "euthanasia of mission" to describe this objective. But the problem persists—and the solving of it presents a challenge to both our theory *and* our practice!

(2) A related problem in which the record of foreign missions is spotty at best is that of the continuance of missionary-initiated ministries, especially "secondary" institutional ministries. That the problem has arisen is understandable, but it could be ameliorated, if not erased.

(3) Finally there is the question of the loss of financial support from the home base of the missionary-evangelist—be that America, Britain, Germany, or wherever. The newly independent church must carry on without the finances and material aids which the missionary-evangelist had supplied. The problem is compounded greatly if an institution such as a clinic or school was closely related to the local church during the church-planting period.

The Withdrawal of the Pioneer Worker(s)

Biblical Principles and Precedents

Leadership Succession in the New Testament

There are several aspects of New Testament teaching which show that there was a succession of leadership in the New Testament:

(1) The preparation of leaders to continue the work.

(2) The symbolism of the laying on of hands (e.g., Acts 13:3).

(3) The types of special gifts the risen Christ gives to His Church—some being "pioneers," others being "consolidators" (Eph. 4:11-13).

(4) The directions given to those in leadership (e.g., II Tim. 2:2).

The Temporary Nature of Paul's Ministry

We have already noted that Paul's ministry was a temporary one, as was the ministry of a number of his team members. It was not the kind of temporary ministry that is confined to some simple preaching and a call to commitment. It resulted in churches. But once a church was born and established, the pioneer worker(s) usually commended the believers to the grace of God and departed for other fields of service (e.g., Acts 14:23; 16:4). Pastor-teachers were then in a position to assume leadership. This was important for the churches. Their members were not to become the wards of one leader (I Cor. 3:4–7). It was also important for the mission, which was not to be abandoned because a church was born.

Relevant Research

Eric Hoffer believes that there is a succession of leadership in growing movements.[1] The qualities of Hoffer's "man of words," "fanatic," and "man of action" may be found in one and the same man, but more often than not, men who begin a movement are not the best qualified to see it through successive stages of development. A study of rapidly growing religious movements reveals that there indeed are various types of leadership and that crises of leadership do occur with the passing of time.[2] Accordingly, Christ has given various types of leaders to His

---

[1]Eric Hoffer, *The True Believer: Thoughts on the Nature of Mass Movements* (New York: New American Library of World Literature, 1958), p. 120.

[2]David J. Hesselgrave, "Nichiren Shoshu Soka Gakkai," in *Dynamic Religious Movements: Case Studies in Rapidly Growing Religious Movements Around the World,* ed. David J. Hesselgrave (Grand Rapids: Baker, 1978), pp. 135–38.

Church. Differing gifts are needed as the local church is born and matures.

Practical Reflection

The time has come to seriously question our usual practice of encouraging successful missionary-evangelist pioneers at home and abroad to take more prestigious pulpits or administrative posts in the missions instead of encouraging them to simply move to new pioneering situations. If Christ has blessed His Church with men and women who are gifted in starting new congregations, would it not be better for them, for the churches, and for unoccupied fields if they were encouraged and supported in a ministry of planting new churches?

Transition in Christian Leadership

Biblical Principles and Precedents

Christ's Appointment of Peter and Paul

Perhaps both Catholics and Protestants are guilty of neglecting part of the picture in their portrayal of leadership in the apostolic church. *Both* Peter and Paul were designated as leaders in the transition of leadership from Christ to His apostles. In Caesarea Philippi Christ made it clear that Peter would play a leadership role in the building of His Church (Matt. 16:18, 19). That Peter carried out his responsibility is clear when one considers the key role he played in acting as the disciples' spokesman on the day of Pentecost (Acts 2:14-40), in opening the door of faith to the Gentiles (Acts 10), and in speaking out at the Jerusalem conference (Acts 15:7-11).

Christ also made it clear that Paul would take a leading part in the continuation and expansion of the Church (Acts 9:1-22, especially vv. 15, 16). That Paul understood and exercised the authority and responsibility that had been given to him is apparent throughout Acts and his Epistles, especially in such passages as Galatians 1:11-24 and Ephesians 3:1-12.

The supernatural wisdom and power of Christ and the Holy Spirit are, of course, apparent in this transition of authority from Christ to His apostles and then to His Church. From a human point of view, two absolutely crucial aspects stand out. First, the leadership role of Peter was announced by Christ and accepted by the other apostles and the Jerusalem church. Second, in spite of some minor misunderstandings, Peter and Paul recognized that both of them had been given places of leadership to be exercised *within specific spheres of responsibility* (Gal. 2:7-9).

Paul's Confidence in the Churches, in Their Leaders, and in the Grace of God

Roland Allen has a most significant insight into the confidence Paul had in the Holy Spirit to direct the local churches.[3] As an Anglo-Catholic, Allen overplays the importance of the sacraments. He perhaps underplays the importance of sound doctrine. But his emphasis on Paul's confidence in the Spirit-led congregation and its leaders is not misplaced. Paul knew that his fledgling congregations would be tested. But he did not believe that his physical presence was critical to their success in standing for truth and moving forward for Christ. He knew that one measurement of faithful service is abiding fruit (John 15:16). Confident that he had been faithful and that the One who had begun a good work would complete it (Phil. 1:6), he could depart from one church after a limited time and begin another. He could speak as though *his* work was done (Rom. 15:18-24), confident that the believers in the churches were evangelizing their environs (I Thess. 1:6-

---

[3]Roland Allen, *The Spontaneous Expansion of the Church* (Grand Rapids: Eerdmans, 1962).

8). His confidence in the churches was matched by his confidence in coworkers on whose shoulders the mantle of leadership was to fall. He was confident that they understood their task and would carry it out faithfully (Titus 1:5).

Relevant Research

The history of religions provides numerous illustrations of the importance of an orderly transition of leadership within religious movements. This is especially true in the case of founders (or pioneers) and their disciples.

When we look at the history of Buddhism, for example, we have a classic example of how important the transition of leadership really is. The record of early Buddhism is not entirely clear, but the case of Nichiren Buddhism in Japan is most instructive. When, in the thirteenth century, the iconoclastic and nationalistic prophet Nichiren died, he did not designate any one of his disciples as their leader. Disagreement and division were the predictable results. When, in the twentieth century, the new Nichirenist lay movement known as Soka Gakkai mushroomed under the leadership of Josei Toda, observers almost universally agreed that it would languish when he died. They did not reckon on Toda's foresight, however. Toda had groomed a disciple, Daisaku Ikeda, and had him waiting in the wings. Upon Toda's death in 1958, and after a smooth transition of authority to a prepared leader, the movement grew as never before!

Students of religion, however, will be aware that *the* classical example is provided by Islam. Because Muhammad died suddenly, he had named no successor (caliph). His followers were left to decide who would be their leader, and the basis upon which he would be chosen. The resultant tensions and schisms have plagued Islam for thirteen centuries!

These illustrations may seem far-fetched to some. After

all, they come from outside the Christian tradition and seem far removed from the local Christian church. The more one reflects on them, however, the more one realizes that the principles involved are universal. And the more one will appreciate Christ and Peter and Paul and perceptive missionary pioneers at home and abroad!

Practical Reflections

When it comes to transition of leadership in the Church, there are two critical concerns:

(1) Bible schools and seminaries need to provide training for the kinds of church leadership required by growing churches. (This is not to minimize the importance of lay leaders.) Precisely at this point the difference between the West and the Third World is most evident. The Christian training institutions in the West prepare comparatively few "pioneers," with the result that there are few workers who are adequately trained for planting new churches. Many Christian training institutions in the Third World prepare evangelists (in the narrow sense of that term) and comparatively few "consolidators," with the result that churches languish for want of adequately trained pastor-teachers. These imbalances are easily explained. In the West the educational focus is on hundreds of churches that need pastoring. In the Third World the educational focus is on thousands of unreached areas that need evangelizing. It is easy to lose sight of the fact that there are thousands of churchless communities in the West and thousands of churches in the Third World.

ME-3 illustration: Missionaries and national leaders in a 30,000-member denomination in central Africa came to a rather rude awakening some years ago. Hundreds of people were making confession of faith and being baptized. Numerous churches were being planted in villages large and small. Amidst the apparent success, however, one great problem persisted despite efforts to solve it. Members were leaving the churches almost as fast as new ones were joining. Changes in local church programs and leadership personnel had little or no effect. Finally, the primary contributing factor became apparent. The training institution for Christian workers was preparing evangelists, those who could gather crowds, preach the gospel, win the lost, and (in some cases) start churches. But it was not training workers who could manage the church, build up believers in the faith, and minister to families in turmoil. The curriculum and practical assignments were then modified. Institutes were held for those in the ministry. Gradually, the local churches have begun to stabilize. Growth has apparently become permanent.

(2) Missionary-evangelists and other leaders in new churches need to prepare themselves and the congregation for a transition in pastoral leadership. In some ways this transition is fraught with the same possibilities for good or ill as is any change in pastoral leadership. After all, successful church-planting missionary-evangelists must do the work of a pastor, and successful pastors must do the work of an evangelist. This first transition is likely to be the most critical, however.

The Continuation of the Ministries

Biblical Principles and Precedents

Paul's confidence was not misplaced. Sometimes members of his team were called upon to continue the ministries in evangelized areas (Titus 1:5). At all times, the leaders and laity in local churches were called upon to communicate the gospel and extend the work in their areas (Phil. 2:15, 16). But Christians are not perfect. Some leaders would fall by the wayside (II Tim. 4:10); some believers would succumb to temptation (I Cor. 10:12); and some of the churches would be in jeopardy (Gal. 3:1). Paul knew that. Still he expressed confidence in the believers (Gal.

5:10), and he and members of his team pressed forward to win converts and establish congregations.

Relevant Research

Most of the research and resultant literature relating to the continuation of ministries initiated by pioneer workers has to do with overseas missions. Furthermore, most of it has to do with rather broad geographical areas and a large variety of ministries. Nevertheless, the conclusions are instructive when applied to local situations at home as well as abroad.

The Western missionary, so welcome in so many places in post-World War II days, became less welcome in the late 1950s and early 1960s. In fact, in 1964 two books, *The Unpopular Missionary*[4] and *Missionary, Go Home*,[5] served to focus attention on the pleas of some nationals and expatriates to discontinue the work of missionaries and bring them home. Church leaders and conclaves called for a moratorium on missions in certain areas of the world. This reversal of the missionary call undoubtedly had its effect. Revolutions, abortive and successful, had an even greater effect. For whatever reason, missionaries were dissuaded from entering some countries and found it impossible to stay in others.

Whatever legitimacy the plea for withdrawal may have had (when pioneers overstay, it is certainly legitimate to ask them to move on!), the results of a nonstrategic discontinuation of missionary ministries were predictable. Already in 1970, Arden Almquist gathered data that motivated him to write *Missionary, Come Back.*[6] He noted

---

[4]Ralph E. Dodge, *The Unpopular Missionary* (Westwood, NJ: Fleming H. Revell, 1964).

[5]James Scherer, *Missionary, Go Home* (Englewood Cliffs, NJ: Prentice-Hall, 1964).

[6]Arden Almquist, *Missionary, Come Back* (Cleveland: World Publishing Co., 1970).

the widespread pleas of leaders and laity in Zaire for missionaries to come back and pick up ministries that had deteriorated or collapsed in their absence. Almquist insisted that the pleas were not limited to Africa nor to medical and educational ministries. He cited, for example, the needs of the churches in Indonesia. And what he said with special reference to Indonesia is most significant for all of us.

> It is recognized by national Christian leadership that unless help is secured for Christians abroad, and soon, much of the harvest may be lost by reversion to the past, or to quasi-Christian sects. Wherever there are sheep without shepherds one hears the cry "Missionary, Come Back!" And where there are shepherds whose flocks are too large for adequate pasturing and watering, the cry is also heard.[7]

The important thing is the *ministry*. Men come and go. The ministry is a continuing thing. It is tempting to stand in lecture halls and make pronouncements. But the history of the last twenty years serves to remind us that, in the final analysis, the important thing is to be out on the fields where men and women are hurting and where there are ministries to be performed.

Practical Reflection

The lessons of the New Testament and of the history of churches and missions are uncomplicated and unequivocal. The ministry of any local church or mission will suffer greatly if the withdrawal of pioneer workers comes either too soon or too late. The baton must be passed to the next runner. When the pioneer leaves the race without passing on the baton, he departs too soon. When he continues to hold the baton until he has exhausted his time and resources, it may be too late.

---

[7]Ibid., p. 58.

ME-3 illustration: Two churches were started by church-planting missionaries in the same Asian city. We will call the churches "A" and "B." The missionary who started Church "A" was especially gifted. Services were crowded, souls were saved, the church flourished. In fact, mission leaders pointed to Church "A" to show what could be accomplished by a hard-working expatriate in a relatively resistant area. The months and years sped by. Just before furlough time a frantic search was made for a national or missionary who could continue the work. Before a replacement was found the missionary left for the United States. Weeks went by. Attendance at Church "A" diminished. Finally, a new worker arrived in the church. But with lesser and different gifts he found it impossible to continue the variegated program inaugurated by his predecessor. The church languished. After a few years of struggle it was dissolved.

The history of Church "B" has been entirely different. With lesser gifts but more foresight, its founding missionary leaned more heavily on his laymen and laywomen. After a relatively short time he encouraged the church to look for a national worker who might eventually take over the work. By furlough time, the ministry of Church "B" was in the hands of this national worker and qualified laymen. The transition was smooth. Today, some twenty-five years later, Church "B" is flourishing with a ministry that reaches well beyond its own community to other parts of the country and even further.

This "tale of two churches" has undoubtedly been duplicated in numerous places. There are countless examples of monuments, on the one hand, to the shortsightedness of God's servants and, on the other, to their foresight and wisdom. We repeat, men with a mission come and go. Churches and their ministries spring to life because they come. Churches and their ministries may long outlive them, depending on when and how they go.

FIGURE 51
Leadership Transition Schedule

A. Time Sequence for Leadership Transition
   1. Projected date of the reassignment of the pioneer worker _____
   2. Projected date of the coming of a new pastor _____
   3. Projected date for initiation of "Steps in the Provision of New Pastoral Leadership" (see below) _____
B. Plans for the Support of New Pastoral Leadership
   1. Source(s) of financial support _____
   _____
   _____
   2. Budgetary provision in the local church _____
   3. Schedule of subsidy reduction (if subsidies are involved) _____
C. Steps in the Provision of New Pastoral Leadership
   1. Preparation of a job description (Date) _____
   2. Recommendations solicited (Date) _____
   3. Résumés solicited and reviewed (Date) _____
   4. Meeting of candidate with church board and congregation (Date) _____
   5. Call issued (Date) _____
D. Items for Consideration in the Preparation and Instruction of the Congregation
   1. Instruction concerning the scriptural role of the pastor in the church. Yes _____ No _____
   2. Instruction concerning scriptural attitudes and responsibilities toward the pastor. Yes _____ No _____
   3. Preparation of the congregation by introducing appropriate variations into the church program. (This is especially important if and when the identity, ministerial style, and aspirations of the incoming pastor become known.) Yes _____ No _____
E. Planning for Continuity of Ministries
   Ministries now dependent on the missionary-evangelist for leadership or expertise:

Ministry	A:	B:	C:
1. Replacement leader's name			
2. Date partial responsibility to be assumed			
3. Date full responsibility to be assumed			

Master Plan Formation

The ministry of the missionary-evangelist is a temporary one in any given location. Of course, not all churches are begun under the leadership of specialists. But more could be and probably should be. And even when they are not, the basic problem of the transition of leadership remains, though the process will, of course, differ somewhat from personality to personality, place to place, and culture to culture.

We will proceed by first pointing out the major items to be considered in forming a master plan for the withdrawal-transition-continuation process and then providing a composite Leadership Transition Schedule (see Figure 51).

Withdrawal of the Pioneer Worker

Plans for withdrawal of the pioneer worker entail two basic aspects:

Local Church Preparation

The leaders and members of the newly-formed local church should not be taken by surprise at the departure of the missionary-evangelist. Theologically, psychologically, and practically they should be prepared for his departure. Otherwise, disappointment and even bitterness may result.

Missionary-evangelist Redeployment

Reassignment for the Christian worker may be no less difficult for him and his family than it is for the church family. Depending on the length of time spent in the target area, the involvement of family members, the availability of housing and services, and so on, moving may be extremely difficult for modern Pauls! Prior understanding as to when and how decisions relative to withdrawal and relocation are reached will go a long way to alleviate the problem. The mobility of the missionary-evangelistic force must be maintained if there is to be a continued outreach.

Leadership Transition

Circumstances differ widely. In ME-1 situations where the church-planter does not continue as pastor, his ministry will terminate before the ministry of the new pastor begins. In many ME-3 situations, a young, aspiring pastor will work with the church-planter for some time before the latter withdraws. Whatever the circumstance, there are two primary aspects of leadership transition that deserve consideration:

The Utilization of Lay Leadership

Blessed is the local church whose leaders have had actual experience in ministering the Word and in administration of the church. That church will be much better prepared to face any eventuality that may attend the transition from missionary to pastoral leadership.

Preparing the Way for the New Pastor

By design, the church-planter can do much to assure the acceptance and support of the new leader. By teaching biblical attitudes toward those who minister the Word, by adjusting the church budget in such a way that pastoral support will be available, by introducing flexibility into the program, by personally demonstrating what it means to "submit to one another in the fear of the Lord"—by these and other such means the way can be prepared for the new pastor.

A word of caution is in order here. These matters are crucial and therefore deserve careful planning. If, for example, the church-planter has outside support, perhaps a corresponding obligation to home missions should be a part of the church budget until the new pastor arrives.

Thus the shock of adding this major new item to the budget can be avoided. If the new pastor's support is to be partially subsidized, plans should be made for that subsidy to come to the *church* (not directly to the pastor) so that responsibility to the congregation is maintained. Even before the new pastor is called, consideration should be given to experientially preparing the congregation for new forms in the worship service. Thus the congregation will be able to adjust to whatever new ideas and ways he may have of doing things.

The Continuation of Ministries

Primary Ministries

If the leaders and ordinary members of the new church fellowship have been active with the missionary-evangelist in discipling ministries, those ministries will likely continue under the new leadership. Continuation should not be taken for granted, however. Whenever possible, plans should be made to orientate the incoming pastor, either directly or indirectly.

Supporting Ministries

Plans for initiating secondary ministries should include their eventual transference to local leadership. In ME-2 and ME-3 situations this is perhaps the most difficult hurdle to keeping missionary-evangelists involved in primary ministries and to keeping a mobile missionary force.

It is no easy task to turn the spiritual results of months (and perhaps years) of self-giving, dedicated ministry over to the care of another. In the face of such a transition, anxiety is to be expected. Will the new leader really care for the flock of God? Will the congregation accept him? Will the attendant ministries be carried on faithfully? Will the church continue to grow? These and many other questions occur to the missionary-evangelist. In one sense, they must have occurred to the Lord Jesus. Certainly they occurred to the apostle Paul as time after time he left fledgling congregations just when he had become most aware of their strengths and weaknesses and, in some ways, had become better prepared to lead them to full maturity in Christ.

How can this anxiety be resolved? What will enable the missionary-evangelist to move on in accordance with his calling? In the final analysis, it will not be the spiritual strength of the congregation, though many of its members may have made great progress in their walk with the Lord. Nor will it be the gifts and dedication of the pastor-elect, encouraging though his reputation might be. In the final analysis, the pioneer worker confidently makes his plans and ultimately moves on because he believes in the grace of God and the power of His Spirit. After doing what he can, he commends the congregation to God and departs.

sixteen

The Relationships Continued

"God be with you... Till we meet at Jesus' feet" is too often interpreted as meaning that we will not meet again until we meet in heaven. In actuality most church-planters have a number of opportunities to meet their congregations again before they are promoted to their pew in the Church Triumphant! Paul did. And how he and the congregations cherished the prospect of those meetings!

But human relationships are fraught with all sorts of possibilities for good and ill. It was so then. It is so now. Happy is the pioneer, therefore, who has thought through the issues and who lays a solid foundation for future relationships with the new congregation. Happy is the pioneer, and happy is the congregation, who build continuing and mutually beneficial relationships on that foundation!

Objectives

Sooner or later, with few exceptions, the local congregation will be forced to come to grips with questions of con-

FIGURE 52
"THE PAULINE CYCLE"

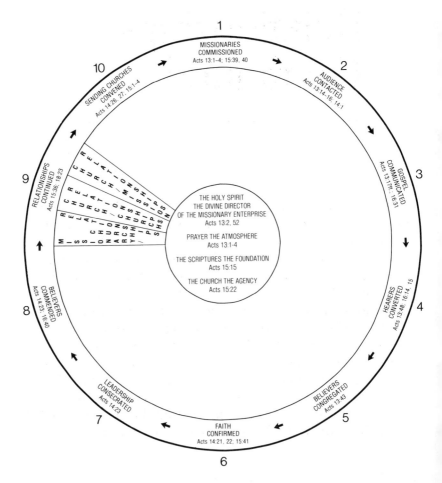

tinuing horizontal relationships. These relationships will be of three types: with departing workers (especially the one who established the church); with other churches (especially the fellowship of churches or denomination which sponsored the church); and with the mission (especially the mission of the departing pioneer worker). If wholesome patterns of church-denomination and church-mission relationships have been initiated before the leave-taking of the pioneer missionary-evangelist, the congregation will be in a much better position to face any difficulties that may attend his departure. If the leaders of the congregation and the pioneer sit down together to pray and discuss what their future relationships ought to be, the congregation will benefit even more. With that in mind we will explore the issues and strive for the following objectives:

(1) To establish between the founding missionary-evangelist and the founded church a continuing relationship which will be spiritually stimulating and mutually rewarding.

(2) To establish between the founded church and the fellowship of churches or denomination a continuing relationship which will strengthen their witness to the world and enhance the spiritual and numerical growth of both.

(3) To establish between the founded church and the founding mission a continuing relationship that will further the worldwide mission of the Church of Christ.

The perplexing and continuing problems that attend these three types of relationships reflect the fact that the Bible does not speak decisively concerning the details of these relationships. It is probably also true that we do not carefully heed what the Bible does have to say. When one adds the widespread reluctance of many Christian workers to deal with these issues until they are forced to do so, that we have problems in these relationships should not come as a surprise.

The Founding Missionary/Founded
Church Relationship

Biblical Principles and Precedents

The relationship that existed between Paul and the churches was manifestly a spiritual one. Even in the case of that great apostle, the relationship could not be characterized as being one of "dominion" (II Cor. 1:24). It is best summed up in that important word *koinōnia* (Phil. 1:5). *Koinōnia* is usually translated "fellowship," but it could be justifiably translated "joint participation" or "partnership" (among other possibilities).

The New Testament gives clear indications of what was involved in true *koinōnia*. We can cite, for example, John's words concerning his relationship to Diotrephes and the church of which he was a member (III John 9, 10); Peter's words to elders (I Peter 5:1–4); and, especially, Paul's detailed descriptions of his interaction with the churches he founded. From Paul's letters we can deduce the major elements in *koinōnia:*

(1) The apostle felt a responsibility for the continued well-being (especially spiritual well-being) of the churches and believers he had fathered in the faith. All of the Pauline Letters bear witness to this. Paul did not wash his hands of the sometimes impure Corinthian Christians once they had said their mutual farewells. He did not write off the churches in Galatia because some of their believers had been hoodwinked by the Judaizers. Rather, he had a genuine and abiding burden for the fledgling churches and their members. So much so that he writes of "the daily pressure . . . of concern for all the churches" (II Cor. 11:28).

(2) The founded churches were expected to give special attention to the words spoken, and the example set, by the apostle, precisely because he had fathered them in the

faith. Listen to Paul's words in I Corinthians 4:15, 16: "For if you were to have countless tutors in Christ, yet you would not have many fathers; for in Christ Jesus I became your father through the gospel. I exhort you therefore, be imitators of me." (Cf. also Phil. 2:1, 2 in this connection.)

(3) The founded churches participated with Paul in his ministry through prayer, gifts, and the sending of helpers (Phil. 2:25; 4:14–16; Col. 4:3). Note, however, that though the apostle greatly appreciated and even solicited some types of partnership, he by no means demanded it nor did he always receive it (Phil. 4:15).

This simple overview does not provide clear answers to many contemporary questions. Paul's position as a special apostle introduces a unique factor into these cases. Obviously, Paul (and John and Peter) possessed an authority that church leaders do not possess today. Quite apart from that authority, however, it seems evident that New Testament *koinōnia* involved a reciprocal concern, respect, and obligation between the apostle and the churches he founded, a relationship that went beyond a handshake and a farewell. It entailed an abiding concern, each for the other, and all for the Christian cause.

Relevant Research

Given the individualism, the kinship and value systems, and the mobility of many Western societies, it is understandable that teacher-student, friend-friend, and even parent-child relationships are considerably different than they are in much of the rest of the world, and also that reciprocity systems are less demanding. The Chinese still live according to the obligations built into Confucius's "five relationships." Filipinos consider *utang na loob* (obligations) as extremely important. The Japanese have an intricate network of obligations.

It is difficult to describe the attitudes and feelings that attend these obligations. They are deep-rooted and extend far past the time when they are easy to fulfill. One has to experience them in each society in order to really understand them. And yet the *basic* feeling is something we all know well.

It is true that obligations of various types deter many from becoming Christians in the aforementioned cultures. That is the dark side of the picture. But it is also true that adherence to the rules governing these relationships makes for stability and qualities of trust that the Church and its leaders should both emulate and model.

Practical Reflection

Upon parting, founders of new churches and the churches themselves must walk a tightrope between two extremes. The first is the tendency on the part of some missionary-evangelists to maintain such close ties with the church (or with friends in the church) that they infringe upon the prerogatives of the new leader. There is the parallel tendency for some churches to remain emotionally and spiritually dependent upon the founding missionary-evangelist to a degree that discourages the new leader.

The other extreme is the tendency of many missionary-evangelists and their churches to part company and practically forget one another. After the first few weeks or months there are negligible communication, little prayer for one another, and minimal mutual concern.

The first extreme (too close ties) is more characteristic of churches in the Third World. The latter extreme (broken ties) is more characteristic of churches in the West. But both extremes can be seen East and West. How much better that, in every culture, we seek a middle ground between the extremes! Before parting let the pioneer worker and the local leaders briefly discuss their future relationship. Not that it needs to be programed. That would undercut the delight of a spontaneous holiday greeting, an invitation to an anniversary gathering, or a gift for a special ministry. But, avoiding extremes, let there be a continuing *koinōnia* within some basic guidelines.

The Founded Church and Its Relationships with Other Churches

Biblical Principles and Precedents

The matter of the relationship between the New Testament churches presents us with numerous unanswered questions. When the Epistles were written, church relationships were in an early stage of development. When, in the second and third centuries, that development became much more formalized and complete, it was not necessarily more exemplary. Are we, then, left to do as we please? Hardly, for however basic and simple they may appear to be, there are biblical principles and precedents, and they constitute a clear indication that, just as believers are to relate to one another in local churches, so local churches are to relate to one another in a larger fellowship which reflects the Church Universal.

The Spiritual Basis of Interchurch Fellowship

It is patently clear that when our Lord said, "I will build My church" (Matt. 16:18), and when He prayed, "that they may all be one" (John 17:21), He had *one* Church in mind. It is tragically true that His builders tend to misconstrue and neglect this clear biblical teaching. Take, by way of example, the common interpretation of I Corinthians 3:16, "Know ye not that ye are the temple of God, and that the Spirit of God dwelleth in you?" (KJV). Most Christians, without so much as a second thought, interpret this to mean that individual Christians are temples of God. Some do interpret the "temple of God" as a reference to the church at Corinth. But note what Henry Alford says about this passage:

> Meyer rightly remarks, that "*naos Theou* is the *temple* of God, not *a* temple of God: for Paul does not conceive . . . of the *various temples* of God, which would be inconsistent with a Jew's conception of God's temple, but of each Christian church as *sensu mystico, the temple of Jehovah.* So there would be not many temples, but many churches, each of which is, ideally, the same temple of God." And, we may add, if the figure is to be strictly justified in its widest acceptation, that all the churches are built together into one vast temple.[1]

The fact that the biblical emphasis on one Church has been used to promote the cause of organizational unity at the expense of other truths does not justify our disregard of this truth and its implications.

Paul and Interchurch Relationships

As far as we know, Paul did not organize the local churches he founded into regional ecclesiastical organizations. Nevertheless, those local churches were not left to themselves. They were bound together in two types of relationships.

First, there was a relationship of *authority.* By virtue of the presence of the apostles, the church at Jerusalem had certain prerogatives. It sent Barnabas to monitor what was happening in the new church at Antioch (Acts 11:22–26). Barnabas stayed on as a teacher in that church (Acts 13:1, 2). Paul went to Jerusalem to consult with the apostles as to his message (Gal. 1:18, 19). When questions were raised in connection with the conversion of the Gentiles, the missionaries went to the Jerusalem church and submitted the issue to its leaders (Acts 15:1, 2).

Second, there was a relationship of *koinōnia* in the body of Christ. Mutual obligations were urged upon them as the

---

[1]Henry Alford, *The Greek Testament,* vol. 2 (Chicago: Moody Press, 1958), p. 495.

proper expressions of their oneness in Christ (Gal. 6:10). The New Testament notes various manifestations of their close fellowship:

(1) The churches founded by the apostles recognized that in Christ they had a common bond with one another—and particularly with the mother church in Jerusalem (Acts 15:1, 2; Rom. 15:26, 27).

(2) The churches regularly sent Christian greetings to each other (Rom. 16:16; I Cor. 16:19, 20; Phil. 4:23).

(3) They collaborated on a project to provide money for the poor saints in the Jerusalem church (Rom. 15:26; I Cor. 16:1-3).

(4) They sent representatives to one another (Acts 11:22, 23, 27; 15:1, 2; I Cor. 16:3, 4).

(5) They supported the apostles' labor in other fields (Phil. 4:15, 16).

(6) They shared letters from the apostles (Col. 4:16).

(7) They encouraged one another by modeling the faith (II Cor. 1:24; 9:2; I Thess. 1:7-10; 2:14).

(8) They cooperated in the common cause of evangelism (I Thess. 1:8).

It is evident that local churches today are not related to any other church in exactly the same way as those first-century churches were related to the Jerusalem church. Churches today do not have a mother church in that sense. But today's churches are authentic churches only to the extent that they evidence subjection to the same apostolic authority by adhering to the faith and practice of the Holy Scriptures. It is this adherence that marks them as part of the Universal Church. Moreover, this adherence will lead to *koinōnia* with other churches under the same authority —a *koinōnia* that will find practical expression in cooperation in good works and glad witness.

Relevant Research

There are at least two lines of research that bear out the importance of supralocal authority and participation.

First, dynamic and growing religious movements of diverse cultures and orientations tend to be decidedly hierarchical in their organization:

The three branches of Caodai, the "apostle" orientation of the New Apostolic Church and Mormonism, the "prophet" orientation of Zionism and Kimbanguism, the president and board of directors arrangement in Soka Gakkai all exhibit authority patterns which are at once definite and graded. Sometimes the organization extends right down to the local levels with an efficiency and explicitness that is reminiscent of the military (Iglesia ni Cristo, Jehovah's Witnesses). On the other hand, the nomenclature used may seem to be democratic and egalitarian (United Pentecostal). In either case the organizations tend to be authoritarian. Lines of authority are seldom blurred or disregarded. Checks and balances there may be, but these seem to be operative mainly at secondary and tertiary levels of leadership. Believers know where real authority lies, and it is usually at the top![2]

Second, the study of distinctly Christian churches in the Third World reveals a similar tendency. In one of the most careful examinations that has been made of the outworking of different approaches to planting churches, Peter Beyerhaus and Henry Lefever conclude:

It seems to be the universal experience of all Protestant missions that the congregational principle cannot be put into practice by itself in the mission-field. Even the independents, as we saw in Anderson's case, have found themselves forced to resort, at least temporarily, to a centralized system in order to guarantee the stability of what they had created. Moreover, episcopacy has a strong appeal in nearly all mission-fields, even where the actual term is not used, as for example in Sumatra. To the student of mis-

---

[2]David J. Hesselgrave, "What Causes Religious Movements to Grow?" in *Dynamic Religious Movements: Case Studies of Rapidly Growing Religious Movements Around the World,* ed. David J. Hesselgrave (Grand Rapids: Baker, 1978), pp. 308–09.

sions that throws a new light on the New Testament pronouncements concerning the problem of church-order.[3]

We must be careful not to jump to the conclusion that episcopal, hierarchical church order is true church order because, all else being equal, it promotes unified belief and action. At the same time, however, we cannot settle for a congregationalism that does no more than mesh with Western democratic and egalitarian ideals. All that we as Christians are allowed to deduce from these studies is that recognizable authority outside of the local group and some measure of subjection to or at least cooperation with that authority seem to be related to effective functioning and growth.

Practical Reflection

Westerners (particularly North Americans) have a cultural bias toward promoting overindependency on the part of the churches they establish. Even when their churches actually belong to a larger fellowship of churches, the likelihood of those churches' assuming an active role in the larger fellowship is not always great. Certain aspects of interchurch relationships, therefore, merit special attention by church-planting personnel.

The Importance of Interchurch Fellowship

There is no substitute for active involvement in an interchurch fellowship. In certain circumstances, individual Christians must survive without the edification provided by fellowship with other Christians. Usually, however, they will be poorer for their isolation. The same is true of congregations. Nothing can replace the deepened faith, en-

---

[3]Peter Beyerhaus and Henry Lefever, *The Responsible Church and the Foreign Mission* (Grand Rapids: Eerdmans, 1964), p. 162.

larged vision, increased sacrifice, and enhanced outreach that participation in a larger fellowship affords.

Churches tied in to a specific denomination will thereby have a feeling of unity and fellowship. In the case of churches with congregational polity and in the case of interdenominational missions, however, the local congregation will be largely dependent upon missionary-evangelists and other leaders for guidance. If this guidance is not forthcoming, one of three things is likely to occur eventually. First, the local congregation may become completely cut off from other congregations. Second, the local group may divide into factions with differing outside loyalties. Third, the congregation may join a suborthodox organization which provides fellowship and unity but at the expense of truth and purity.

ME-1-3 illustration: A well-known missionary organization which is engaged in evangelizing and discipling all around the world has run head-on into this problem. Because it raises funds on an interdenominational basis, it feels duty-bound not to set up anything resembling a fellowship of churches or a denomination. Consequently, new groups of believers are left to work out interrelationships largely on their own. Some of them join together in what amounts to area-wide fellowships of independent churches—a denomination of sorts. Many others have fallen into one or another of the three traps mentioned above.

ME-3 illustration: The small but rapidly growing Evangelical Free churches in Japan merit careful study. Urged and guided to form themselves into a viable national organization from the first, they went considerably beyond their parent body in the United States in effecting cooperation and fellowship. Out of this cooperation has come a program for starting new congregations by sending personnel and providing seed money (often tens of thousands of dollars) from existing congregations. This is usually done with no thought of repayment but in the anticipation that when it has grown sufficiently, the new congregation will participate in the same kind of outreach. This kind of generosity and cooperation has resulted in an extremely high level of per capita stewardship and comparatively rapid growth in a land which many regard as resistant to the gospel.

The Uniqueness of the Relationship Between the Founded Church and the Founding Denomination or Fellowship

As the Head of the Church, Christ rules the churches. He does so primarily through the Holy Spirit-inspired Word which He gave to and through the prophets and apostles. Ultimately, every duly constituted congregation is responsible before God to abide faithful to that Word. It cannot escape that responsibility by simply deferring to a founding denomination or mother church.

On the other hand, it is not too far-fetched to assume that if the individual who "fathers" believers in the faith has some special prerogatives, the fellowship that "mothers" a congregation has some special prerogatives also. And the resultant relationship has some very significant benefits. Not only does the new church have a ready-made opportunity to realize a wider fellowship in the gospel. It also enjoys the steadying influence and helpful monitoring that such a relationship can provide. Just as the hazards of the shoreline are left behind a departing ship, so newer churches face difficulties that diminish as progress is made. The local church is far less likely to flounder near the shore if it is able to link up with the Universal Church through a sponsoring denomination or fellowship. For that reason, constitutional and practical reinforcements for this kind of initial and continuing relationship should be provided.

Relationships Between Churches and Missions

In recent years one of the most extensively discussed questions in mission circles has been that of the relationship between the missions and the churches that result from their labors. On the one side are to be found the proponents of fusion or merger. They insist that *mission* is the responsibility of the *Church*, that missions have no basis for maintaining their separate existence, and that missionary personnel and organizations should be incorporated into the churches they establish.[4]

On the other side are to be found the proponents of separation. They insist that a primary purpose for the organizing of missions has been to evangelize the world and plant new churches; that if missions are merged with the churches they establish, this ministry will be impeded or aborted; and that missions must maintain a position of equal partnership with the churches in order to carry out their proper function.

In between these polar positions, all sorts of compromises have been proposed.

Biblical Principles and Precedents

Even a cursory reading of the Bible reveals that Christ ordained the Church (and, therefore, the churches) and gave it a mission. That the apostles and the churches carried out their mission in the first century is equally clear. It is impossible to make the same kind of a case for mission organizations. Paul's team affords the closest New Testament parallel to modern mission agencies. But the differences between Paul's team and the large interdenominational missions of the modern era are probably greater and more numerous than are the similarities.

What, then, can be concluded on the basis of the New Testament? Can we not say that Christ builds the Church, that every believer is made a member of that Church, that the apostles had a special authority in that Church, and

---

[4]Cf. Stephen Neill, *Creative Tension* (London: Edinburgh House Press, 1959).

that Christ's mission in the world was to be carried out by apostles and believers in the churches as they were led by the Holy Spirit? The Bible, then, does not allow for a missionless church or a churchless mission. It *requires* that churches be engaged in mission and that they send out missionaries. It *allows* for organization among those going forth in missionary service. Organized missions plant churches, but they do not supplant churches.

Relevant Research

Historical and pragmatic cases can be made for the importance of elitist fellowships of Christians. It has been pointed out that one reason for the retarded beginnings in Protestant missions after the Reformation was that the Reformers rejected the Catholic orders that had been in the forefront of the missionary enterprise of the Roman Church. Thus, even when ecclesiastical difficulties and theological questions that discouraged missionary-evangelistic activities had been partially resolved, the organizational vehicles for world mission were not present. Protestants had to begin by building their own "orders" which, for the most part, cut across ecclesiastical (denominational) lines.

From examples like that of the Protestant start in the mission enterprise it has been concluded that modalities (vertically-structured organizations that include men and women, young and old—such as churches and denominations) *need* sodalities (horizontally-structured organizations that are made up of people with special expertise or interests—such as missions, evangelistic associations, and other parachurch organizations). As Ralph Winter expresses it, "Churches need missions, because modalities need sodalities."[5]

---

[5]Ralph Winter and R. Pierce Beaver, *The Warp and the Woof: Organizing for Mission* (South Pasadena, CA: William Carey Library, 1971), p. 62.

Historically, mission agencies have played a major role in carrying out the mission of the Church. The Church and missions must work together. Arguments used to support the existence of missionary organizations that are separate from (rather than "within" and "under") the organized Church are somewhat less than convincing.

Practical Reflection

Missionary-evangelists (and the missions) are often caught in the middle between the churches which sent them and the churches which they helped to plant. In some cases, churches as such do not send them at all. In any case the issues are complex because the missions must walk a line which fulfills their responsibility both to those who sent them and those who subsequently host them. We believe that the issues can be resolved only when we keep in view the permanency of the Church and the temporary nature of the mission organizations. When this perspective is adopted, mission agencies may remain as partners of the churches while the latter grow and mature. Even so staunch a churchman as Harvie Conn has concluded as much:

> In the awesome complexity of transition between the initiation of evangelistic work in an area, and forming of the structure of the church, the patterns implicit in terminology like "partnership of mutuality" and "cooperation of autonomous equals" are serviceable, as much so as in the transition of a North American home mission work from preaching point to formal organization as a structured body of Christ. But ultimately, the biblical call to unity in the worldwide fellowship Christ has instituted is a call to the consideration of the legitimacy of separate structures.[6]

_____

[6]Harvie M. Conn, "Church-Mission Relationships," mimeographed manuscript for the Reformed Missions and the Theology of Church Growth Consultation, March 24-26, 1975, at Westminster Theological Seminary, p. 18.

FIGURE 53

Basic Patterns of Relationship
Between Church and Mission

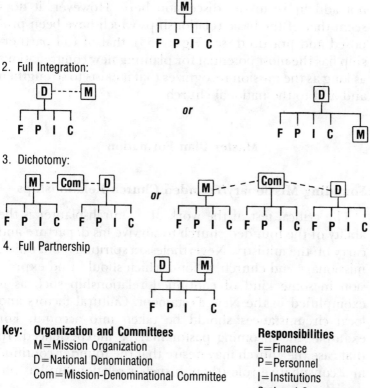

1. Paternalism:

2. Full Integration:

   or

3. Dichotomy:

   or

4. Full Partnership

Key: **Organization and Committees**
   M=Mission Organization
   D=National Denomination
   Com=Mission-Denominational Committee

   Responsibilities
   F=Finance
   P=Personnel
   I=Institutions
   C=Local Congregations

Conn's call for ultimate integration of church and mission is understandable in the light of the paternalism of many missions in the past and the New Testament emphasis on the Church. However, we must not forget two factors. First, most missions exist under the aegis of sending churches. Second, as long as governments allow missions the freedom to evangelize and extend the frontiers of the Church, the responsibility and opportunity to do so should not be forfeited in order to integrate with receiving churches which do not have a vision for that God-given task.

The relationship of field missions and national (and local) churches has been a topic of much debate. We will not add more to the discussion here. However, it does seem that of the basic relationships which have been proposed and practiced (see Figure 53), that of full partnership has the most potential for planting new congregations as long as the mission recognizes that it exists to strengthen and add to the national church.

Master Plan Formation

Founding Missionary/Founded Church Relationships

The critical test of the work of a church-planter is the ability of the founded church to survive his departure and carry on the ministry. Nevertheless, a spiritual bond unites missionary and church, a bond which should find expression in some kind of continued relationship such as is exemplified in the New Testament. Cultural factors and local circumstances should be taken into account. For example, the incoming pastor may be inexperienced. In that case the church may desire that the founder continue in a consultative role (though such a relationship has potential problems).

In a spirit of cooperation and concern, then, let the missionary-evangelist and church leaders discuss future relationships. Avoiding extremes, let them first determine the type of relationship that they want to establish. This can best be done by thinking in terms of the degree of relationship desired (see Figure 54).

Second, the church-planter and church leaders would

FIGURE 54

Continuum of Founder/Church Relationships

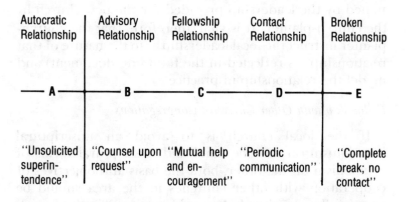

Autocratic Relationship	Advisory Relationship	Fellowship Relationship	Contact Relationship	Broken Relationship
— A ——	—— B ——	—— C ——	—— D ——	—— E
"Unsolicited superintendence"	"Counsel upon request"	"Mutual help and encouragement"	"Periodic communication"	"Complete break; no contact"

do well to project in some detail the form that their relationship will take in the immediate future. For example, if the church decides to support a new effort to be undertaken by the missionary-evangelist, the extent of this support should be clear. Again, if the missionary-evangelist is expected to visit the church periodically, it would be well to spell out the frequency and purpose of such visits. Of course, this kind of planning is not meant to rule out those spontaneous expressions of Christian love which mean so much to the family of God. Rather, such planning is merely to insure that the continuing relationship, whatever forms it might take, will be built on mutual understanding and respect.

Church/Church Relationships

The master plan should include provision for interchurch relationships of two basic types: those with the sponsoring denomination or fellowship of churches and those with other Christian congregations.

Relationship with the Sponsoring Denomination

The kind of relationship which the local church will have with the sponsoring denomination will be determined by the leadership provided for the new church by the church-planter. It is vital, therefore, that the church-planter instruct the local leadership as to the nature of that relationship (as reflected in the founding document) and model the relationship in practice.

Fellowship with Other Christian Congregations

If the local church is to avoid an unscriptural isolationism on the one hand and unscriptural forms of ecumenism on the other, both the basis and objectives of cooperation with other churches in the area should be prayerfully considered. A simple statement in the founding document or official record as to the essential items of faith upon which cooperation and fellowship will be based will go far toward averting future dissension or confusion in the local church. To a somewhat lesser extent, the initiation of certain types of cooperation will be important. Consider, for example, cooperation in the following areas:

(1) Evangelistic efforts
(2) Worship services
(3) Special occasions on the church calendar (e.g., Good Friday and Easter)
(4) Community projects

Church/Mission Relationships

The relationship between the mission and the national church is generally a matter decided on a nation- or area-wide basis, not at the local level. However, the missionary-evangelist has the responsibility to instruct and guide the local congregation in the fulfillment of its role in the larger scheme of things.

Our Lord said, "I chose you, and appointed you, that you should go and bear fruit, and that your fruit should remain" (John 15:16). Long after the church-planting missionary has departed, the planted church will live and work within the framework of the relationships dealt with in this chapter. If those relationships are both spiritual and strategic, there is a great likelihood that the fruit of the church-planting labors will remain.

PART FIVE

The Sending Church and the Christian Mission
(Continued)

seventeen

The Sending Church Convened

Almost without exception missionary-evangelists who are successful in planting new churches have the backing of sending churches. Why? Because missionary-evangelists sent by Christian churches (as opposed to those who are sent by individual Christians or institutions, or those who go on their own initiative) tend to be churchmen. They are church-oriented rather than campaign-oriented and program-oriented. But there is another reason. To be successful, church-planters—like other servants of God—need encouragement and prayer. And they may need counsel and finances. What better source could one find than the sending church?

In Part Four we were concerned with the new, emerging church. We assume, however, that during the church-planting period, the missionary-evangelist has been in communication with the church(es) that commissioned, sent, and supported him. At certain times—perhaps at a missionary conference or school of mission—the members of the sending church should hear a personal report. It

FIGURE 55
"THE PAULINE CYCLE"

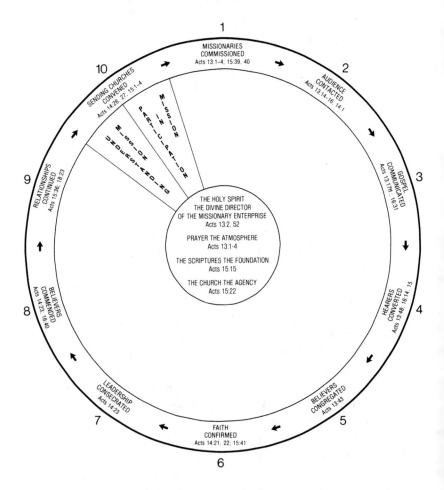

1 MISSIONARIES COMMISSIONED Acts 13:1-4; 15:39, 40

2 AUDIENCE CONTACTED Acts 13:14-16; 14:1

3 GOSPEL COMMUNICATED Acts 13:17H; 16:31

4 HEARERS CONVERTED Acts 13:48; 16:14, 15

5 BELIEVERS CONGREGATED Acts 13:43

6 FAITH CONFIRMED Acts 14:21, 22; 15:41

7 LEADERSHIP CONSECRATED Acts 14:23

8 BELIEVERS COMMENDED Acts 14:23; 16:40

9 RELATIONSHIPS CONTINUED Acts 15:36; 18:23

10 SENDING CHURCHES CONVENED Acts 14:26, 27; 15:1-4

MISSION PARTICIPATION
CONGREGATIONS INVOLVED

THE HOLY SPIRIT
THE DIVINE DIRECTOR
OF THE MISSIONARY ENTERPRISE
Acts 13:2, 52

PRAYER THE ATMOSPHERE
Acts 13:1-4

THE SCRIPTURES THE FOUNDATION
Acts 15:15

THE CHURCH THE AGENCY
Acts 15:22

would be hard to imagine anything more stimulating to a congregation than to hear firsthand how God has used the personnel they have sent, the prayers they have offered, and the other provisions they have made for the establishment of churches in new areas!

Objectives

Definite objectives should be set for the meeting (conference, convention, rally, school of mission, or whatever) where the church-planter reports to the sending church. Whatever frills may be thought necessary, nothing should obscure the grand truth that, through His dedicated people and blessed Holy Spirit, Christ is building His Church. Bringing citizens of the kingdom together around the King's business, the local church leaders should have two objectives in mind:

(1) To achieve a thorough understanding of what God has accomplished through the missionary-evangelist and how this fits into His purpose for the Church.

(2) To achieve a full participation of all Christians in the missionary efforts of the local church.

It should be borne in mind that the only way to determine whether or not these objectives are being reached is to devise some method of testing understanding and monitoring participation.

Understanding the Church's Mission

There are two essential elements in understanding the Church's mission. First, the members of the sending congregation should understand the mission of the Church in biblical terms as presented in Part One of this book. Second, believers should understand exactly what has been accomplished through the work of their missionaries, and how it has been accomplished.

Biblical Principles and Precedents

Of course, the biblical prototypes of the kind of reporting which we have in mind are the Antioch and Jerusalem missionary conferences. The Lukan record of the return of Paul and Barnabas to Antioch after the first missionary journey is succinct and stimulating:

> And when they had spoken the word in Perga, they went down to Attalia; and from there they sailed to Antioch, from which they had been commended to the grace of God for the work that they had accomplished. And when they had arrived and gathered the church together, they began to report all things that God had done with them and how He had opened a door of faith to the Gentiles. And they spent a long time with the disciples. (Acts 14:25-28)

The focus of the Jerusalem conference was somewhat different (Acts 15:1-30). At that conference the concern was to understand how the work of the apostles in planting churches among the Gentiles fitted into the larger plan of God.

Paul also returned to Antioch after his second missionary journey (Acts 18:22) and to Jerusalem after his third journey (Acts 21:17-19). He sent Epaphroditus back to the Philippians with instructions that they should "receive him in the Lord with all joy, and hold men like him in high regard" (Phil. 2:29). He sent Tychicus and Onesimus to Colossae so that the Colossians might be informed and encouraged (Col. 4:7-9). A prominent note in all of these meetings was that of encouragement, joy, and praise to God for what He had done.

Relevant Research

American Opinion About Organized Religion

A 1977 study revealed a considerable degree of skepticism as to organized religion's "honesty, dependability,

FIGURE 56

American Opinion About Various Key Groups

How would you rate the following groups in:

	Honesty, Dependability, Integrity?			Ability to Get Things Done?		
	Poor	Average	Good	Poor	Average	Good
The White House	23%	55%	17%	29%	54%	9%
The Supreme Court	19%	41%	33%	19%	45%	25%
U.S. Military	19%	53%	21%	16%	51%	22%
Educators	14%	56%	23%	19%	57%	14%
Organized Religion	14%	48%	30%	16%	53%	19%
Medical Profession	14%	53%	28%	9%	52%	29%
Science and Technology	4%	46%	41%	5%	45%	38%
Large Business	25%	60%	9%	10%	54%	25%
Broadcast News Media (TV news, radio news)	15%	51%	26%	8%	45%	35%
Print News Media (news magazines, news- papers)	15%	58%	21%	9%	51%	29%

and integrity," and "ability to get things done."[1] The ratings achieved by organized religion and some (not all) of the other groups included in the questionnaire are given in Figure 56 so that a comparison can be made. If we can assume that "organized religion" is more or less synonymous with the Christian church, it becomes apparent that churches have to "prove themselves" in these areas. At least, this is so as far as the general public is concerned.

The Opinions of Christian Youth Regarding the Christian Mission

The opinions held by some five thousand youthful delegates to the 1967 Urbana Missionary Convention are still pertinent (though enthusiasm for the Church has increased significantly since then).[2] In fact, no similar survey of so large a mission-oriented group of evangelical youth has been undertaken since that time. Of the scores of questions and responses in the survey, several speak clearly to the need for the kind of instruction and reporting we are advocating here. (It should be noted that 85 percent of the respondents were church members, and 93 percent attended church regularly.)

First, when the delegates were polled as to what they regarded as the primary missionary occupation, "personal evangelists" rather than "church-planters and developers" was the number one choice. In fact, many delegates selected "technicians and engineers" as most important. For full results see Figure 57.

Second, in answer to the question, "If you were going to be a missionary, which would you most like to be?" about

---

[1] *The Study of American Opinion, 1977*, Marketing Concepts, Inc., 1235 N. Avenue, Nevada, Iowa.

[2] Paul F. Barkman, Edward R. Dayton, and Edward L. Gruman, *Christian Collegians and Foreign Missions: An Analysis of Relationships* (Monrovia, CA: Missions Advanced Research and Communications Center, 1969).

FIGURE 57

Primary Missionary Occupation-
Urbana 1967 Survey Result*

Question: If all of the following kinds of missionaries are needed on a given missionary field, but only one kind would be permitted to remain, which one should remain?

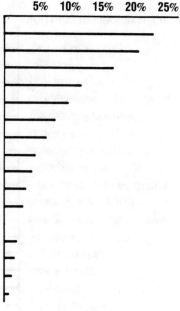

PRIMARY MISSIONARY OCCUPATION   5%   10%   15%   20%   25%

Personal evangelists
Church-planters and developers
Technicians and engineers
Bible teachers
Physicians and nurses
Mass evangelists
Translators and linguists
University student workers
Non-professional missionaries
School teachers
Radio program and production
Missionary journalists and printers
Agricultural workers
Anthropologists
Aviation and radio-phone network

Note: The responses averaged 2.1 answers.

*Based on Paul F. Barkman, Edward R. Dayton, and Edward L. Gruman, *Christian Collegians and Foreign Missions: An Analysis of Relationships* (Monrovia, CA: Missions Advanced Research and Communications Center, 1969), p. 65.

FIGURE 58

Desired Missionary Occupation—
Urbana 1967 Survey Result*

Question: If you were going to be a missionary, which would you most like to be?

DESIRED MISSIONARY OCCUPATION	5%	10%	15%	20%	25%	30%	35%

Personal evangelism
Education
Medical work
Student/youth work
Non-professional missionary
Journalism, literature work
Linguistics and translation
Missionary anthropology
Church-planting, development
Radio & TV, engineering
Aviation, radio-phone network
Radio & TV, programing
Mass evangelism
Children's work
Social work
Agricultural work

Note: Occupations stated this way in the original survey.

*Based on Paul F. Barkman, Edward R. Dayton, and Edward L. Gruman, *Christian Collegians and Foreign Missions: An Analysis of Relationships* (Monrovia, CA: Missions Advanced Research and Communications Center, 1969), p. 79.

five times as many delegates chose to be in education as chose to be in church-planting and development. Figure 58 gives the complete results.

Of course, we are not saying that the various missionary occupations listed in the questionnaire are not worthy. However, the responses do indicate the need for instruction as to what the basic mission of the Church is. They also point up the importance of communicating the excitement of what is actually happening around the world as missionary-evangelists develop churches made up of people who have been reconciled to God in Christ and therefore have a new relationship to one another and the world around them.

Practical Reflection

The annual missionary conference held by many churches is certainly not the only way to teach and promote mission. Many other missionary meetings and emphases are needed throughout the church year. But attendance at, and interest in, the missionary conference is a fairly accurate measurement of the mission pulse in most churches. It may be instructive, therefore, to focus on its state of health and suggest a way of revitalizing it:

> Is the mission conference still a relevant part of the local church program? Missionaries frequently stop by my office while "on the circuit," and give vent to various frustrations related to conferences. One evangelical mission leader said to me, "Dave, I've almost given up on missionary conferences in the churches. They're like treadmills, always covering the same ground and seemingly going nowhere."
>
> These critics are not professional crepehangers who would be happy with the sudden demise of mission conferences. Quite the contrary. They want an infusion of new vitality, wider participation, more "get up and go." They would be among the first to appreciate the appraisal of the pastor who said, "Without the annual missionary conference down through the years, our program of outreach would have died on the vine!"

The fact remains that many fear the mission conference may be suffering from a malady similar to that which incapacitated the evangelistic services and Bible conferences in many churches a decade or two ago....

What can be done about these problems? Let us assume that we have a concerned pastor, a mission committee which is ready to go to work, and a congregation with allegiance to our Lord Christ who started this vast enterprise and wills its continuance and consummation!

First, Scripture and strategy must be in clearer focus. I am convinced that Bible emphasis is a necessary condition for a successful conference. The whole mission enterprise needs to be grounded in the revealed purpose of God. Sympathy for men in their poverty and diseases is noble, but not enough. There are too many heathen who are wealthy and well! Nothing less than the will of God is sufficient basis for a world-encompassing self-sacrificing mission. Mission is in the Bible from Genesis to Malachi, and from Matthew to Revelation. God the Father is the Sender, and the Son is the Sent One, and the Spirit is the Missionary Spirit. The successful mission conference must be set in the context of a continuing preaching and teaching emphasis on what God says about mission.

And then we come to strategy. We are in the twentieth century. "Reports from the field" are important, but to be up-to-date they must be more than a report of "the work." ... Christians have been urged to pray and give if they cannot go as missionaries. An increasing number of contemporary Christians remain unchallenged by the approach. They find little compulsion to support that which they do not understand or that of which they do not feel themselves to be a real part. A credibility gap has emerged—not because the average Christian does not trust the missionary, but because he is unable to enter into mission problems and possibilities with real understanding.

The credibility gap can be closed. Real issues and realistic plans must be discussed. Reports must be factual with maps, charts, and graphs that show clearly where, how, why, and to what extent the church of Christ is growing. When people "see" they will interact.[3]

---

[3]David J. Hesselgrave, "The Mission Conference Treadmill: How to Get Off," *World Vision*, September 1972, pp. 12–13.

Participation in the Church's Mission

Biblical Principles and Precedents

The fundamental biblical principle related to the sending church's participation in mission is found in II Corinthians 8:1–5:

> Now, brethren, we wish to make known to you the grace of God which has been given in the churches of Macedonia, that in a great ordeal of affliction their abundance of joy and their deep poverty overflowed in the wealth of their liberality. For I testify that according to their ability, and beyond their ability they gave of their own accord, begging us with much entreaty for the favor of participation in the support of the saints, and this, not as we had expected, but they first gave themselves to the Lord and to us by the will of God.

The reference, of course, is to the provision made for the poverty-stricken saints in Jerusalem. The Macedonians had given far above the expectation of the apostle. Why? What was their motivation? The obvious answer is love—not just love for the Jerusalem saints, but love for the Lord. *They gave of their means to others because they had given themselves to the Lord!* The Macedonian Christians had acted upon the truth that Paul had tried to drive home in his first letter to the Corinthian Christians: "Do you not know that . . . you are not your own? For you have been bought with a price" (I Cor. 6:19, 20).

Here, then, we have the mainspring of actual participation in God's great program for His Church on earth. This accounts for the fact that when the church members in Jerusalem were subjected to suffering at the hands of Saul the persecuter and were scattered, they "went about preaching the word" (Acts 8:4). It accounts for the fact that when, after his missionary campaigns throughout Asia Minor, Macedonia, and Greece, Paul the persecuted insisted upon returning to Jerusalem despite warnings of impending suffering, the believers in Caesarea said, "The will of the Lord be done," and started down the road with him (Acts 21:14-16). And it accounts for the fact that, in spite of lapses and failures, great numbers of ordinary believers were involved in one way or another in the great mission spearheaded by the apostle.

Relevant Research

There is much evidence in the field of comparative religions that indicates the importance of lay involvement at the cutting edge of religious movements. It is important to note that some of the really successful religious movements of our time are lay movements entirely. Out of the numerous studies that could be cited, we choose but one.

In the United States an outstanding example is Bahai. Since 1960 this movement has grown rapidly (though not rapidly enough to justify its claim of being the fastest growing religion in the world). In slightly more than ten years (from 1960 to 1971), Bahai membership in the United States increased from just under 10,000 to over 100,000, and the number of assemblies from about 200 to 837. One of the important factors in this growth was the strategy of encouraging small groups of believers to band together and emigrate to new communities where they functioned as embryonic assemblies.[4]

Practical Reflection

We live in an unusual day. Consider how easy it is to travel throughout the Mediterranean lands where our

---

[4]William J. Petersen, *Those Curious New Cults* (New Canaan, CT: Keats Publishing Co., 1973), p. 182.

Lord and His apostles carried out their mission. In a matter of hours we can motor from Dan to Beersheba—a distance that once took days of exhausting travel on animal or by foot on the part of our Lord. In two or three hours we can fly over seas and lands which required weeks and months of treacherous travel on the part of the apostle Paul. The technology of modern transportation and communication makes it possible for ordinary Christians to participate in the worldwide mission of the Church with a facility never dreamed of in the first century. Yet to many Christians, mission is little more than responding to pleas for money to support missionary-evangelists and sustain the needy. If the field is the world, let believers in new churches as well as older ones be encouraged to actively participate in claiming additional territory for Christ, whether it be near at home or far away.

The possibilities for active participation in the mission of the Church today are almost unlimited. Consider a few:

(1) Churches can establish relationships with emerging churches at home or abroad on the pattern of "sister cities." Communication can flow back and forth. Visits can be exchanged.

(2) Young Christians can establish pen-pal relationships with young people in pioneer areas.

(3) Foreign nationals can be invited into the homes of local Christians. Many of them can be won to Christ and will become witnesses in their home areas.

(4) Teams of local Christians gathered from one or several churches can be sent out to aid in pioneer work at home and abroad.

(5) Groups of local Christians can relocate and become the vanguard of a church in a new area.

(6) Retirees and specialists can go to a pioneer area at their own expense in order to aid the work of Christ.

ME 1-3 illustration: One of the secrets of the success of the Southern Baptist Convention in establishing new churches has been their program of "evangelizing and congregationalizing."[5] And one of the secrets of that program has been the preparation and involvement of teams of lay persons in reaching a target area. Lay people of sponsoring churches are deployed in home visitation, special meetings, Bible study groups, and so forth. In fact, teams of lay persons have often been utilized in carrying out a special witness in sections of our country far from their home, and even in mission fields abroad. This kind of commitment and involvement goes a long way to explain why the Southern Baptists evidenced continued growth during a time when many other large denominations experienced a decline in membership.

Prayer for guidance ascended to the Lord of the Church. Potential areas for a new work were surveyed and evaluated. Pioneer workers were selected and sent. Plans were carefully laid. Then, contacts were made; the gospel was communicated; converts were won; believers were congregated; faith was confirmed; leadership was consecrated; the church was commended to the grace of God; and the missionary-evangelists were relocated. From the beginning it was in their hearts that, once established, the new churches would become the bases for the prayers, plans, and participation essential to enter still other territories for Christ both at home and abroad. And so the Pauline Cycle has been and will be repeated, on and on, over and over, until Christ comes again and the Church Militant becomes the Church Triumphant. Maranatha!

---

[5]Cf. *Evangelizing and Congregationalizing: Guide for Establishing New Churches and Missions* and *Associational New Work Campaign* (Home Missions Board, Southern Baptist Convention, n.d.).

Bibliography

Allen, Roland. *Educational Principles and Missionary Methods.* London: Robert Scott, 1919.

———. *Missionary Methods: St. Paul's or Ours?* Grand Rapids: Eerdmans, 1962.

———. *The Spontaneous Expansion of the Church.* London: World Dominion Press, 1927.

———, and Paton, Donald. *The Ministry of the Spirit.* Grand Rapids: Eerdmans, 1962.

Almquist, Arden. *Missionary, Come Back.* Cleveland: The World Publishing Co., 1970.

Anderson, Efraim. *Churches at the Grass Roots.* London: Lutterworth Press, 1968.

Anderson, Rufus. *To Advance the Gospel.* Edited by R. Pierce Beaver. Grand Rapids: Eerdmans, 1967.

Ayres, Francis O. *The Ministry of the Laity.* Philadelphia: Westminster Press, 1962.

Bannerman, D. Douglas. *The Scripture Doctrine of the Church.* Grand Rapids: Eerdmans, 1955.

Baumann, Dan. *All Originality Makes a Dull Church.* Santa Ana, CA: Vision House Publishers, 1976.

Bavinck, J. H. *An Introduction to the Science of Missions.* Translated by David H. Freeman. Grand Rapids: Baker, 1960.

Benjamin, Paul. *The Growing Congregation.* Cincinnati: Standard Publishing, 1972.

Bennett, Charles. *Tinder in Tobasco.* Grand Rapids: Eerdmans, 1968.

Benson, Donald. *How to Start a Daughter Church.* Quezon City, Philippines: Filkoba Press, 1972.

Beyerhaus, Peter, and Lefever, Henry. *The Responsible Church and Foreign Mission.* Grand Rapids: Eerdmans, 1964.

Bradshaw, Malcolm R. *Church Growth Through Evangelism-in-Depth.* South Pasadena, CA: William Carey Library, 1969.

Braun, Neil; Boschman, P. W.; and Yamada, T., eds. *Experiments in Church Growth: Japan.* Kobayashi City, Japan: Church Growth Association, 1968.

Brow, Robert. *The Church: An Organic Picture of Its Life and Mission.* Grand Rapids: Eerdmans, 1968.

Brown, Arthur Judson. *The Why and How of Foreign Missions.* New York: Eaton and Mains, 1908.

Brown, Stanley C. *Evangelism in the Early Church.* Grand Rapids: Eerdmans, 1963.

Busia, K. A. *Urban Churches in Britain.* London: Lutterworth Press, 1966.

Church Expansion Handbook. New York: American Baptist Home Mission Societies, 1958.

Clark, Charles Allen. *The Korean Church and the Nevius Methods.* Unpublished doctoral dissertation, University of Chicago, 1929.

Clark, J. W. Sidney. *The Indigenous Church.* London: World Dominion Press, 1923.

Coleman, Robert E. *The Master Plan of Evangelism.* Westwood, NJ: Fleming H. Revell, 1963.

Cook, Harold R. *Historic Patterns of Church Growth.* Chicago: Moody Press, 1971.

_____. *Missionary Life and Work.* Chicago: Moody Press, 1959.

_____. *Strategy of Missions.* Chicago: Moody Press, 1963.

Dana, H. E., and Sipes, L. M. *A Manual of Ecclesiology.* Kansas City: Central Seminary Press, 1944.

Davies, J. Q. *Worship and Mission.* New York: Association Press, 1967.

Davies, W. D. *A Normative Pattern of Church Life in the New Testament: Fact or Fancy?* London: James Clarke and Co., n.d.

Davis, John Merle. *New Buildings on Old Foundations.* New York: International Missionary Council, 1945.

Dobbins, Gaines S. *The Churchbook.* Nashville: Broadman Press, 1951.

Dodge, Ralph E. *The Unpopular Missionary.* Westwood, NJ: Fleming H. Revell, 1964.

Engel, James F., and Norton, H. Wilbert. *What's Gone Wrong with the Harvest? A Communication Strategy for the Church and World Evangelism.* Grand Rapids: Zondervan, 1975.

Fiers, Alan Dale. *This Is Mission.* St. Louis: Bethany Press, 1953.

Gerber, Vergil. *God's Way to Keep a Church Going and Growing.* Glendale, CA: Gospel Light Publications, 1973.

————, ed. *Missions in Creative Tension.* South Pasadena, CA: William Carey Library, 1971.

Getz, Gene. *The Measure of a Man.* Glendale, CA: Regal Books, 1974.

————. *Sharpening the Focus of the Church.* Chicago: Moody Press, 1974.

Green, Michael. *Evangelism in the Early Church.* Grand Rapids: Eerdmans, 1970.

Greenway, Roger S. *Guidelines for Urban Church Planting.* Grand Rapids: Baker, 1976.

————. *An Urban Strategy for Latin America.* Grand Rapids: Baker, 1973.

Grimley, John, and Robinson, Gordon. *Church Growth in Central and Southern Nigeria.* Grand Rapids: Eerdmans, 1966.

Hamilton, Keith. *Church Growth in the High Andes.* Lucknow, India: Lucknow, 1962.

Hay, A. R. *New Testament Order for Church and Missionary.* Audubon, NJ: New Testament Missionary Union, 1947.

Hesselgrave, David J. *Communicating Christ Cross-Culturally.* Grand Rapids: Zondervan, 1978.

————, ed. *Dynamic Religious Movements: Case Studies of Rapidly Growing Religious Movements Around the World.* Grand Rapids: Baker, 1978.

Hiscox, Edward T. *The Hiscox Guide for Baptist Churches.* Valley Forge, PA: Judson Press, 1964.

Hodges, Melvin L. *Build My Church.* Springfield, MO: Assemblies of God, 1957.

————. *A Guide to Church Planting.* Chicago: Moody Press, 1973.

————. *The Indigenous Church.* Springfield, MO: Evangelical Publishing House, 1953.

Hoffer, Eric. *The True Believer: Thoughts on the Nature of Mass Movements.* New York: New American Library of World Literature, 1958.

Hollis, Michael. *Paternalism and the Church.* London: Oxford University Press, 1962.

Idowu, Bolaji. *Towards an Indigenous Church*. London: Oxford University Press, 1965.

Jackson, Paul R. *The Doctrine and Administration of the Church*. Des Plaines, IL: Regular Baptist Press, 1968.

Jenkins, Daniel. *The Protestant Ministry*. Garden City, NY: Doubleday, 1958.

Kane, J. Herbert. *Twofold Growth*. Philadelphia: China Inland Mission, 1947.

Kelley, Dean M. *Why Conservative Churches Are Growing*. New York: Harper and Row, 1972.

Kennedy, D. James. *Evangelism Explosion*. Wheaton, IL: Tyndale House, 1970.

Knight, William Henry. *Missions in Principle and Practice*. Nashville: Sunday School Board of the Southern Baptist Convention, 1929.

Kraemer, Hendrik. *From Mission Field to Independent Church*. London: SCM Press, 1955.

Kuiper, R. B. *The Glorious Body of Christ*. London: Banner of Truth Trust, 1966.

Küng, Hans. *Structures of the Church*. New York: Thomas Nelson, 1964.

Lapham, Henry A. *The Bible as a Missions Handbook*. Cambridge: W. Heffer and Sons, 1925.

Laubach, Frank C. *How to Teach One and Win One for Christ*. Grand Rapids: Zondervan, 1964.

Lawson, E. LeRoy, and Yamamori, Tetsunau. *Church Growth: Everybody's Business*. Cincinnati: Standard Publishing Co., 1971.

Leeming, Bernard. *The Churches and the Church: A Study of Ecumenism with a New Postscript*. Second edition. Westminster, MD: Newman Press, 1963.

Lees, Harrington C. *St. Paul and His Converts*. London: Robert Scott, 1910.

Lindsay, Thomas M. *The Church and the Ministry in the Early Centuries*. Second edition. London: Hodder and Stoughton, 1903.

Lindsell, Harold. *Barriers to Church Growth*. Grand Rapids: Eerdmans, n.d.

————. *Missionary Principles and Practice*. Westwood. NJ: Fleming H. Revell, 1955.

Longenecker, Harold L. *Building Town and Country Churches*. Chicago: Moody Press, 1973.

McCall, Duke K., ed. *What Is the Church? A Symposium of Baptist Thought*. Nashville: Broadman Press, 1958.

McGavran, Donald. *The Bridges of God.* New York: Friendship Press, 1955.

———. *Church Growth in Jamaica.* Lucknow, India: Lucknow, 1962.

———. *Church Growth in Mexico.* Grand Rapids: Eerdmans, 1963.

———. *How Churches Grow.* New York: Friendship Press, 1959.

———. *Understanding Church Growth.* Grand Rapids: Eerdmans, 1968.

———, ed. *Church Growth and Christian Mission.* New York: Harper & Row, 1965.

———, ed. *Eye of the Storm: The Great Debate in Mission.* Waco, TX: Word Books, 1972.

MacLeish, Alexander. *Jesus Christ and the World Christian Missionary Principles.* London: Lutterworth Press, 1934.

MacNair, Donald J. *The Growing Local Church.* Grand Rapids: Baker, 1973.

McQuilkin, J. Robertson. *How Biblical Is the Church Growth Movement?* Chicago: Moody Press, 1973.

Mains, David R. *Full Circle.* Waco, TX: Word Books, 1971.

Manson, T. W. *Ministry and Priesthood: Christ's and Ours.* Richmond: John Knox Press, 1958.

Marshall, Thomas William M. *Christian Missions: Their Agents and Their Results.* Second edition. Two volumes. New York: D. & J. Sadlier and Co., 1864.

Mavis, W. C. *Advancing in the Smaller Local Church.* Grand Rapids: Baker, 1968.

Miller, Paul. *Group Dynamics in Evangelism.* Scottdale, PA: Herald Press, 1958.

Missionary Methods—Candidate Seminar Manual No. 2. Cleveland: Baptist Mid-Mission, July 1964 revision. See the articles by Gordon D. Mellish ("Pioneering") and Denzel L. Osburn ("The Indigenous Church").

Montgomery, H. H. *Principles and Problems of Foreign Missions.* Westminster: Society for the Propagation of the Gospel, 1904.

Munro, Harry C. *Fellowship Evangelism Through Church Groups.* St. Louis: Bethany Press, 1951.

Nederhood, J. H. *The Church's Mission to the Educated American.* Grand Rapids: Eerdmans, 1961.

Nee, Watchman. *The Normal Christian Life.* Washington, DC: International Students Press, 1962.

Neill, Stephen. *Creative Tension.* London: Edinburgh House Press, 1959.

Nevius, John. *Planting and Development of Missionary Churches.* Philadelphia: Presbyterian and Reformed, 1899.

Nida, Eugene A. *Message and Mission: The Communication of Christian Faith.* New York: Harper and Row, 1960.

Norbie, Donald L. *New Testament Church Organization.* Chicago: Christian Libraries, 1955.

Olson, Gilbert. *Church Growth in Sierra Leone.* Grand Rapids: Eerdmans, 1969.

Packer, J. I. *Evangelism and the Sovereignty of God.* Chicago: Inter-Varsity Press, 1965.

Palmer, Donald C. *Explosion of People Evangelism.* Chicago: Moody Press, 1974.

Peill, S. G., and Rowlands, W. F. *Church Planting.* London: World Dominion Press, n.d.

Pentecost, Edward. *Reaching the Unreached.* South Pasadena, CA: William Carey Library, 1974.

Perry, Lloyd Merle, and Lias, Edward John. *A Manual of Pastoral Problems and Procedures.* Grand Rapids: Baker, 1964.

Pickett, J. Waskom. *Christian Mass Movements in India.* New York: Abingdon, 1933.

_____. *Christ's Way to India's Heart.* Lucknow, India: Lucknow, 1960.

_____. *Church Growth and Group Conversion.* Lucknow, India: Lucknow, 1962.

_____. *The Dynamics of Church Growth.* New York: Abingdon, 1963.

Planning and PERT (Program Evaluation and Review Technique). Monrovia, CA: Missions Advanced Research and Communication Center, 1966.

Porter, H. Boone, Jr. *Growth and Life in the Local Church.* South Pasadena, CA: William Carey Library, 1974 reprint.

Randall, Max W. *Profile for Victory: New Proposals for Missions in Zambia.* South Pasadena, CA: William Carey Library, 1970.

Read, William. *New Patterns of Church Growth in Brazil.* Grand Rapids: Eerdmans, 1966.

Read, William R.; Monterroso, Victor M.; and Johnson, Harmon A. *Latin American Church Growth.* Grand Rapids: Eerdmans, 1969.

Reese, J. Irving. *A Guide for Organizing and Conducting a Baptist Church.* Elyria, OH: J. Irving Reese Publications, 1962.

Richards, Lawrence O. *A New Face for the Church.* Grand Rapids: Zondervan, 1970.

_____. *A Theology of Christian Education.* Grand Rapids: Zondervan, 1975.

Richardson, William J., ed. *The Modern Missionary Apostolate.* New York: Maryknoll Publications, 1965.

Ritchie, John. *Indigenous Church Principles in Theory and Practice.* New York: Fleming H. Revell, 1946.

The Role of the "Diakonia" of the Church in Contemporary Society. New York: World Council of Churches, 1966.

Ronan, Hoffman. *Pioneer Theories of Missiology.* Washington, DC: Catholic University of America Press, 1960.

Ross, Byron W. *Training Lay Workers.* New York: Christian and Missionary Alliance, n.d.

Rowland, Henry. *Native Churches in Foreign Fields.* New York: The Methodist Book Concern, 1925.

Rowlands, W. R. *Indigenous Ideals in Practice.* London: World Dominion Press, n.d.

Saunders, J. Roscoe. *Men and Methods That Win in the Foreign Fields.* New York: Fleming H. Revell, 1921.

Schaller, Lyle E. *Hey, That's Our Church.* New York: Abingdon, 1975.

Scherer, James A. *Justinian Welz: Essays by an Early Prophet of Mission.* Grand Rapids: Eerdmans, 1969.

―――. *Missionary, Go Home.* Englewood Cliffs, NJ: Prentice-Hall, Inc., 1964.

Schmidt, Otto Henry. *St. Paul Shows Us How.* St. Louis: Concordia, 1950.

Schuller, Robert H. *Your Church Has Real Possibilities.* Glendale, CA: Regal Books, 1974.

Schweizer, Edward. *Church Order in the New Testament.* Naperville, IL: Alec R. Allenson, Inc., 1961.

Scopes, Wilfred, ed. *The Christian Ministry in Latin America and the Caribbean.* New York: Commission on World Mission and Evangelism, World Council of Churches, 1962.

Shearer, Roy. *Wildfire: Church Growth in Korea.* Grand Rapids: Eerdmans, 1966.

Smith, Ebbie C. *God's Miracles: Indonesian Church Growth.* South Pasadena, CA: William Carey Library, 1970.

Snyder, Howard A. *The Problem of Wineskins: Church Structure in a Technological Age.* Downers Grove, IL: Inter-Varsity Press, 1975.

Speer, Robert G. *Missionary Principles and Practices.* New York: Fleming H. Revell, 1902.

Street, T. Watson. *On the Growing Edge of the Church.* Richmond: John Knox Press, 1965.

Subbama, B. V. *New Patterns for Discipling Hindus.* South Pasadena, CA: William Carey Library, 1970.

Sunda, James. *Church Growth in the Central Highlands of West Guinea.* Lucknow, India: Lucknow, 1963.

Swanson, Allen J. *Taiwan: Mainline Versus Independent Church Growth.* South Pasadena, CA: William Carey Library, 1973.

Taylor, John V. *The Growth of the Church in Buganda.* London: SCM Press, 1958.

Thorwall, LaReau N., and Bender, Edgar J. *Growth Through Body Building.* (Typewritten, 1974)

Tippett, A. R. *Church Growth and the Word of God.* Grand Rapids: Eerdmans, 1970.

_____. *Verdict Theology in Mission Theory.* Lincoln, IL: Lincoln Christian College Press, 1969.

_____, ed. *God, Man, and Church Growth.* Grand Rapids: Eerdmans, 1973.

Trueblood, Elton. *The Company of the Committed.* New York: Harper and Row, 1961.

Vicedom, G. F. *Church and People in New Guinea.* New York: Association Press, 1961.

Wagner, C. Peter. *Frontiers of Missionary Strategy.* Chicago: Moody Press, 1971.

_____. *Your Church Can Grow.* Glendale, CA: Gospel Light Publications, 1976.

_____, ed. *Church Mission Tensions Today.* Chicago: Moody Press, 1972.

Wasson, Alfred. *Church Growth in Korea.* New York: International Missionary Council, 1934.

Weber, Hans-Ruedi. *Salty Christians.* New York: Seabury Press, 1963.

Weld, Wayne. *An Ecuadorian Impasse.* Chicago: Department of World Missions, Evangelical Covenant Church of America, 1968.

White, James F. *Protestant Worship and Church Architecture.* New York: Oxford University Press, 1964.

Winter, Gibson. *The Suburban Captivity of the Churches.* New York: The Macmillan Company, 1962.

Winter, Ralph, and Beaver, R. Pierce. *The Warp and the Woof: Organizing for Mission.* South Pasadena, CA: William Carey Library, 1971.

Wold, Joseph Conrad. *God's Impatience in Liberia.* Grand Rapids: Eerdmans, 1968.

Woodson, Leslie. *Evangelism for Today's Church.* Grand Rapids: Zondervan, 1973.

Worley, Robert C. *Change in the Church: A Source of Hope.* Philadelphia: Westminster Press, 1971.

Yamamori, Tetsunao. *Church Growth in Japan.* South Pasadena, CA: William Carey Library, 1974.
———, and Lawson, E. LeRoy. *Introducing Church Growth.* Cincinnati: Standard Publishing Co., 1975.
Yoder, J. H. *As You Go: The Old Mission in a New Day.* Scottdale, PA: Herald Press, 1961.

Index

SUBJECT INDEX

Index

SCRIPTURE INDEX